Studies in Economic Transition

General Editors: **Jens Hölscher**, Reader in Economics, University of Brighton; and **Horst Tomann**, Professor of Economics, Free University Berlin

This series has been established in response to a growing demand for a greater understanding of the transformation of economic systems. It brings together theoretical and empirical studies on economic transition and economic development. The postcommunist transition from planned to market economies is one of the main areas of applied theory because in this field the most dramatic examples of change and economic dynamics can be found. The series aims to contribute to the understanding of specific major economic changes as well as to advance the theory of economic development. The implications of economic policy will be a major point of focus.

Titles include:

Lucian Cernat
EUROPEANIZATION, VARIETIES OF CAPITALISM AND ECONOMIC
PERFORMANCE IN CENTRAL AND EASTERN EUROPE

Irwin Collier, Herwig Roggemann, Oliver Scholz and Horst Tomann (*editors*)
WELFARE STATES IN TRANSITION
East and West

Bruno Dallago (*editor*)
TRANSFORMATION AND EUROPEAN INTEGRATION
The Local Dimension

Hella Engerer
PRIVATIZATION AND ITS LIMITS IN CENTRAL AND EASTERN EUROPE
Property Rights in Transition

Hubert Gabrisch and Rüdiger Pohl (*editors*)
EU ENLARGEMENT AND ITS MACROECONOMIC EFFECTS IN
EASTERN EUROPE
Currencies, Prices, Investment and Competitiveness

Oleh Havrylyshyn
DIVERGENT PATHS IN POST-COMMUNIST TRANSFORMATION
Capitalism for All or Capitalism for the Few?

Jens Hölscher (*editor*)
FINANCIAL TURBULENCE AND CAPITAL MARKETS IN TRANSITION
COUNTRIES

Jens Hölscher and Anja Hochberg (*editors*)
EAST GERMANY'S ECONOMIC DEVELOPMENT SINCE UNIFICATION
Domestic and Global Aspects

Mihaela Kelemen and Monika Kostera (*editors*)
CRITICAL MANAGEMENT RESEARCH IN EASTERN EUROPE
Managing the Transition

Emil J. Kirchner (*editor*)
DECENTRALIZATION AND TRANSITION IN THE VISEGRAD
Poland, Hungary, the Czech Republic and Slovakia

David Lane and Martin Myant (*editors*)
VARIETIES OF CAPITALISM IN POST-COMMUNIST COUNTRIES

Tomasz Mickiewicz (*editor*)
CORPORATE GOVERNANCE AND FINANCE IN POLAND AND RUSSIA

Tomasz Mickiewicz
ECONOMIC TRANSITION IN CENTRAL EUROPE AND THE
COMMONWEALTH OF INDEPENDENT STATES

Milan Nikolić
MONETARY POLICY IN TRANSITION
Inflation Nexus Money Supply in Postcommunist Russia

Julie Pellegrin
THE POLITICAL ECONOMY OF COMPETITIVENESS IN AN
ENLARGED EUROPE

Stanislav Poloucek (*editor*)
REFORMING THE FINANCIAL SECTOR IN CENTRAL
EUROPEAN COUNTRIES

Gregg S. Robins
BANKING IN TRANSITION
East Germany after Unification

Johannes Stephan
ECONOMIC TRANSITION IN HUNGARY AND EAST GERMANY
Gradualism and Shock Therapy in Catch-up Development

Johannes Stephan (*editor*)
TECHNOLOGY TRANSFER VIA FOREIGN DIRECT INVESTMENT IN
CENTRAL AND EASTERN EUROPE

Hans van Zon
THE POLITICAL ECONOMY OF INDEPENDENT UKRAINE

Adalbert Winkler (*editor*)
BANKING AND MONETARY POLICY IN EASTERN EUROPE
The First Ten Years

Studies in Economic Transition
Series Standing Order ISBN 0–333–73353–3
(*outside North America only*)

You can receive future titles in this series as they are published by placing a standing
order. Please contact your bookseller or, in case of difficulty, write to us at the address
below with your name and address, the title of the series and the ISBN quoted above.

Customer Services Department, Macmillan Distribution Ltd, Houndmills, Basingstoke,
Hampshire RG21 6XS, England

Varieties of Capitalism in Post-Communist Countries

Edited by

David Lane

and

Martin Myant

First published 2007 by
PALGRAVE MACMILLAN
Houndmills, Basingstoke, Hampshire RG21 6XS and
175 Fifth Avenue, New York, N.Y. 10010
Companies and representatives throughout the world

PALGRAVE MACMILLAN is the global academic imprint of the
Palgrave Macmillan division of St. Martin's Press, LLC and of Palgrave
Macmillan Ltd. Macmillan® is a registered trademark in the United States,
United Kingdom and other countries. Palgrave is a registered trademark
in the European Union and other countries.

ISBN–13: 978–1–4039–9641–1
ISBN–10: 1–4039–9641–5

This book is printed on paper suitable for recycling and made from fully
managed and sustained forest sources.

A catalogue record for this book is available from the British Library.

A catalogue record for this book is available from the Library of Congress.

10   9   8   7   6   5   4   3   2
16   15   14   13   12   11   10   09   08   07

Printed and bound in Great Britain by
Antony Rowe Ltd, Chippenham and Eastbourne

Contents

List of Figures

List of Tables

List of Abbreviations

ASRK	Agency on Statistics of the Republic of Kazakhstan
BEEPS	Business Environment and Enterprise Performance Survey
BCDTU	Belarusian Congress of Democratic Trade Unions
BiH	Bosnia and Herzegovina
CCP	Chinese Communist Party
CEB	Council of Europe Development Bank
CEEC	Central and East European countries
CIS	Commonwealth of Independent States
CME	Coordinated market economy
ČSÚ	Český Statistický Úřad (Czech Statistical Office)
CPI	Consumer Price Index
EAKL	Eesti Ametiühingute Keskliit (Confederation of Estonian Trade Unions)
EBRD	European Bank for Reconstruction and Development
EIRO	European Industrial Relations Observatory
EIU	Economist Intelligence Unit
ESC	Economic and Social Council
EP	Employment protection
EPL	Employment protection legislation
ETTK	Eesti Töändjate Keskliit (Estonian Employers' Confederation)
EU	European Union
FBiH	Federation of Bosnia and Herzegovina
FDI	Foreign direct investment
FOB	Free on board
FPI	Foreign portfolio investment
FTUB	Federation of Trade Unions of Belarus
GDP	Gross Domestic Product
GDR	German Democratic Republic
GERD	Gross Domestic Expenditure on R&D
GSE	Georgian Stock Exchange
GTZ	Gesellschaft für Technische Zusammenarbeit
HRIDC	Human Rights Information and Documentation Center
ILO	International Labour Organization
IMF	International Monetary Fund
IOM	International Organization for Migration

IPB	Investiční a poštooní banka (Investment and Post Office Bank)
ISIC	International Standard Industrial Classification
JSC	Joint-stock company
KZT	Kazakhstan Tenge (Kazakhstan currency)
LME	Liberal market economy
NACE	Nomenclature Statistique des Activitiés économiques dans le Communauté Européenne (Statistical Classification of Economic Activities in the European Community)
NGO	Non-government organization
NSCG	National Securities Commission of Georgia
OECD	Organisation for Economic Cooperation and Development
OPEC	Organization of Petroleum Exporting Countries
PIF	Privatization Investment Fund
PPP	Purchasing Power Parity
R&D	Research and Development
RCA	Revealed comparative advantage
RMB	Renminbi (Chinese currency)
RS	Republika Srpska
SAA	Stabilization and Association Agreement
SASAC	State Asset Supervision Administration Commission
SCF	State-controlled fund
SF banks	System forming banks
SITC	Standard International Trade Classification
SMIC	State Medical Insurance Company
SME	Small and medium-sized enterprise
SOE	State-owned enterprise
TALO	Teenistujate Ametiliitude Keskorganisatsioon (Estonian Employees' Unions' Confederation)
UK	United Kingdom
UN	United Nations
UNCTAD	United Nations Conference on Trade and Development
UNDP	United Nations Development Programme
UP	Unemployment protection
USAID	United States Agency for International Development
VET	Vocational Education and Training
VoC	Varieties of Capitalism
WTO	World Trade Organization
ZSSS	Zveza Svobodnich Sindikator Slovenije (Association of Free Trade Unions of Slovenia)

Notes on the Contributors

Will Bartlett is Reader in Social Economics at the University of Bristol. His recent research has been into economic and social development and post-war reconstruction in South-East Europe and he has carried out several research projects on the role of small businesses in promoting sustainable development in the region. Recent publications include *Croatia: Between Europe and the Balkans* (London: Routledge, 2003).

Clemens Buchen studied economics at the European University Viadrina in Frankfurt (Oder). He currently works as a research assistant at the Department of Economics of the European Business School in Wiesbaden. In his doctoral research he studies emerging economic systems in Eastern Europe.

Ken Charman is an economist specializing in transition economies. He has been a policy adviser to governments in Eastern Europe and the Middle East since 1993, and has lived and worked in Kazakhstan, Belarus and Syria. He has an MBA and a PhD (Economics) from London Business School and is a member of the London Business School Centre for New and Emerging Markets, and the Centre for Euro-Asian Studies, University of Reading. He has published a number of articles on economic transition and on joint-venture activity in transition economies.

Barbara Christophe is a political scientist at the European University of Viadrina in Frankfurt (Oder). Her research work concentrates on nationalism, state-building, ethnic conflicts and local-level politics in the post-Soviet space. She has conducted intensive field work in Lithuania, Georgia and Kyrgyzstan. At the moment she is conducting a comparative research project on the dynamics of hybrid regimes in Georgia, Ukraine and Kyrgyzstan.

Philip Hanson is Professor of the Political Economy of Russia and Eastern Europe (Retired Emeritus) and an Associate Fellow of the Royal Institute of International Affairs Russia and Eurasia Programme. His research interests include comparative economic systems, the Soviet and Russian economies and the economics of transition. He has recently been working on business–state relations in Russia and on the assessment of Russian economic policies. Recent publications include *The Rise and Fall of the Soviet Economy* (Harlow: Pearson Education, 2003).

Mark Knell studied economics at the New School for Social Research, New York. He is Senior Research Fellow at the Norwegian Institute for Studies in Research and Education – Centre for Innovation Research (NIFU STEP) in Oslo and has been a consultant to several UN agencies. Mark has published extensively on the transition economies and is currently doing research on technology, innovation and economic growth in the European context.

Julia A. Korosteleva is a Research Assistant (Statistician) in Politics at Glasgow University, working on an ESRC-funded project. After three years' experience of work as a Senior Economist in one of the Belarusian banks, Julia has undertaken a Doctoral Degree at the Department of Economics and International Development, University of Bath, UK. Her research interests lie in the field of transition economics and financial development and economic growth.

David Lane is Senior Research Associate in the Faculty of Social and Political Sciences at the University of Cambridge. He is currently the recipient of a Leverhulme Research award to study the relationship of class to transformation in Ukraine and Russia. His recent books include: *The Legacy of State Socialism* (editor and contributor) (Maryland and Oxford: Rowman and Littlefield, 2002) and *Russian Banking: Evolution, Problems and Prospects* (Cheltenham, UK; Northampton, MA, USA: Edward Elgar, 2002) (editor and contributor).

Martin Myant is Professor in the Paisley Business School, University of Paisley. He has written extensively on economic and political development in East-Central Europe, particularly the Czech Republic. Among his recent publications is *The Rise and Fall of Czech Capitalism: Economic Development in the Czech Republic since 1989* (Cheltenham, UK; Northampton, MA, USA: Edward Elgar, 2003).

Vlad Mykhnenko worked on, and completed, a PhD at Darwin College, University of Cambridge, from October 1999 to May 2005, comparing the forms of capitalism in Poland and Ukraine. He subsequently worked as an International Policy Fellow, Open Society Institute, Budapest and has been working since February 2005 as a Research Fellow in the Centre for Public Policy for Regions, University of Glasgow, Scotland.

Rudi Schmidt, Professor of Sociology, has held university and research posts at the Universities of Berlin, Erlangen and Jena. He was Chair of the Sociology of Work Committee of the German Sociological Association 1991–3 and is a member of the Commission for the Study of the Social and Political Change in East Germany from 1991 to 1996. Research interests include the sociology of work, industrial relations, the modernization of industry and production systems and transition societies in East-Central Europe.

Martin Srholec is a post-doctoral research fellow in the Centre for Technology, Innovation and Culture (TIK) at the University of Oslo. He has published in the areas of innovation studies, economic growth and international trade and investment. His current research interests include patterns of innovation and entrepreneurship at the micro-level and the role of global production networks for economic development.

Elizabeth Teague is an analyst of Russian politics with the Foreign and Commonwealth Office, London. She has also worked for Radio Free Europe/ Radio Liberty in Munich, as an adviser to the OSCE High Commissioner on National Minorities in The Hague, for the Jamestown Foundation and for the UK Ministry of Defence. She graduated from the Universities of Surrey and Birmingham. The views expressed here are personal and should not be taken as representing those of the UK Government.

Jeanne Wilson is Professor of Political Science at Wheaton College in Norton, MA, and a research associate at the Davis Center for Russian and Eurasian Research at Harvard University. Her research interests include the politics of transition in China and Russia and Russian–Chinese relations. She is the author of *Strategic Partners: Russian–Chinese Relations in the Post-Soviet Era* (Armonk, NY: M.E. Sharpe, 2004), and is currently working on a research project examining the impact of internationalization on domestic policy in Russia and China.

Introduction

All the former state socialist countries have, over recent years, transformed or reformed their economies. This book addresses the question of how far they have changed into capitalist systems and, if so, what kind of capitalism they have developed, or are developing. The collection of papers has been the subject of two conferences of participants. The first, organized by David Lane, constituted the Thirteenth Research Seminar of the Managing Economic Transformation (MET) Network, supported by the Jean Monnet Centre for Excellence, and held at the University of Cambridge, 12 March 2004. The second workshop was organized by Martin Myant at the University of Paisley on 23 and 24 September 2005, supported by the university's Business School. The contributors were asked to consider how far the societies in transformation from state socialism carry a common footprint from their communist pasts, or whether other factors have led to divergences in the kinds of capitalism that are emerging. An initial framework is provided by the considerable literature on the 'varieties of capitalism' in advanced economies, but it becomes clear that even these different frameworks need to be applied flexibly and sensitively. It also becomes clear that comparisons between countries using accessible quantitative indicators reveal only part of the story. Legal and institutional frameworks can appear similar between countries and yet have very different meanings in the different contexts; the quantitative data also do not address the role of causal factors. This is revealed by a study of development in individual countries alongside the attempt to make generalizations across countries.

The book is divided into four sections. There are two introductory chapters which outline different approaches to the 'varieties of capitalism' paradigm and consider comparatively the types of society which have emerged after the fall of state socialism. The following three parts of the book are case studies of a range of post-communist societies, chosen to cover a range of different geographical locations. In each case, the authors have studied the extent to which the country fits into the 'varieties of capitalism' framework. On the basis of the discussion in Chapter 1, we have organized the chapters under three different headings, representing the extent to which an initial analysis would suggest that the societies have transformed. In Part II, we focus on those countries which have made a fairly successful transition; by this we mean, have constructed a competitive market economy with private property. In Part III, we define a number of 'hybrid' economies. By 'hybrid' we mean economies which have concurrently more than one form of coordination: they include substantial components of the institutions and processes of the former state socialist societies (such as significant state property) in conjunction with mechanisms adopted from market economies. In Part IV, we consider two 'statist' societies. These might also be considered in some sense to have hybrid parts; here, however, the degree of economic and political change is at a qualitatively lower level and significant institutional structures of state socialism continue. They are therefore statist, but operate in a market framework. The Appendix, prepared by Vlad Mykhnenko, contains a comprehensive collection of economic and social indicators for the period of transformation.

In the introductory chapter, David Lane considers the criteria by which one may distinguish modern capitalism from other types of capitalism as described by Marx, Weber and Schumpeter. Against this background he outlines the transition from state socialism. While market systems based on private ownership have been constructed in all but three of the former state socialist societies discussed here, he defines a gap between the central European former socialist societies and those in the heartland of the former USSR. A major problem for all the former socialist societies is the low level of internally sourced investment and capital accumulation. All have relatively low levels of stock market capitalization. They all differ from Western modern capitalism by having higher levels of state ownership and control of the economy. He contends that the Central European societies have developed the preconditions of modern capitalism; in this they have been strongly influenced by the conditionality of the European Union and other international economic institutions. A second group of countries form a hybrid or mixed type of uncoordinated capitalism. Not only do they have low levels of domestically sourced investment, but they also lack the psychological, political and societal preconditions to support a modern type of capitalism. He contends that a state-led type of social formation is a possible way for these societies to develop.

A third group of countries (illustrated by Belarus and China in the present collection) have not made the breakthrough to a capitalist-type system. They remain in the mould of statist societies and are likely to continue to do so, unless propelled in another direction by exogenous forces.

Mark Knell and Martin Srholec consider the post-state socialist countries in the context of other major industrialized ones. In defining the type of capitalism, they focus on three major components: institutional arrangements of social cohesion, labour market regulation and business regulation. They find that social cohesion in general is linked to the level of development. Most of the post-communist countries fall into a group of low GDP and liberal forms of social coordination. Remarkably perhaps, they find that Russia is even more liberal than the USA. For labour market regulation, there is a mixed picture, with Ukraine being highly regulated and Russia being more liberal. In terms of business regulation, there is again a spread of countries ranging over the liberal-coordinated range, with Russia, Lithuania and Hungary being more 'liberal' than the USA. Strategic coordination differs greatly between different countries. Both the introductory chapters make the point that there is no one single model of a 'post-state socialist economy'. Knell and Srholec point out that the footprint of state socialism is a major determinant of the character of the economy developed after transformation.

Clemens Buchen studies two small countries, Estonia and Slovenia. These he contends, despite similarities in the period of state socialism, now form two contrasting states as far as their forms of coordination are concerned. He considers comparatively five aspects in terms of different types of coordination: industrial relations; corporate governance; inter-firm relations; social security; and vocational training. He also addresses the important question of the extent to which comparative institutional advantage influences the development of different types of economic activity. Overall, his conclusion is that Slovenia, with a 'stakeholder' approach, is moving towards a corporatist's type of economy, with a complement of institutions, something like its neighbours, Germany and Austria. Estonia, on the other hand, is more individualistic; it has more decisively jettisoned Soviet-style norms and has greater similarities with the Anglo-American model.

Rudi Schmidt studies the unique case of the former German Democratic Republic which lost its own political identity when united with the Federal Republic. He emphasizes the great economic differences which persist between the two areas of Germany. The East has the character of a depressed area, with high levels of unemployment and low wages, and it is lacking in investment. The provisions of the German welfare state have to be made available to the citizens in the East. Thus the former Western Germany acts as a conduit for economic and social transfers to the East giving it the character, in the opinion of many, of a dependency economy. Schmidt points out that it has been impossible to 'export' the West German model. Again the historical model of state socialism, compounded by the conditions of transition, brings its own footprint to the construction of the East German economy. The East German economy is unattractive to foreign investment and is likely to be dependent on the West for a considerable time. Paradoxically, the conditions in the East are more favourable to the Anglo-American model, and are likely to push the former Western areas in that direction.

The Czech Republic is often considered one of the most successful state socialist countries to have transited to capitalism. Martin Myant's study focuses on the particular features of construction of capitalism. His chapter brings out the fact that even the Czech Republic has not reached a settled form of capitalist society. The early years of transformation were concerned with the creation of a capitalist class. He points out that privatization, in itself, is not a sufficient condition for the creation of capitalism; it may lead to a class whose main intent is to become rich from wealth ownership. Czech development involved a number of stages. First, there was an attempt to create a 'Czech' version of capitalism – based mainly on Czech ownership. This was followed by extensive encouragement of foreign ownership of capital and inward investment, giving rise to a more 'European' type of capitalism. This was contingent with the political move to join the European Union, which set accession standards and in turn influenced the developments taking place. Myant, however, is unable to fit the evolving system into any of the recognized paradigms of capitalism. He notes some movement to the liberal market economy (LME) model in respect of wage bargaining; however, in the sphere of social policy, the society is strongly social-democratic.

Vlad Mykhnenko compares Poland and Ukraine. In terms of economic reform indicators, Poland would appear to be a consolidated market economy, having met the requirements for entry to the European Union. Mykhnenko, however, finds many similarities. Both are 'mixed' or 'weakly coordinated' market economies. He compares five different aspects of the evolving economies: product-market regulation, the wage–labour nexus and labour-market institutions, the financial system and corporate governance, the social protection sector, and the education and knowledge sector. In the product market field, both countries have high regulation and are comparable to the Mediterranean model as suggested by Bruno Amable. Poland has moderate employment protection compared to Ukraine's high level. Ukraine is more in line with a neo-corporatist system. In both countries there is an undeveloped financial system. Both countries have a minimum-universal system of social protection. Overall, neither of the countries has adopted features of the Anglo-American model of capitalism and both have adopted a form of 'social market' regulated capitalism. As in other chapters in this book, the varieties of capitalism paradigm provide only limited explanations of developments, and Mykhnenko points to the role of historical legacies, the types of industrial assets and 'global power networks'.

Philip Hanson and Elizabeth Teague consider Russia. They do not find existing varieties of capitalism very useful to explain developments; rather they would point to a Weberian form of 'political capitalism'. The absence of supportive structures associated with a 'liberal market economy' is crucial in Russia. The society lacks an adequate financial system, an independent judiciary and government efficiency. The state is of supreme importance, particularly since the advent of President Putin. Russia, unlike the other states described in this book, is also dependent on natural resources and large companies running them. This sector provides the state with the largest share of its income. The privatization process, in the early years of transformation, was accompanied by widespread corruption and was widely regarded as illegitimate. State control over resources is not only popular but crucial for the maintenance of state power. Hanson and Teague also point to the international context and the interdependencies of markets and finance for the natural resources sector. However, they consider that such forces are unlikely to have a short-run effect, and will take a long time to affect the nature of the political economy.

Barbara Christophe's study of Georgia highlights many of the factors which make the 'varieties of capitalism' approach difficult to apply to, and even irrelevant to, at least some of the post-socialist countries under transition. The macro-features of economic change have been rapid and massive decline – deindustrialization, disinvestment and ruralization. Essentially, the economy lacks a coherent set of institutions. She points to the effects of competing donor organizations which have provided significant economic resources and have shaped the forms of regulation taken by the donor recipients. In Georgia, attempts to 'import' copies of German and American institutions have implanted contradictory and conflicting norms. The institutions have not succeeded in forming an incentive structure. An alternative paradigm of political capitalism is postulated, though it in turn is considered to be faulted, on the grounds that 'political capitalism' is usually applied to pre-modern societies. In the modern society of Georgia, it is contended that the political elites *cultivate* a perverse and parasitic order of capitalism having the form of 'organized chaos'.

Kazakhstan is also considered, by Ken Charman, to be a dual-type economic structure. He points to two parallel developments. First, the move to markets has some features of the liberal market economy (LME) model. He notes that the formal rules on corporate governance, inter-firm relations, employment, industrial relations, training and education and the absence of a strong supportive social policy look similar to those in the LME societies. However, the formal rules lack effective implementation by an independent judiciary. Unlike the LME model, the banking system is undeveloped, as is the stock exchange, as a mechanism of economic coordination. The second set of developments lies in the role of the state. This maintains a strong hold through ownership and control of major strategic industries: energy, transport and communications. The President's office functions as a major economic coordinating body with control over investment, legal enforcement and provision of social services. The state effectively channels resources from energy profits to the social infrastructure. Charman suggests that the political economy is moving to a system of a *state*-led liberal economy. This is unlike the state-led capitalism in which the state interacts with capitalist corporations, but one in which it (by virtue of ownership of strategic industries, and control of legal enforcement) plays a hegemonic role. Charman contends that such a system might be followed by other oil-rich economies, such as Azerbaijan and Turkmenistan.

Will Bartlett, in his chapter on the Western Balkans, reminds us that war was a concomitant of transformation for Croatia, Bosnia and Herzegovina, Serbia and Kosovo, Macedonia and Albania. The Western Balkans then relied on international and donor aid for assistance, which in turn led to policy transfer and uncoordinated advice. The upshot is that the institutions in these countries are not complementary or compatible. Even with the more pluralistic approach of Bruno Amable, the Western Balkans does not fit into any of the conventional boxes of different types of capitalism. He examines the countries of the West Balkans from the standpoint of the five criteria utilized by Amable: product market; labour market; financial-intermediation; social security system and protection and education. Despite the fact that four of the five countries started from a fairly similar staring point, as constituent parts of Yugoslavia, the upshot, he suggests, is three types of capitalist economies. Despite their many inconsistencies and ambiguities, Croatia and Macedonia, he contends, are evolving towards a continental European model. The second group, Albania and Kosovo, appear to be moving towards a liberal market economy.

However, it has its own specific character; there is more scope for the operation of organized crime and a stronger reliance on informal institutions. The third group, Serbia, Montenegro, Bosnia and Herzegovina, has more similarities with the Mediterranean model described by Amable, with the added presence of black market activities.

The final section of the book concludes with the study of two states which have maintained many of the components of the traditional system of state socialism. Belarus is discussed by Julia A. Korosteleva, who concludes that it fits none of the typologies of capitalist economies suggested by either Hall and Soskice or Amable. She contends that it is state capitalist. This not only involves state ownership but also limitations on profits in the private sector. The government coordinates investment, manages demand and sets low interest rates, thus stimulating credit expansion. Capital flows and foreign exchange are controlled and tariffs protect trade. In many ways the processes of the former planned economy continue. However, the enterprises previously subordinated to state ministries were turned into joint-stock companies with the government maintaining a dominant ownership interest. The state also maintained its control over strategic decisions, irrespective of the share of ownership and controlled prices and profit margins. Economic policy was not based on the IMF-type of monetary stabilization, but favoured the maintenance of full employment in which it succeeded in keeping unemployment at very low levels, and labour was employed at centrally determined wage levels. The banking system functioned as state agents and the stock exchange mainly dealt in government securities. Social protection continued largely under state control and secured low rates of poverty and relatively equal income distribution. The system in Belarus, therefore, is not a market-driven economy and cannot be considered in existing paradigms of the 'variety of capitalism' types.

Jeanne Wilson points out that while China is officially a 'socialist market economy' it has moved towards legitimating private property. However, it remains a state governed by the Communist Party. Its somewhat ambiguous dualism – a socialist state with aspects of capitalism – is distinctive because of its remarkable economic growth and progress. While the 'varieties of capitalism' approach is not directly applicable to China, Wilson considers it useful to clarify different components in the transformation process. Some of the reform mechanisms in China are consistent with the liberal market economy model, whereas others – the quest to establish large-scale conglomerates – appear closer to the Asian model. Other features include a commitment to globalization, while maintaining a strong role for the state. As in other post-communist states, the state, rather than the firm, is a crucial form of coordination, as well as being a transformative agent. Not only has the state led institutional changes towards the market and the global economy, but it has also designated 'pillar' industries of strategic importance and sheltered them from market competition: hence bureaucratic as well as market forms of coordination continue side by side. The thrust of reforms, it is contended, are in the mould of the liberal market economy: privatization, liberalization of trade, encouragement of FDI and fiscal reform. A major difference, however, is the absence of the market as a determinant of capital allocation, a role still performed, to a considerable extent, by the political leadership.

The picture that emerges is of considerable diversity among the post-communist countries, but there are also a number of identifiable common themes. The first is the implication of the initial absence of capitalists and of matching forms of financial intermediation. The extent to which these gaps have been filled varies between countries. It was not resolved by the processes of privatization and destatization – unlike some other elements of a market system such as price liberalization which proved relatively straightforward. Nor was it a simple matter to create an effective legal framework. Even when laws were imported from mature market economies, the institutional structures of a modern system of financial intermediation, dependent on trust and habits built up over a long time period, could not emerge quickly. 'Importing' from the West also had its own problems: donor organizations often advocated incompatible systems of laws.

A second common theme is the nature of political life, in the broadest sense, to include both the behaviour of those in power and the wider participation of citizens and representative organizations. A number of countries retained regimes that were, to varying degrees, authoritarian and repressive. This hampered the development of features of a coordinated market economy, as described by Hall and Soskice, in which voluntary cooperation between actors is important. It also precluded the development of an independent legal system that is required for a standard liberal market economy. However, it sat reasonably comfortably with low levels of labour protection and freedom for smaller businesses, albeit with some apparently unnecessary regulation that may at least benefit state officials. There is, then, frequently an appearance of features familiar from a liberal market economy alongside substantial differences in the development of the business sphere.

Countries that have come closer to the 'standard' democratic model may have a basis for something closer to a coordinated market economy. Labour legislation often reflects restrictions from the past and the subsequent influence of the European Union and structures have been created for permanent consultation with trade unions and employers' representatives. There are, then, some coordinated market economy elements, but differences in the business sphere overrule any such easy classification. Many of the contributors, in emphasizing the role of the state, turn to earlier versions of 'political capitalism' and current types of 'state capitalism' to capture the peculiar features of transformation of the former state socialist societies.

A third common theme is the unsettled, and often provisional, appearance of features that are often used as indicators in the variety of capitalism literature. These societies are still undergoing substantial changes. The outcome, in most cases, will be a variety of capitalism. Some features may already be clear, but the variety, to varying degrees, has still to take a definite shape. The various contributions confirm that transformation is taking place, but a transition to what remains uncertain.

Part I
The 'Varieties of Capitalism' Paradigm and Post-Communist Countries

1
Post-State Socialism: A Diversity of Capitalisms?*

David Lane

The disintegration of the state socialist societies in the early 1990s left ambiguous the type of political and economic order which was to replace them. Their fall was not a consequence of the classical pattern of revolution, in which an alternative *ex ante* economic system was postulated in the political policy of the reformers. The major systemic changes advocated by the reformers were the removal of the dominant Communist Party and its replacement by democratic forms and a move to markets in place of centralized planning. There was no major claim that capitalism would form an alternative economic and political system. Only after the Communists had left power was capitalism publicly advocated as a means to further democracy and public well-being. The new leaders in these societies, in alliance with those in the hegemonic capitalist world, set out to create, on the ashes of state socialism, a social system having a capitalist market economy, a polyarchic polity and a pluralist civil society. Such intentions, however, left problematic the component parts of the type of capitalism which might be constructed and the ways that a system transfer could be effected on the institutions of state socialism. The most favoured economic model is that of neo-liberalism, the Anglo-American type of capitalism, which was adopted by the major policy makers. (On the components of this policy, see Williamson 1990).

The focus of this book is the type of political economy which has been created: other aspects – polyarchy and civil society – are the topics of other works. Moreover, as some commentators have contended that 'capitalism' is not the outcome of the 'social transformation' (see particularly Zaslavskaya 1999: 149; see also Chapters 9, 11 and 12 by Julia Korosteleva, Jeanne L. Wilson and Barbara Christophe) of post-socialism, it is necessary to define in a more analytical manner what we mean by the term and the forms it may take.

The papers in this book take as a vantage point the growing literature on Varieties of Capitalism (Hall and Soskice 2001; Amable 2003). It is contended, however, that the Varieties of Capitalism approach does not capture the dynamics of the economic systems in the countries undergoing transformation. The divergences from these approaches and the peculiarities of the former state socialist societies are shown in many of the following chapters as well as in this one. These theories are predicated mainly on the advanced stable industrialized countries of the OECD. Capitalism, however, may take many different forms.

Modern capitalism

Even before the Varieties of Capitalism debate, which has evolved in the late 1990s, many have recognized different types of capitalism, and the ways modern capitalism evolved from other formations. Weber and Marx differentiated between booty capitalism, merchant capitalism, modern capitalism, monopoly capitalism and state capitalism; also, 'pariah' capitalism, pursued by marginal trading groups (such as Jews or Parsees in non-capitalist formations) (Gerth and Mills 1948: 66–7). The major distinction for Weber was between 'political capitalism' and modern capitalism. In the former, opportunities for profit are derived from 'the exploitation of warfare, conquest and the prerogative of political administration' (Gerth and Mills 1948: 66); profits are made from various forms of political domination. This is what many contemporary untheorized commentaries on 'mafia capitalism' and bureaucratic domination have in mind[1] when they consider the post-socialist countries. This approach is discussed below in Chapter 7 by Philip Hanson and Elizabeth Teague, and Chapter 9 by Barbara Christophe.

Modern capitalism was defined by Weber as 'the pursuit of profit and forever renewed profit, by means of continuous, rational, capitalistic enterprise' (Weber 1970: 17). By rational economic conduct he meant the making of profit and, for the labourer, the maximization of income. Capitalism is predicated on a market, formally free labour and a psychological predisposition to adopt rational economic conduct, the 'ethos of the capitalist economic system, the spirit of capitalism'. This entails the avoidance of spontaneous spending for enjoyment and the continual reinvestment of profits for accumulation of capital. Similarly, Marx emphasized the role of accumulation. For Marx, the capitalist mode of production involved the continual growth of the forces of production: this was ensured by the extraction of surplus value (profit) through market competition of autonomous productive units (capitals).[2]

The institution of private ownership of property in a market system is crucial. It is not only Marxists who regard the institution of private property as the cornerstone of capitalism, but also many ideologists of capitalism, such as Frank H. Knight and Ludwig von Mises. A capitalist class predicated on rights of ownership of property and of the proceeds of production gives the necessary incentive to accumulate capital. The implication here for the post-communist societies is that a capitalist class had to be created, and formed relatively early in the period of transition to capitalism.

Exchange of commodities and services for profit cannot exist without markets. They promote the efficient exchange of goods and services and the creation of surplus which may be used for investment: 'The market mechanism is a form of economic organization in which individual consumers and business interact through markets to determine the central problems of economic organization' (Samuelson and Nordhaus 1985: 234). Market systems involve the spontaneous activities of individuals and groups in the advancement of their own interest(s). Freedom is a characteristic of market systems because it allows the opportunity for individual choice and activity. Autonomous subsystems are defining features of a market system which constitute civil society. The state has an important but restricted role in the coordination of economic and social life; it cannot suppress entrepreneurship, the market and private ownership of property. The dynamic process of capitalism is the institutionalization of capital investment, or the accumulation of capital. In the ideology of the 'Washington consensus', which guided the transition process, private property, markets, pluralism and civil society are interrelated components of a capitalist system.

To promote accumulation, a banking system and entrepreneurship are required. In Schumpeter's definition: 'Capitalism is that form of private property economy in which innovations are carried out by means of borrowed money, which in general, though not by logical necessity, implies credit creation'; and the individuals who carry out these innovations 'we call entrepreneurs' (cited in Bottomore 1985: 36).

For both Weber and Marx, the economic system and economic institutions were the critical variables, but capitalism and the capitalist mode of production are not limited to economic institutions. Analysis has to understand the ways the economy is embedded in political and social institutions which provide leadership and legitimacy, scientific innovation, social cohesion and/or forms of division and conflict. Important components promoting cohesion in society are the state, class and ideology. A sociological interpretation would consider the integrative mechanisms in society, the institutions which maintain cohesion: a value system, a dominant bourgeois class, and institutions (such as the state) promoting social, political and economic coherence.

I would therefore propose to define modern, really existing, capitalism as: a system of production taking place for global market exchange, utilizing money as a medium which determines differentials of income, levels of investment and the distribution of goods and services; productive assets are privately (collectively or individually) owned, and profit leading to accumulation is a major motive of economic life. The state, which is embedded in a more or less pluralistic society, establishes an effective system of law, securing private property and rights of owners over the proceeds of production. There is a dominant legitimating ideology of polyarchy, which entails competition between parties and groups for influence over the legislature and executive arm of state government and a sphere of autonomy, civil society (including the economy), between the individual (or family) and the state. Individual states are located in a global market which itself exerts autonomous pressures on, and limits the power of, states.

In a more structural sense, one might define an 'ideal type' of modern capitalism as having eleven major features, which all capitalist countries share to a greater or lesser extent, as set out in Table 1.1.

Not all 'actually existing' capitalist countries share these features to the same extent or pattern, which forms the basis of the Varieties of Capitalism approach. Marx is rarely recognized as a forerunner of theories of 'divergent capitalisms' but, when comparing German capitalism to British capitalism, he pointed to the 'incompleteness' of capitalist development, and to the 'passive survival of antiquated modes of production' in the former country (Marx 1956: 9). Also he noted the ways in which the needs of social solidarity modified the interests of capital and led to the growth of socialistic elements within early British capitalism.[3]

By the twenty-first century, the analysis of capitalism has taken other forms. There are three major approaches: Peter Hall and David Soskice (2001), David Coates (2000) and Bruno Amable (2003). These writers point to a number of different 'paradigms' of capitalism, each with their specific features and complementarities. The models give insight into the different forms taken in the post-state socialist countries which, I contend, are consolidating into different groups of societies but quite unlike those defined by these authors.

The work of Hall and Soskice takes as a defining factor the ways in which the activities of firms are coordinated. They consider two ideal types of coordination of modern capitalism: liberal market (LME) and coordinated (CME) (sometimes referred to as 'organized') market economies. The

Table 1.1 Components of modern capitalism

Economic:
1. Private ownership of the means of production
2. Market monetary exchange of commodities for profit, leading to renewed accumulation of capital
3. Competition between units of capital (firms, companies)
4. Wage labour

Psychological:
5. Entrepreneurs with the propensity to invest to accumulate capital
6. A work orientation on the part of the population

Political:
7. An appropriate type of government – one with limited powers over the economy and ownership but sufficient to maintain economic and political stability
8. A system of law able to enforce private ownership of property and a free market system

Societal:
9. Ideology – the values of accumulation and private property
10. Civil society giving rise to autonomy of individuals with rights to combination and to the alienation of assets
11. A class structure derived from position in the economic order (1, 2 and 4 above)

liberal market model applies in the 'Anglo-Saxon' societies – the USA, UK, Canada, Australia and New Zealand. Firms here operate through competitive markets in all areas of economic life, with price signals, supply and demand being crucial economic indicators. There is a high level of complementarity between institutions and processes. Such economic systems have high levels of stock-market capitalization, low levels of employment protection, high levels of paid employment and high income inequality. The economy is characterized by mergers and acquisitions which are facilitated through the stock exchange, trade unions are weak and labour is insecure. The market is the primary instrument of economic coordination.

In the second form of economy (CME), firms are coordinated through many non-market relationships. They include network monitoring based on exchange of private information, and collaborative (rather than competitive) relationships within and between firms. For Peter Hall and David Soskice, Germany, Denmark, France and Japan are examples of such systems. They have high rates of employment protection, low stock-market capitalization, relatively lower numbers of working hours and relatively low differentials of income inequality. Company takeovers are relatively rare and trade unions secure the interests of labour. Companies are coordinated through vertical or horizontal associations of firms. While Hall and Soskice point to differences within subtypes of these economies (for example, Japan and Germany on the one hand and Britain and the USA on the other), the similarities between the coordinating mechanisms and complementarity between them point to two generic types of economy.

There are many criticisms of these approaches, even by writers who adopt the Varieties of Capitalism framework, though only two major ones are discussed here. (For more detail see: Whitley 1999; Morgan, Whitley and Moen 2005.) First, the analysis considers only one feature of capitalist economies – the coordination processes of firms. Important and illuminating as this is, being derived from only one dimension of capitalism it conflates into one model very different kinds of societies, when other measures are used. For instance, Japan and Germany have very different types of state provision and dissimilar participation in the international economy. Britain, Canada and the USA also have significant differences with respect to welfare and global reach. Second, the industrial profile (high-tech, primary producers) exposure to the world economy, the 'driving forces' (companies, classes, the state) of accumulation, the forms of innovation and education, as well as types of ownership and control provide other criteria – and give different combinations of countries. David Coates (1999; 2000) and Bruno Amable (2003) extend the analysis to include product-market competition, wage-labour and labour-market institutions, the financial intermediation sector and corporate governance, social protection and the welfare state (Amable 2003: 14). Like the work of Hall and Soskice, these typologies have institutional complementarities. Different groups of societies have congruent economic, political and social institutions: they hold together as coordinated systems of capitalism.

Amable devises five types of capitalism. A *market-based* one is equivalent to Hall and Soskice's liberal market economy. The distinguishing features of the *social-democratic* model (similar to Coates's 'labour'-led capitalism) are moderate employment security, a high level of social welfare, widespread labour retraining and a coordinated wage-bargaining system. The *Continental European* system is similar to the social democratic model, but the welfare state is less developed, the financial system facilitates long-term corporate strategies, wage bargaining is coordinated, and labour retention is less possible than in the social-democratic type. The *Mediterranean model* has more employment protection and less social provision than the Continental European model; a workforce with limited skills and education does not allow for the implementation of high wages and high skills in industrial strategy. The *Asian model* (a variant of Coates's 'state'-led capitalisms) is 'highly dependent on the business strategies of the large corporations in collaboration with the State and centralized financial system'(Amable 2003: 15). Labour is protected through possibilities of retraining and careers within corporations. There is an absence of social protection and also sophisticated financial markets; stability is provided by the large corporation. Amable's model is summarized on Figure 1.1.

A feature shared by all these approaches is that they are predominantly concerned with advanced capitalist countries with relatively high levels of market development and have a long history as capitalist countries. Even Coates's Asian model includes countries such as Singapore (27th in world rank of GDP) and Korea (52nd), which are currently higher than any former state socialist society, except Slovenia (46th). All the components of capitalism (though taking different forms) defined in Table 1.1 above are more or less in place.

The social formation preceding modern capitalism is widely recognized as having a formative influence on its character. The post-communist transformation is different from those considered by Marx and Weber for many reasons: state socialist societies were already advanced forms of industrial society though they lacked markets, money and banks (as instruments of accumulation) and private property. In an institutional sense, under state socialism, there was neither a capitalist class predisposed to accumulation, nor even a critical ideology sympathetic to capitalist norms.

Table 1.2   Five types of modern capitalism

Type	*Country*
Liberal Market	Australia, Canada, UK, USA
Asian	Japan, Korea
Continental European	Switzerland, Netherlands, Ireland, Belgium, Norway, Germany, France, Austria
Social-Democratic	Denmark, Finland, Sweden
Mediterranean	Greece, Italy, Portugal, Spain.

Criteria:
Product markets: (regulated, deregulated)
Labour markets: (flexible, regulated)
Finance: (stock markets, banks, property ownership)
Welfare: (extent and type of welfare state)
Education: (extent and public/private type)

Source: derived from Amable (2003: 173–5).

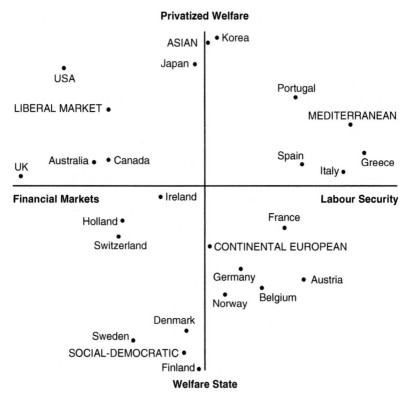

Figure 1.1   Amable's five models of capitalism
Source: based on *Amable* (2003: 173–7).

In the transformation of the post-socialist societies, non-capitalist features are taken from quite a different mould. They had forms of ownership and coordination quite unlike capitalist market societies. In the absence of a free market, the government was the major coordinator of the economy through extensive public ownership of resources, complete control over the issue of money and the direction of investment. Government direction largely determined levels of employment, wages, and division between personal and collective spending. The social basis of pluralistic democracy – a bourgeoisie and the private ownership of assets – did not exist. Pluralistic parliaments had no function.

The state socialist societies, as a whole, had achieved relatively high levels of income and human development.[4] A notable feature of these states was that the Human Development Index had a ranking usually above the ranking of gross domestic product, indicating that resources had been channelled by the state to provide for education and health.[5] This reflected the weakness of the market and the positive role of the state in directing resources to human development. Of course, the state socialist societies were behind the top echelon of industrial states but they all had an advanced industrial base, high literacy and educational attainment and average life expectations of over seventy years – a consequence of adequate housing, food and health care. The 'legacy of socialism' provided a footprint quite different from that which Western capitalist societies have evolved.

In post-communist economies, as well as other developing ones, many components of capitalism are compromised by alien features – non-market economic relationships, the absence of a complementary ideology, of classes of entrepreneurs and capitalists. They are 'transiting', as it were, to capitalism. Analysis, then, must grasp not only the *type* of capitalism, but the *extent* to which capitalism has been constructed.

To determine the scale of capitalism, we need to consider: the extent of private ownership of assets; the presence of a free market and price liberalization; the accumulation of capital; exposure to, and participation in, the global economy; mechanisms for the coordination of capitalist firms; levels of income redistribution and inequality. (In this chapter and generally in this collection, the psychological, political and ideological have been excluded). We consider the ways that the heritage of a state-planned, low-wage employment economy have affected the outcomes.

Policy and economic outcomes of transformation

An assumption of many reformers was that the Soviet Union and other state socialist societies were politically and ideologically bankrupt and presented a *tabula rasa* on which an advanced form of capitalism could be created. The initial policy of marketization and privatization was legitimated by a neo-liberal policy. Advisers from the West advocated a transition to an Anglo-American type of capitalism. Lipton and Sachs (1992: 350–4), two major policy advisers, called for a 'comprehensive' reform process. There were three major policies. First, was the creation of market competition based on 'deregulation of prices, free trade, full liberalization of the private sector and the demonopolization of the state sector' (Lipton and Sachs 1992: 351). The second was a drive to privatization of state property. A significant part of industry could be denationalized immediately: small and medium enterprises, particularly in retail trade. Longer-term strategy was to destatify the state sector. The third policy was to handle disruptive effects of short-term unemployment and poverty; the World Bank would provide support. It was optimistically hoped by Western advisers that the effects of these changes would be positive and that the population would receive immediate benefits, thereby raising levels of support for the policy of markets and the introduction of capitalism. Neo-liberal thinking strongly emphasizes individual property rights and this has been the policy priority of Western advisers. The divesting of state property has been one of the major objectives of the transition process. The neo-liberal argument, as noted by Knight and von Mises above, is that private ownership is an essential initial component: it increases profitability, sales and the utilization of capital (World Bank 1996: 49). Politically and socially, it is a necessary condition for the creation of a capitalist class, the *gravitas* of a capitalist system. To what extent then has a neo-liberal system of capitalism been built on the ashes of communism, and what type of capitalism has arisen?

By 2002, price liberalization was either comprehensive or with only a small number of administered prices comparable to Western market economies. Only Belarus, Turkmenistan and Uzbekistan fell below these levels (EBRD 2003: 16). Most of the transition countries had a private sector contributing more than 60 per cent of their GDP (here and following data taken from EBRD 2003: 16). Privatization[6] of 50 per cent or more of large-scale companies accounted for only six of the twenty-seven countries, another fourteen had achieved a 25 per cent level; for small-scale privatization, the figures were much higher: twenty-one had reached the levels of advanced industrial economies, and another four had comprehensive programmes ready for implementation.

The private sector's share of GDP includes estimates, drawn from both official and unofficial sources, of the extent of informal or unreported economic activity. These figures, even for the most advanced countries, still show a considerable level of state ownership and production: even the most privatized (Hungary, Slovakia, Czech Republic and Estonia) had, in 2002, 20 per cent of GDP from the state sector.

Combining private sector share of GDP and extent of privatization, we may divide the post-state socialist countries into three major blocks as shown in Table 1.3. The top group with levels of privatization scores of over 8 and GDP private sector over 75 per cent contains Slovakia, Hungary, Estonia, Czech Republic, Poland, and Lithuania. A second group of states has 60 or more per cent of GDP originating from the private sector and a privatization score of 6.5 or more; this group includes Bulgaria, Albania, Latvia, Russia, Armenia, Slovenia, Ukraine, Romania, Kyrgizia, Croatia, Macedonia, Georgia and Kazakhstan. A third group, with relatively little

Table 1.3 Private sector share of GDP and privatization index by countries

	Low	Medium	High
High		Lat	Slovak Hun Est Cze Pol Lith
Medium	Mold	Bul Alb Rus Arm Sloven Ukr Rom Kyr Croa Mac Geo Kaz	
Low	Aze Taj Bos Uzb Serb Turkm Belor		
	Low	Medium	High

(vertical axis) **Private sector % of GDP**

Privatization index

privatization or schemes only in preparation, and 60 per cent or less of private production in GDP includes Azerbaijan, Moldova, Tajikistan, Bosnia, Uzbekistan, former Yugoslavia, Turkmenistan and Belorussia. The incidence of privatization and the output of the private sector are highly correlated with a Pearson's *r* of 0.92.

Stock-market capitalization and the provision of credit

One of the major components of the Anglo-American model of capitalism is the open trading of companies on the stock exchange. In 2003, Hong Kong has the highest stock-market capitalization of 456.1 (expressed as a percentage of GDP) followed by Switzerland with 226.7; UK at 134.4, the USA with a figure of 130. Figure 1.2 shows the post-communist

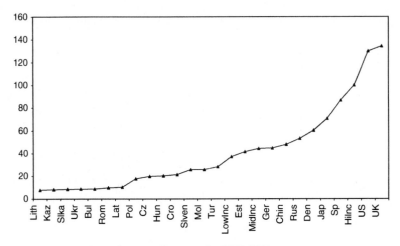

Figure 1.2 Stock-market capitalization (% GDP) 2003

countries, with significant other comparisons (Hong Kong and Switzerland are excluded from the figure).

Other countries of the 'coordinated economies' type are very much lower: Germany's rating is 44.9 and Japan 54.4. Russia and China are the only countries to be ranked above the average for middle-income countries. Russia is exceptional and its rank is based on a relatively small number of very large companies in the primary sector. (This point is developed in Chapter 7 by Hanson and Teague.)

The average figure for the former state socialist societies was only 29.7 in 2003 – a figure just above average of the 'very low income' countries (27.3). Most of the post-socialist countries are below the level of low-income countries. At the bottom end of the scale are Lithuania, Kazakhstan, Slovakia and Ukraine, with indexes under 10. One might conclude that the stock market as a coordinator of the economy (in Hall and Soskice's terms) can be ruled out for all the post-socialist societies. China is the one with a significant level: a relatively high stock-market capitalization and 1,384 firms listed in 2004. Russia has 215 firms, less than Turkey with 296, and the UK with 2,311 and the USA with 5,295 (data from World Bank 2005).

A key variable in capitalist development is the level of investment both domestically and from the world market. The provision of credit to the private sector is a key indicator of the propensity of a capitalist system to

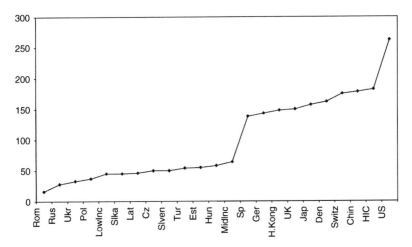

Figure 1.3   Domestic credit formation 2003 (% GDP)
Source: World Bank (2005).

invest. The amount of domestic originated credit to the private sector
(expressed as a percentage of GDP) is shown in Figure 1.3.

In high-income countries the average level of domestic credit to the private sector, as a percentage of GDP, in 2003 was 182; for middle-income
countries 64.3. The average for the post-socialist countries was 37.7; this
is below even the average for low-income countries, which was 45.3.
Domestic credit, of course, includes advances to the domestic sector as
well as small businesses; most investment for companies originates from
internal sources. These data then show both the underdevelopment of the
banks as well as the low levels of consumer credit. The banks were not
functioning to create credit, which is a major factor in the rise of modern
capitalism (for Russian banks, see Lane 2002: ch. 1, esp. 15–17).

Figure 1.3 brings out the striking international differences between
the levels of domestic credit to the private sector: all the industrial countries are clustered to the right-hand side of the chart, all have credit to
GDP ratios of over 150, with a remarkable 262 in the USA: China is also
in this category (178). For the European transition countries, only
Hungary is near the level of middle-income countries (64) and Poland,
Romania, Ukraine and Russia are below the levels of even the low-income
countries. For the post-socialist societies as a whole, the very low levels
of internal investment and accumulation indicate a serious drawback to
their quest to become modern Western-type capitalist countries.

The global dimension

When one turns to foreign investment as a proportion of gross capital formation in the private sector, Table 1.4 shows a quite different picture. For high-income countries, the proportion of capital formation derived from FDI averages around a fifth: Japan is less than 1 per cent, while the UK is exceptional with a high (25.8%) level. China (10.1%) is lower than the average (13.2%) for middle-income countries. Central and Eastern European post-socialist countries (Czech Republic, Croatia, Hungary, Estonia, Poland, Slovakia, Latvia, Kazakhstan, Moldova, Bulgaria, Lithuania,

Table 1.4   Foreign direct investment as percentage of capital formation

Japan	0.6
Slovenia	2.7
Belarus	3.5
Russia	3.6
Low-income countries (average)	3.9
Turkmenistan	6.8
Latvia	8.4
Germany	8.5
China	10.1
Ukraine	10.3
Middle-income countries (average)	13.2
Turkey	13.4
Romania	13.7
East European and Caucasus	13.8
Spain	14.5
Poland	15
USA	15.1
Hungary	17.2
Lithuania	17.3
High-income countries (Average)	19.2
Denmark	21.2
Slovakia	22.6
Bulgaria	25.1
United Kingdom	25.8
Georgia	27.1
Czech Republic	28.9
Croatia	31.4
Moldova	31.5
Estonia	35.2
Kazakhstan	47.9

Source: World Bank (2003: tables 5.1 and 5.2).

Romania and Georgia) all have higher proportions of investment coming from abroad than middle-income countries do; and all (except Belarus and Slovenia) have a very much higher dependency than even low-income countries (average of 3.9).

Data for 1998–2000 indicate that Bulgaria, Moldova and the Czech Republic had over 30 per cent of gross fixed capital formation from FDI flows, and Latvia, Lithuania and Croatia were between 20 and 30 per cent (United Nations 2002: 70). Countries with a very low FDI as well as low rates of domestic investment are Ukraine, Georgia, Turkmenistan, Belarus, Russia and Slovenia. The low level of foreign investment as a share in capital formation is lower than one might expect: this may reflect the bunching of investment for big projects and also the high level of capital export.[7]

Foreign Direct Investment for 2003 for selected countries is shown in Table 1.5. In line with the discussion above, Japan has a very low level of Foreign Direct Investment (FDI), whereas the UK has a higher than average one for high-income countries. The former state socialist countries have a mixed profile: Estonia and Hungary receiving a considerable amount compared to Poland, Ukraine and Czech Republic. Kazakhstan attracted a very high level (as in Table 1.4), reflecting investment in oil. Foreign direct investment has declined in recent years following the end of privatization sales.

Foreign direct investment is only one aspect of the role of globalization; also of importance is the contribution of foreign investment to GDP product and employment and the structure of exports. One informative index here is the transnationality index. This is an average of four different components of transnational activities: FDI inflows as a percentage of gross fixed capital formation for the previous three years (which overcomes somewhat large inward takeovers or projects in any one year); inward stocks as a percentage of FDI in the given year (2000), value added of foreign affiliates as a percentage of GDP in a given year, and employment of foreign affiliates as a percentage of total employment (United Nations 2003: 6). The composition of exports measured in terms of primary and manufactured goods is a good indicator of modernization of the economy.

Developed and developing countries do not differ on average in terms of their transnationality indexes: for the former it is 21 and for the latter 20.05. The indexes for former state socialist countries are much lower, with an average index of 13. Again there are important differences between the different blocks of countries. There is a small group of countries with a very low participation rate: Russia, Belarus, Ukraine have an index below 5. At the other end of the scale are Czech Republic (24), Estonia (25) and

Hungary (27) with rates above that of the average of high-income countries (21). These figures are probably explained by the low foreign ownership in the first three countries – even in the energy extraction industries (due to legal restrictions), and very high levels of foreign ownership in the second. Consequently, the three former Soviet republics have much less dependency on international trade. If one considers the proportion of employment by foreign affiliates (as a proportion of all employment), Hungary has a figure of 27.4 per cent and Latvia 10.4 per cent; the figures for Russia, Ukraine and Belarus are 1.6, 0.7 and 0.3 per cent respectively (United Nations 2002: 275)[8] – for Belarus, the lowest in the world.

The former state socialist societies have an export profile most similar to low-income countries. As a proportion of merchandise exports, primary commodities represent 45 per cent of low income countries' exports, and in the Central and East European countries and former Commonwealth of Independent States (CIS), the figure is 42 per cent; high-income

Table 1.5   Foreign direct investment in selected countries, 2003

	FDI as % of GDP
USA	3
UK	8.6
Germany	4.2
Japan	1
Denmark	9.3
China	4.5
Turkey	0.9
Belarus	1
Czech Rep	3.2
Estonia	14.1
Hungary	10.2
Kazakhstan	9.3
Poland	2.5
Slovakia	4.3
Slovenia	4.8
Russia	5
Ukraine	2.9
High-income Countries (average)	5.2
Middle-income Countries (average)	3.4
Low-income Countries (average)	1.5

Source: World Bank (2005: table 6.1).

countries, on the other hand, have an average in this category of only 15 per cent and middle-income 35 per cent. There are, however, important differences between the post-communist countries. Bulgaria, Lithuania, Latvia, Russia, Moldavia, Kazakhstan and Turkmenistan constitute a group with a share of primary exports higher than the middle-income countries. At the other end is a group with primary exports below the average level of high-income countries: these include Slovenia (the lowest with 10 per cent), Czech Republic, Hungary, Slovakia (15 per cent) – just below the United Kingdom (with 17 per cent).

I plot the combinations of countries in Figure 1.4.

We note only four countries with low primary exports similar to the profiles of high-income industrialized countries: Czech Republic, Hungary, Slovakia, Slovenia; of these, however, the first two have a very high

Transnationality index				
High (more than 20)	Czech Hungary HIGH-INCOME countries (average)	Estonia		
Medium (10–19)	Slovakia	EAST EUROPE (average) Latvia Lithuania Bulgaria Croatia Romania Poland	Moldavia	
Low (less than 10)	Slovenia	Belarus	Russia	Ukraine
No data		LOW-INCOME countries (average) MIDDLE-INCOME countries (average)	Kazakhstan Turkmenia	
	Low (0–10)	Med (15–49)	High (50–)	No data

Primary sector share of exports

Figure 1.4   Transnationality index and primary exports

dependency on foreign investment. At the other end of the scale are four countries with exports over the level of even low-income countries: Moldova, Russia, Kazakhstan and Turkmenia. Finally, a third group of countries have a very low level of dependency on foreign investment: Slovenia, Belarus, Russia and Ukraine. Of these Russia, Kazakhstan, Ukraine, Moldavia and Turkmenia would appear to be countries with a high level of export of primary commodities but with low levels of gross domestic product and investment generated by FDI. These countries are even more dependent on primary sector exports than even low-income countries; countries with a similar level of primary sector exports include, Colombia, El Salvador, Egypt, Morocco and Senegal.

Post-state socialist economic recovery and growth

How then have these developments impacted on the recovery, growth and equity of the post-communist economies? One must qualify the use of the quantitative data shown here. They do not show the processes which took place during the transformation period and, of course, do not show the qualitative changes at the micro level (see King 2003). The objective of the analysis is to utilize the macro-level data, to illustrate and explore comparisons between countries. Figure 1.5 shows first, the level of GDP in the transition countries in 2002, taking 1989 as the base year (100). Secondly, it plots the extent of the private sector for each country, the straight line is the trend line averaging out private sector development. Most of the transition countries were at a lower level of GDP in 2002 than they were at the beginning of the reforms (i.e. below the base of 100), though seven countries (Poland, Slovenia, Albania, Hungary, Slovakia, Uzbekistan and Czech Republic) exceeded the 1989 level. They are followed by thirteen countries at between 70 per cent and 95 per cent of their former level. A third group of countries (Russia, Azerbaijan, Tajikistan, Serbia, Ukraine, Moldova and Georgia) have fallen to between 38 per cent and 65 per cent. Comparing the 2001 rankings on the Human Development Index with those in 1990, nearly all the post-state socialist societies had considerable falls.[9]

There is a positive but not very strong link between GDP recovery and extent of the private sector. The Pearson correlation is +0.26. The trend line has only a shallow upward slope: in other words, as private sector development increases, so does GDP, but only very slightly overall. The chart also brings out deviations between the two variables. There are two countries where private sector growth has been quite substantial but GDP growth is very low (Georgia, Ukraine) and a similar tendency is apparent

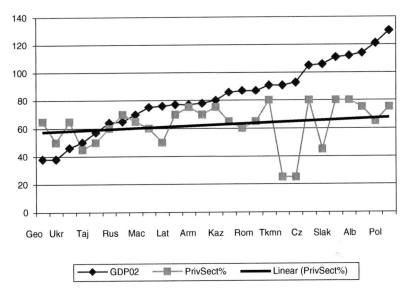

Figure 1.5   GDP (2002) and extent of private sector
Source: EBRD (2003: 18).

in Russia, but to a lesser extent. The cases of Turkmenistan and Belarus are also interesting: here the share of the private sector is the lowest of all the transitional societies, but GDP recovery is in the second group of countries. Uzbekistan and Bosnia Herzegovina have similar but not so severe profiles. Finally, Slovenia (Slen) has a private sector below the trend line but has the second highest level of GDP.

One might make two conclusions from these statistics. First, private sector growth (and privatization) has been pursued with vigour by all but three countries; GDP recovery, however, is not very strongly related to extent of the private sector or privatization. Second, some of those countries which have the lowest levels of private sector growth have not experienced a significantly lower level of GDP growth. State coordination, at least in the first phase of transition, would appear to be at least as successful as market coordination. These points are taken up in more detail in Chapters 8, 11 and 12 on Kazakhstan, Belarus and China.

Income inequality and its correlates

In addition to growth and efficiency, equity is a major component of economic development. One might expect that levels of privatization and

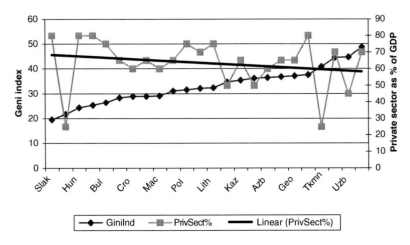

Figure 1.6   Inequality and the private sector

the development of a market economy might have the effect of increasing income inequality. The level of private sector development plotted against inequality is shown in Figure 1.6, using data from 2002.

There is a somewhat uneven relationship between the strength of the private sector and levels of inequality, with a slight tendency for the development of the private sector to be associated with lower levels of inequality. The Pearson correlation coefficient here is −0.185. Similar results are found if we test the association between privatization rank and inequality – the lower the level of privatization, the higher the level of inequality: the Pearson's r is −0.181. The Russian case illustrates a low level of privatization but high levels of inequality. This is related to the privatization of valuable natural resource assets (oil) leading to massive incomes in this sector, the general impoverishment of the society as a consequence of unemployment and depression giving rise to a large stratum of very poor people (see King 2003). Two countries have asymmetric profiles: Belarus has a very lowly developed private sector but one of the lowest levels of inequality whereas Turkmenistan with a similar private sector development has a high level of inequality (data derived from UNDP 2003: 282–5). China is not shown on the graph; as Wilson's chapter in this collection shows (Chapter 12), though poverty has decreased there, inequality has risen as reform measures have taken root.

One might conclude that in the more successful transition countries (Hungary, Czech Republic) the privatization of assets in place of state coordination leads to a labour market raising wage levels and providing employment. However, there are other contextual factors which would need to be examined to explain other cases. Belarus, for example, clearly has a state sufficiently strong to maintain low-income differentials. At the other end of the spectrum, Turkmenistan has not developed the private sector and has either been unwilling or unable to prevent high-income differentials which are probably due to the peculiarities of a primary sector exporting economy. The top five primary sector exporting countries (Kazakhstan, Moldova, Azerbaijan, Turkmenistan and Russia) all have very high Gini coefficients. The correlation between share of primary exports and inequality is very high at +0.689. This is probably explained by the low labour costs and low labour saturation in primary production industries, and high incomes from oil exports being retained by few people, as a consequence of privatization. Possibly, the 'Dutch disease' syndrome, in which a high exchange rate may depress agriculture and manufacturing and consequently lead to unemployment, may be at work in these countries.

The move to stock market capitalization in Western countries is associated with greater inequality of incomes. Here data are available for only fifteen of the post-communist countries and they support the findings of Hall and Soskice. The correlation is high between level of inequality and stock market capitalization at +0.43. Hence, while privatization and the growth of a private sector as such do not increase inequality, stock market capitalization does, probably because it depresses wage levels and increases shareholder profit. While the absolute level of stock market capitalization has been shown to be comparatively low, it is probably associated with a neo-liberal policy, which favours income 'incentives', legitimating inequalities. It also places greater reliance on individualism, and reduces levels of support for the poor.

Conclusions

Following the disintegration of state socialism, a market system based on private ownership and production for profit has been constructed in all but three of the former state socialist societies. Whether these countries have moved to a modern capitalist system is open to question. The consequences of transformation have led to three blocks of post-state socialist countries: two of which are market-oriented and have large private sectors and one cluster of transition 'laggards' which preserve statist economies. Despite the significant policies of destatization, the post-communist societies all share a higher level of state control than market capitalist countries and most have stock market capitalization at the levels of 'low income countries'. The average amount of internally sourced investment for the post-state socialist societies is even below the average for low-income countries. For some, foreign direct investment has been much higher, though this, to a considerable extent, has been due to the privatization of state assets and may not continue at this rate. Some countries (including Ukraine) have both low domestic and foreign investment which gives rise to deindustrialization and de-development. This pattern also applies to Russia to some extent but is mediated by investment in the oil and gas sector.

A similar overall pattern can be detected with respect to the export profile which is similar to low-income countries, though again there is an important divide between the Central European countries and those in the heartland of the former Soviet Union. Private sector development and level of privatization have been shown to be only slightly positively correlated to GDP recovery between 1989 to 2003. However, private sector development and levels of privatization both affect income inequality in the same direction: the higher the measure of private sector development and privatization, the lower the inequality. Stock market capitalization (as in Anglo-American capitalism) is correlated with high-income inequality. However, as the levels of stock market capitalization are relatively low, it may be contingent on associated factors: such as a strong neo-liberal ideology and sector concentration. Here of great importance are the levels of gross national income and non-primary sector exports. Those countries that are poor and have high primary product exports (energy) have very high rates of income inequality. The form privatization has taken may lead to relatively few owners in extractive industries, such as oil, giving rise to great wealth on the one hand and, because of relatively low employment rates and ineffective redistribution policies, to poverty on the other.

Economics is concerned, not only with efficiency, but also with equity. The move to the market and private ownership has significantly diminished equity in the post-communist states – though with the exception of those bordering on the European Union. In terms of social development, the post-communist states have fallen in the world rankings of human development.

One might identify several areas in which all, or nearly all, of the former state socialist countries diverge from the advanced Western ones: they all have a higher level of state ownership and control of the economy and have serious deficiencies in the levels of internally sourced investment. I would suggest that two major types of capitalism are developing. Weber's claim that modern capitalism is distinguished by 'the pursuit of profit and forever renewed profit, by means of continuous, rational, capitalistic enterprise' (Weber 1970: 17; see also King 2003; Lane 2002) applies to the first group but not to the second. The first is closest to the continental type of market capitalism, though it is more state-led. Countries here include the central European countries, Slovenia, Czech Republic, Poland, Hungary, Slovakia and Estonia – all new members of, and having had borders with, the European Union. They are approaching the levels of OECD countries with respect to marketization and privatization, they also have a very positive participation in the global economy. But all have a low level of stock market capitalization and more developed welfare states, making them distinct from the Anglo-American countries. They also have a much lower level of internal accumulation than advanced capitalist countries. Some, but not all, have very high exposure to the global market which acts as an exogenous source of economic change. They resemble, and are likely to identify with, the continental European system as they all have embedded welfare states derived from the state socialist period. Economic coordination here is not through stock exchange capitalism, but is dependent on the state and also on companies with an international presence. Another sub-group is composed of Lithuania, Croatia, Latvia, Romania and Bulgaria which have made a relatively successful move to a market system, though with lower levels of privatization and greater state coordination. Despite low levels of economic accumulation, these societies possess most of the other components of advanced capitalism. Tutored by the conditionality requirements of the EU and the IMF, they have developed not only the economic preconditions of capitalism, but also the political and societal: an appropriate type of government, a civil society and an emerging bourgeois class structure.

A second model is that of a hybrid state/market uncoordinated capitalism. This is a relatively economically poor group which has had an unsuccessful period of transition: Russia, Ukraine, Kazakhstan, Georgia, Turkmenistan and Moldova. These countries have exceedingly high income differentials, and high levels of poverty and unemployment. They have the characteristics of low-income, primary sector exporting countries, with a very low integration into the global economy. They have particularly low levels of domestically sourced investment, though those with a large energy sector have significant foreign direct investments. While they have pursued privatization and market monetary exchange, they lack the psychological, political and societal preconditions necessary to support modern capitalism. The initial period of privatization and destatization led to a weakening of the state and consequently to a period of 'chaotic capitalism'. A chaotic social formation may be defined as a social and economic system which lacks institutional coordination and promotes social fragmentation: goals, law, governing institutions and economic life lack cohesion. Its characteristics are uncertainty about the future, elite disunity, the absence of a dominant and mediating class system, criminalization and corruption, rent-seeking entrepreneurs, inadequate political interest articulation and an economy in decline characterized by inflation, unemployment and poverty.[10] Georgia, as described in Chapter 9 of this volume by Barbara Christophe, is a case study.

Reliance on the state is probably the only way these societies may develop a modern industrial advanced society. State-led capitalism might ensure accumulation. In countries with natural resources, the state would channel economic rents earned from export-oriented industries to support the modernization of the economy and would also channel resources to the private sector through state institutions and banks. Social cohesion in such societies would be provided by a culture steeped in nationalism, and social solidarity would be maintained by a welfare state. The state through political patronage and rule application to a considerable extent supplants an independent legal system. Kazakhstan, as described in Chapter 8 by Ken Charman, is a good example of such 'state-led' capitalism.

Countries in the third group – Uzbekistan, Belarus and Turkmenistan – have not made the breakthrough to a capitalist system: these countries are not driven by market forces, have relatively low levels of private ownership, and have preserved from state socialism high levels of state control, economic coordination and rule enforcement.

They are likely to remain statist economies. These last two groups of countries still preserve major elements of state bureaucratic control, and may be moving in the direction of a form of state capitalism. The footprint of state socialism may 'fit' better into a pattern of cooperative state-led capitalism. State capitalism, in which the state, either directly or through state-owned corporations, operates on internal and world markets, and bureaucratically determines the level and direction of capital accumulation, provides a type of political economy quite different to that which has been tried in the other 'transition societies'. It calls for further discussion in the context of the Varieties of Capitalisms paradigm. While the first and third group of countries have a relatively high and imperfect level of complementarity between their institutions, the second does not and remains in a transitionary state, between market- and state-led economies. Political forces within and outside these societies seek to propel them in the direction of one or the other. In Russia, the Ministry of Economic Development and Trade and the Ministry of

Finance confront the 'power ministries' and social ministries led by President Putin. Criticisms from the liberal viewpoint are summarized by Hanson and Teague in Chapter 7 or the current volume. The Russian leadership, which is generally following the course advocated here, is confronted by very powerful external interests: the IMF, the World Bank, OECD, the European Union, foreign companies seeking profitable investments, sources of materials and markets. The smaller, economically less well-endowed countries of central Europe have had little option but to enter the global marketplace. Russia provides an alternative: production is local in character and regional companies and political actors have considerable scope for action independently of the global economy. With the important exception of the extractive industries, the globalization of finance has had relatively little impact on Russia. The physical endowment of the country can ensure wealth and provide the basis for a corporate economy which could manage better the restructuring of state socialism.

Notes

* An earlier version of this chapter appeared in *Competition and Change*, 9, 227–47, September 2005, published by W.S. Maney & Sons, Leeds.

1. Andrey Piontkovski has opined that 'Putinism is the highest, concluding stage of the capitalism of bandits and officials in Russia, the natural and logical mutation of the preceding Yeltsin model', <http://www.gazeta.ru/2003/12/25/snovymgodomt.shtml>.
2. This is 'a continuous connected process, of reproduction, [which] ... reproduces capitalist relationships: on the one side, the capitalist, on the other the wage-labourer' (Marx, 1958: 578).
3. For instance he noted the role of the factory laws (The Ten Hours Bill) in England which limited the length of the working day as well as the role of the state in sanitation and housing.
4. Data used are life expectancy at birth, adult literacy, mean years of schooling and gross domestic product. Based on data for the 1980s (before the fall of state socialist regimes), seven countries were ranked in the top UNDPs 'high human development' category of fifty-three states (Czechoslovakia (ranked 27), Hungary (30), USSR (31), Bulgaria (33), Yugoslavia (34), Poland (41) and Albania (49)), the rankings are out of a total of 163 countries (UNDP 1991: 119–21).
5. The USA, Denmark, Germany, Turkey and only Romania from the socialist states all had negative deviations (human development rank being below their GDP rank), whereas Hungary, Yugoslavia, Poland and Albania (and especially China) had very significant positive ones.
6. The EBRD estimated the extent of privatization, on a scale with 0 being no privatization and 4.5 (4+ in original) being comparable to advanced industrial

countries. The data are shown separately for large-scale and small-scale privatization (two scales 0 to 4+). I have aggregated into one scale – being a total of nine (I have translated the original – and + signs to −0.5 and +0.5). The definition of a 'private' company includes companies which are not part of the state sector, but they certainly include companies in which various government agencies (local authorities, ministries) hold stakes.

7. World Bank 2003, Table 5.2. This is a three-year average.
8. These data are not given in the 2003 edition.
9. Only Poland had a higher rank than Thailand. These precipitous falls cannot be explained by changes in the database or statistical calculations. In 1990, the USSR was 31; in 2001 its two most populous states, had fallen to 75 (Ukraine) and 63 (Russia), whereas Hungary, Yugoslavia, Poland and Albania (and especially China) had very significant positive scores.
10. I developed this concept in an earlier article covering the initial period of transformation in the Russian Federation (Lane 2000).

References

Amable, Bruno (2003) *The Diversity of Capitalism* (Oxford: Oxford University Press).
Bottomore, Tom (1985) *Theories of Modern Capitalism* (London: Allen and Unwin).
Coates, David (1999) 'Models of Capitalism in the New World Order: the UK Case', *Political Studies*, 47, 643–60.
Coates, David (2000) *Models of Capitalism* (Cambridge: Polity).
EBRD (2003) *Transition Report* (London: European Bank for Reconstruction and Development).
Gerth, H.H. and C.W. Mills (1948) *From Max Weber* (London: Routledge and Kegan Paul).
Hall, Peter A. and David Soskice (2001) *Varieties of Capitalism* (Oxford: Oxford University Press).
King, Larry (2003) 'Shock Privatization; The Effects of Rapid Large-Scale Privatization on Enterprise Restructuring', *Politics and Society*, 31, 3–30.
Lane, David (2000) 'What Kind of Capitalism for Russia? A Comparative Analysis', *Communist and Post-Communist Studies*, 33, 485–504.
Lane, David (ed.) (2002) *Russian Banking* (Cheltenham, UK and Northampton, MA: Edward Elgar).
Lipton, David and Geffrey Sachs (1992) 'Creating a Market Economy in Eastern Europe: the Case of Poland', Brookings Papers on Economic Activity, Vol. 1, 1990. Extract in David Kennett and Marc Lieberman, *The Road to Capitalism* (New York and London: Dryden Press), 350–4.
Marx, K. (1956) *Capital*, Vol. 1 (Moscow: Foreign Languages Publishing House).
Marx, K. (1958) *Capital*, Vol. 3 (Moscow: Foreign Languages Publishing House).
Morgan, G., R. Whitley and E. Moen (2005) *Changing Capitalisms? Internationalization, Institutional Change and Systems of Economic Organization* (Oxford: Oxford University Press).
Samuelson, Paul and William Nordhaus (1985) *Economics* (New York: McGraw-Hill).
United Nations (2002 and 2003) *World Investment Report* (New York and Geneva: United Nations).

UNDP (United Nations Development Programme) (1991) *Human Development Report 1991* (New York and Oxford: Oxford University Press).

UNDP (United Nations Development Programme) (2003) *Human Development Report 2003* (United Nations: UNDP).

Weber, M. (1970) *The Protestant Ethic and the Spirit of Capitalism* (London: Unwin Books).

Whitley, R. (1999) *Divergent Capitalisms: The Social Structuring and Change of Business Systems* (Oxford: Oxford University Press).

Williamson, John (1990) 'What Washington Means by Policy Reform', in J. Williamson (ed.), *Latin American Adjustment: How Much has Happened?* (Washington, DC: Institute for International Economics).

World Bank (2005) *World Development Indicators* (World Bank: Washington DC).

World Bank (2003) *World Development Indicators* (World Bank: Washington DC).

World Bank (1996) *World Development Report: From Plan To Market* (Oxford: Oxford University Press).

Zaslavskaya, T. (1999) 'Transformatsionny protsess v Rossii: sotsiostrukturny aspekt', in *Sotsial'naya traektoriya reformiruemoy Rossii* (Novosibirsk: Nauka).

2
Diverging Pathways in Central and Eastern Europe

Mark Knell and Martin Srholec

In this chapter we analyse the patterns of production regimes in a large sample of countries using the Varieties of Capitalism (VoC) approach. The main focus is on the post-socialist countries from Central and Eastern Europe and the former Soviet Union, but we also include advanced market economies from Western Europe, North America and Asia for comparative purposes. We begin in the first section by making several constructive comments that place the approach in the broader context of institutional economics. We then analyse some of the relevant patterns in the context of different modes of coordination, following the work of Hall and Gingerich (2004). This analysis shows that the post-socialist countries are spread across the spectrum, reflecting both historical backgrounds and their individual development strategies. The following section elaborates on the industrial relations systems in more detail. A final section contains some further comments and reflections on the VoC approach.

Toward a political economy of production regimes

The VoC perspective has helped to reaffirm the importance of institutions and institutional change. Following Hollingsworth and Boyer (1997) and Soskice (1999), this approach considers a production regime that includes not only the technical structure, but also its organization of production and the market-related institutions, or rules of the game, that affect how economic actors structure and organize their relationships. However, one weakness of the approach is that it has great difficulty allowing adequately for institutional change. This weakness becomes even more pronounced when considering the transformation of the post-socialist economies from a command economy to a more market-oriented one. One important defining feature of the first phase of this transition, marked by rapid economic decline, was the sweeping changes made to the overall institutional framework. These changes created new variants of capitalism, though not in a fully developed form, because informal constraints, such as routines, customs, traditions and conventions, needed more time to develop. Nevertheless, by the mid 1990s, changes to the incentive system embodied in the institutional framework put the post-socialist economies onto a different path of economic growth (Gehrke and Knell 1992) and path of institutional change (North 1990), creating potentially new variants of capitalism.

This difficulty in incorporating change originates in the 'new Keynesian' economic thinking that underpinned the VoC approach (e.g. Carlin and Soskice 1990). In the 1990s, it incorporated numerous contributions from different disciplines, mainly political economy and sociology (Hall and Soskice 2001), but was still built around the approach familiar in economic theory, which starts from the assumption that an institutional framework is fixed and unchanging and markets are imperfectly competitive. Thus there may be different possible institutional frameworks – unlike in neoclassical economic theory where there should be only one variety of capitalism, typified by liberal markets – but it is not clear how institutions change, or what happens when they change.

There have been different approaches to the elements that are considered important within an institutional framework. Soskice (1999) includes the financial system, the industrial relations system, the education and training system and the system of intercompany relations. Adloph Löwe (1976) adds a fifth distinct element, the historical context, including cultural and ethical-religious traditions. 'Institutions' in this context are defined by Löwe (1977: 52) as the 'crystallization of routinised behaviour conforming to established rule'. Behaviour becomes routine after new rules and customs are embedded in society.

Different institutional frameworks create different varieties of capitalism which can be seen as the range of economic means available for attaining a particular goal, such as a higher standard of living. Löwe (1977) develops this with an analysis centring on determining the optimal path of economic growth. There may be many possible paths of economic growth that could be described as desirable, each one having its own advantages and weaknesses and specific type of organization and institutional arrangement (Boyer and Hollingsworth 1997). Chapter 3 by Clemens Buchen and previous publications (Damijan and Knell 2005) argue that Estonia and Slovenia provide good examples among the post-socialist economies of different means towards the same aim.

However, as Soskice (1999) suggests, the importance of interlocking complementarities may limit the number of feasible institutional frameworks. In other words, countries can follow different paths of economic growth towards the same goal but the constellation of complementary institutional configurations may be limited. Hall and Soskice (2001) apply this idea by distinguishing between two modes of coordination, one based on liberal markets and the other on strategic coordination. There should be scope for more. Indeed, Löwe allows for a more flexible version of complementarities in which performance of the system (i.e. growth and prosperity) depends on 'the interlocking of innumerable microdecisions' and on 'the concordance of these microdecisions with the required macroprocesses' (1976: 17). That appears as an invitation to view complementarities less rigidly than in the Hall and Soskice approach and possibly to seek new and novel forms in societies undergoing substantial transformations.

Changing the institutional arrangements can also be an important way to move the economy onto a different growth path. In most instances, institutions will change very slowly because they are deeply embedded in society. But there are episodes in history when there have been major shifts in the institutional arrangements and the way firms are managed, such as the recent transformation in the post-socialist countries. This transformation reflects the sudden change of the dominant group in power and the way this group changed the rules of the game over a relatively very short period of time (Amable 2003: 68). Most, if not all, socio-political groups, including those members of the *nomenklatura* who saw it as an opportunity for financial gain, supported both the collapse of the command economy and the subsequent transformation. Initially the groups pushing for liberal reforms dominated policy circles in most of the post-socialist economies, which gave the momentum to the path of institutional change. Those groups and individuals disadvantaged by the new social system of production have expressed a political demand for institutions typical of coordinated market economies. The following sections provide a comparative analysis of where the social systems of production are after a decade of systemic change in the post-socialist countries.

Measuring the diversity of production regimes

Differences in production regimes can be viewed in the VoC approach as a continuum that runs from market coordination to strategic coordination, incorporating the areas as outlined in Chapter 1. While this view may limit the way we can explore the issue of diversity, it also focuses our analysis on the institutional framework associated with different types of coordination.

The main problem is to identify and obtain relevant indicators for enough countries to make the analysis possible. We adopt the methodology followed by Hall and Gingerich (2004) and use factor analysis to group together variables with similar characteristics. Factor analysis produces linear combinations of variables that are most correlated with one another and least correlated with other variables (OECD 2005). One problem with the analysis of Hall and Gingerich (2004), however, is that they have too few observations to make the analysis plausible. They include only twenty OECD countries and none of the post-socialist economies of Europe and Asia. It is not generally recommended to conduct a factor analysis on a sample of fewer than fifty observations. Our analysis includes fifty-one countries, and includes most of the post-socialist economies of Europe and Asia and the advanced economies for comparative purposes.

By including a larger set of countries, we limit the number of indicators for which relevant data are available. The selection of indicators is based on Soskice (1999), Hall and Soskice (2001) and Hall and Gingerich (2004). Taking our data constraints into consideration, we consider the three different types of institutional arrangements of social cohesion, labour market regulations and business regulations. We measure social cohesion or redistribution by inequality (the Gini coefficient), taxation (the highest marginal tax rates on personal and corporate income) and public spending (the share of government expenditure in GDP). Labour market regulation is given by a set of indicators developed at the World Bank, which gives survey-based information on regulation of employment. Regulation of business activity is based on the same source from the World Bank, which provides information on regulation of market entry and exit and the transfer of property rights. The relative roles of stock markets and banks in transferring capital between borrowers and lenders are obtained from the World Development Indicators. Table 2.3 on page 56 defines the indicators used in the factor analysis and provides sources for the indicators.

Our analysis focuses on evidence roughly over the 2001–4 period as many indicators from national accounts and surveys of the qualitative aspects became available only recently for the post-socialist countries. To categorize the post-socialist countries within the varieties of capitalism framework, we group together variables with similar characteristics, which reflect the salient aspects of the national production regimes. Results of the factor analysis provide a base for grouping of the variables. The analysis suggests that three different aspects of the institutional arrangements should be distinguished. Table 2.1 shows factor loadings, which are correlation coefficients between the variables and the three principal factors detected by the factor analysis. The higher is the loading, the more the

Table 2.1   Results of the factor analysis

	Factor loadings		
	Social cohesion	Labour market regulation	Business regulation
Gini coefficient	−0.61	0.11	0.01
Highest marginal personal income tax rate	0.63	0.26	−0.39
Highest marginal corporate income tax rate	0.44	0.15	−0.08
Government final consumption expenditure (% of GDP)	0.40	−0.10	−0.11
Difficulty of hiring workers index	0.15	0.50	0.36
Difficulty of firing workers index	−0.23	0.56	0.31
Costs of firing workers (weeks of wages)	0.08	0.70	0.19
Rigidity of working hours index	0.13	0.65	−0.09
Number of start-up procedures to register a business	−0.20	0.31	0.69
Time to resolve insolvency (years)	−0.09	−0.06	0.47
Number of procedures to register property	−0.29	0.36	0.45
Stock market relative to baking sector in the financial system	0.07	−0.04	−0.63
Eigenvalue after rotation	1.35	1.82	1.73
% of the sum across eigenvalues after rotation	28	38	36
Number of observations	51		

Note: Varimax normalized rotation; the highest loading for each variable is marked by grey shading.
Source: Table 2.2 on page 52.

principal factor represents the variable. In the table, the first principal factor has high loadings of the variables on inequality, taxation of income and public spending, so that it reflects 'social cohesion'. Difficulties in hiring-and-firing workers and labour market rigidity are grouped into the second principal factor, which is then labelled 'labour market regulation'. Obstacles to entry and exit, property rights transfer and use of equity markets relative to banks comprise the third factor of 'business regulation'.

Accordingly three composite indicators can be constructed by using factor-scoring coefficients as weights for the variables. Apart from the highest correlation, some variables are also (at least modestly) correlated to other principal factors. But weighting such a variable into more than a single composite would lead to an ambiguous interpretation of the composites. So, to keep the analysis lucid, each variable only appears once in the composite for which it has the highest loading. The factor analysis suggests a balanced distribution of the variables with four indicators in each composite, as indicated by grey shading in Table 2.1. We therefore calculate the composite indicators as sums across the relevant variables. Since some of the indicators are negatively correlated to the composites – a higher Gini coefficient reflects lower social cohesion – these variables have to be summed into the composites with a reversed scale. The variables also have to be put on a common scale, standardized by deducting the mean and dividing by the standard deviation, before combining them into the composites. This implies that the resulting indexes are centred on zero with standard deviation equal to unity.

Empirical evidence on the varieties of capitalism

Given the construction of the composites, liberal market economies are expected to appear with low scores, while the coordinated market economies will have high scores on each of the three factors. Figures 2.1 to 2.4 present results for the individual countries. Table 2.4 provides a full overview of the results. Since we include advanced as well as post-socialist countries in the sample, each of the composites are plotted on the horizontal axis against development level of a country given by GDP per capita (in purchasing power parity) on the vertical axis. The GDP figure for Serbia and Montenegro, in the absence of official figures in the World Development Indicators, is the average of other countries of the former Yugoslavia, weighted by their populations. The dotted lines show sample averages and divide the figures into four quadrants with below/above average scores.

Figure 2.1 reveals that the scores for social cohesion are strongly related to the level of development. Most countries appear in the upper-right and lower-left quadrants, suggesting that the most advanced countries tend to maintain relatively high levels of equality, income taxation and levels of public spending, while the opposite holds for most of the post-socialist countries. The main outliers are the United States, Ireland, Canada and Switzerland, which maintain markedly more liberal welfare systems as compared with other high-income countries. Belarus and Bosnia and Herzegovina, Croatia and the Czech Republic are also outliers as they keep relatively high state involvement. One reason why most of the post-socialist countries appear on the liberal end of the spectrum is that they chose a liberal path of transition to a market economy. Policy advice

46

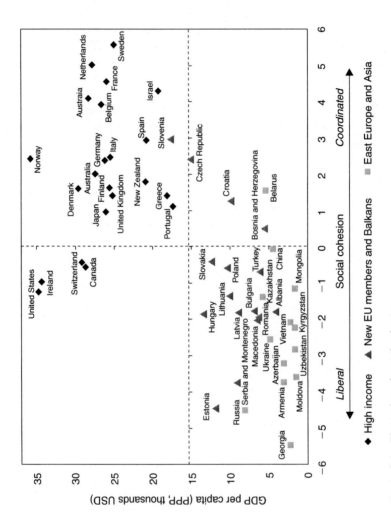

Figure 2.1 The index of social cohesion

from the international financial institutions and liberal market economists pointed to the American model (Djelic 1998), which eventually put
most of the economies well beyond the United States on the liberal side.
The developed economies appear in an order similar to previous studies
(Hall and Soskice 2001), with Sweden as the most coordinated market
economy and the United States as the most liberal market economy.

Figure 2.2 plots the regulation of the labour market against GDP per
capita. In this figure the level of development is not as important. As suggested in the literature, the Anglo-Saxon economies tend to have fewer
barriers to employee turnover than the coordinated market economies.
But, unlike previous studies, the southern European economies appear
as extreme coordinated economies, whereas the Scandinavian countries
are more moderate. This may be a consequence of not having data on the
system of wage bargaining. Nevertheless, the Scandinavian countries have
recently introduced liberal labour market regulations. Many of the post-
socialist countries have also liberalized their labour markets, with Slovakia
on the far end of the liberal spectrum, but many others maintain relatively
high employment protection. Yet, few of these countries can be considered
coordinated in the sense of Hall and Soskice (2001), again perhaps because
the composite indicator does not include information about wage bargaining. Like the more developed southern EU member states, there is
some tendency for the Balkan countries to appear more coordinated.
Overall, there appears to be only a weak relationship between labour market regulation and the development level of countries ($R^2 = 0.12$).

Figure 2.3 shows results for the index of business regulation against
GDP per capita. There appears to be a strong link to the level of development in this composite, though in the opposite direction to the composite of social cohesion. A majority of the advanced countries maintain
relatively flexible regulation of business activity and/or have relatively
developed stock markets as compared with the post-socialist countries.
France, Italy, Greece, Portugal and Israel appear above average in the
composite score. This may be a consequence of not including data on
corporate governance in the index. The overemphasis on business regulations may mask qualitative differences in company organization. A
general tendency towards a liberal approach to taxation and social
systems has not been matched by a move towards a liberal environment
for business in the post-socialist countries. Many of these countries continued to maintain a strong state bureaucracy well after the collapse of
central planning. The data suggest that the only exceptions are Russia,
Lithuania, Hungary and Estonia. However, the score for Russia is dominated

48

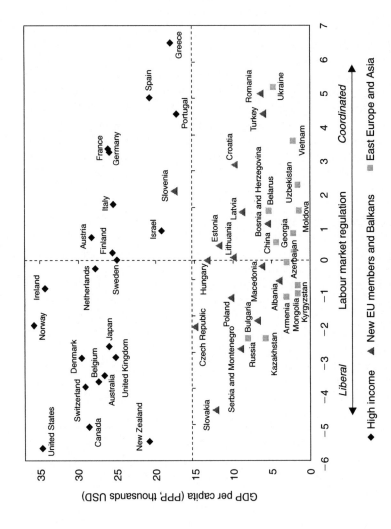

Figure 2.2 The index of labour market regulation

49

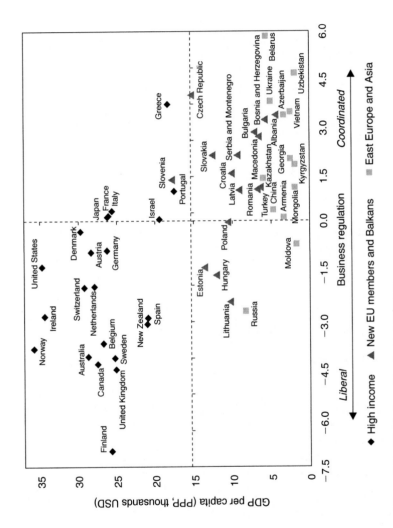

Figure 2.3 The index of business regulation

by the relative importance of the stock market in the economy. The score would be around zero if this were excluded from the composite. Finland is on the extreme edge of liberal market economies for the same reason.

Finally, we can sum up the three composites into a simple overall index of coordination which should provide us with a broad ranking of countries along the liberal market versus coordinated market spectrum. Figure 2.4 gives the results. The distribution of developed countries roughly corresponds to the grouping established in the VoC literature. In the group of former socialist countries, Belarus, Ukraine, Slovenia and Croatia seem to be the prime examples of countries with prevailing strategic coordination, while Russia, Estonia and Armenia come out as the main examples of liberal economies.

Selected aspects of industrial relations

The index of labour market regulation is meant to distinguish the nature of industrial relations across the liberal and coordinated spectrum. Although the VoC literature puts forward rules of hiring and firing workers and regulation of working hours as important features of industrial relations in a national system, there are other more qualitative aspects that should be acknowledged as well (Hall and Soskice 2001; Hall and Gingerich 2004). These include various features of a collective bargaining system, frequency of labour disputes and the organization of vocational training in firms. It was not possible to include these indicators of industrial relations in the factor analysis because reliable statistics are not available for most countries of the former Soviet Union, but there is data for the OECD countries as well as for some non-member European states.

Table 2.2 provides an overview of the industrial relations systems of the high-income and selected post-socialist economies. We have divided the sample into these two broad groups of countries and ranked them according to our index of labour market regulation. A commonly used indicator of industrial relations is the role of trade unions in the economy. The Scandinavian countries and Belgium maintain the highest union density with membership exceeding 50 per cent of the workforce, while in almost all of the other high-income countries less than a third of the workforce is organized. From this point of view the Scandinavian countries and Belgium would appear much closer to the coordinated edge of the labour market index, if we included this data in our composite indicator.

51

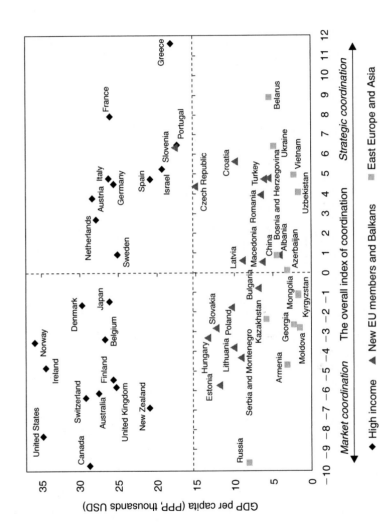

Figure 2.4 The overall index of coordination

Table 2.2 Detailed data on industrial relations in selected countries

Period	Index of labour market regulation 2001–4	Union density in % 2002	Collective bargaining coverage in % 2002	Wage-bargaining levels			Influence of tripartite consultations on wage bargaining 2004	Days lost due to strikes and lockouts per 1,000 2001–3	Enterprises with CVT courses in % 1999
				Inter-sectoral 2004	Sectoral 2004	Firm 2004			
High-income countries									
Greece	6.5	33	70	(XXX)	XXX	X	No	–	9
Spain	4.9	15	83	X	XXX	X	Yes	62.4	28
Portugal	4.4	24	83	–	XXX	X	–	6.5	11
Germany	3.3	25	68	–	XXX	X	No	2.0	67
France	3.2	10	93	X	XX	XX	No	–	71
Italy	1.7	35	83	–	XXX	X	Yes	45.4	23
Austria	0.7	37	98	–	XXX	X	No	–	71
Finland	0.2	76	93	XXX	X	X	Yes	14.2	75
Sweden	0.0	81	93	–	XXX	X	No	23.9	83
Netherlands	-0.2	23	83	X	XXX	X	Yes	–	82
Ireland	-0.9	44	–	XXX	X	X	Yes	14.7	56
Norway	-1.9	54	73	XX	XXX	X	Yes	11.2	81
Japan	-2.6	22	18	–	–	XXX	–	–	–
Denmark	-2.9	74	83	X	XXX	X	No	19.1	88
United Kingdom	-2.9	31	33	–	X	XXX	No	13.2	76
Belgium	-3.5	56	93	XXX	X	X	Yes	–	48

Australia	-3.6	25	83		–	–	–	18.5	–
Switzerland	-3.8	18	43		–	–	–	2.2	–
Canada	-5.0	28	32		–	–	–	–	–
New Zealand	-5.4	23	28		–	–	–	9.1	–
United States	-5.6	13	14		X	XXX	–	6.8	–
Post-socialist countries									
Romania	5.0	–	–	(XXX)	X	XXX	Yes	0.7	7
Slovenia	2.1	41	100	XXX	X	X	Yes	–	33
Latvia	1.5	30	20	–	X	XXX	Yes	0.4	26
Estonia	0.4	14	30	(XXX)	X	XXX	Yes	–	47
Lithuania	0.1	15	10	(XXX)	X	XXX	Yes	–	21
Hungary	0.0	20	33	(XXX)	X	XXX	Yes	0.4	24
Poland	-1.1	15	43	–	X	XXX	Yes	0.1	26
Bulgaria	-1.8	–	30	X	XXX	X	No	–	17
Czech Republic	-2.0	27	28	–	X	XXX	Yes	–	61
Slovakia	-4.5	36	53	–	XXX	X	No	0.0	–

Notes: X = existing level of wage bargaining; XX = important, but not dominant level of wage bargaining; XXX = dominant level of wage bargaining; (XXX) = bargaining on national minimum wage; CVT = Continuing Vocational Training; in some cases the latest year available is reported – see the original sources for details. The last column refers to firms with ten or more employees.

Sources: EIRO (2004; 2005); Eurostat (2005); ILO (2005); OECD (2004).

Union density is relatively low in the post-socialist countries included in the table, except for Slovakia and Slovenia. This figure was close to 100 per cent before the collapse of central planning because union membership was compulsory in most countries.

Collective bargaining coverage can substantially exceed union membership as agreements typically affect the wages and labour conditions of workers not organized in unions. Because of this Scandinavia does not appear so exceptional in the European context. It is striking to see the difference between the high-income European countries when compared with the United States, Canada, New Zealand and Japan. The United Kingdom and Switzerland are the main exceptions with collective bargaining coverage close to levels found in the non-European liberal market economies. In Austria and Slovenia the coverage is close to 100 per cent because of obligatory membership in employer organizations, which act on behalf of their members in collective bargaining. The collective bargaining coverage is lower in most of the other post-socialist countries, but it is noticeably higher than union density in Poland and Slovakia.

Another important aspect of industrial relations is the degree of centralization of wage bargaining. This is typically carried out at the company level in economies with liberal labour markets, such as in the United States, United Kingdom and Japan. Multi-employer bargaining institutions are strong in most high-income European countries, with most agreements negotiated at a sectoral level, but some at the inter-sectoral level. By contrast, wage bargaining in the majority of the post-socialist countries is usually at the company level, with the exception of Bulgaria and Slovakia, where it is at the sectoral level and Slovenia, where it is at the national level. Yet, bargaining on the minimum wage remains at the national level in Hungary, Estonia, Lithuania and Romania, which is not the case in other European countries, with the single exception of Greece.

Tripartite consultations at the national level, which include the government, are often closely connected with collective bargaining. These consultations influence negotiations in almost all of the post-socialist countries, but are important in only about half of the high-income countries. Fewer days lost to strikes and lockouts in the post-socialist economies suggest that unions have less power than in the high-income countries. Causes could be cultural or economic, but are likely to be the outcome of the transition process itself. Even the liberal market economies tend to have more labour disputes than the post-socialist countries.

Strategic coordination of labour markets influences the acquisition of skills in the economy because long job tenures encourage investment in company- or industry-specific skills. Sophisticated and highly institutionalized systems of vocational training are complementary to other institutions typical for coordinated market economies. Table 2.2 provides evidence on the extent of firms' involvement in continuing vocational training courses. This applies to more than two-thirds of firms in most high-income European countries. Vocational training is most widespread in the Scandinavian countries with strong industry-level training systems, which also illustrates the coordinated nature of their industrial relations systems. Less than a third of firms are involved in vocational training in Spain and Italy and only about 10 per cent in Portugal and Greece. Similarly, vocational training is also weak in the post-socialist countries, except in the Czech Republic, which has a strong tradition of firms' involvement in training system, and to a lesser extent Estonia.

Concluding remarks

This chapter has provided a comparative analysis of the social systems of production in the post-socialist countries. They appear across the spectrum with Belarus, Ukraine, Slovenia and Croatia being among the most coordinated, and Russia and Estonia the most liberal. This reflects the diversity of the paths of economic growth and institutional change that took place after the collapse of the command economy, but the current analysis cannot explain why countries followed a particular path. Indeed, a weakness of the VoC approach is that it does not adequately take into account institutional change. One of the reasons for the diversity is that the institutional arrangements in these economies varied historically, creating path dependence in the transformation process. At the same time the depth of change differs across various types of institutions.

Our results suggest that the market economies that emerged in most of the post-socialist countries appear to be even more liberal than the United States, at least as far as size of the public sector, income tax burden and income inequalities are concerned. Although these broad 'rules of the game' changed fundamentally, business regulation remains relatively rigid as compared to high-income countries, which suggests that the fabric of state bureaucracy tends to change much more slowly. Labour market regulation is more evenly spread across the liberal and coordinated spectrum in the post-socialist countries.

Table 2.3 Definitions and sources of the data

Indicator and definition	Scaling	Source of data and methodology	Period
GDP per capita, PPP (constant 2000 international USD): gross domestic product per capita converted to international dollars using purchasing power parity (PPP) rates. An international dollar has the same purchasing power over GDP as the US dollar has in the United States.	thousand of USD	World Bank (World Development Indicators 2005)	Av. 2001–03
General government final consumption expenditure: all government current expenditures for purchases of goods and services (including compensation of employees). It also includes most expenditures on national defence and security, but excludes government military expenditures that are part of government capital formation.	% of GDP	World Bank (World Development Indicators)	Av. 2001–03
Highest marginal personal income tax rate: the highest rate shown on the schedule of tax rates applied to the taxable income of individuals.	%	Heritage Foundation (Index of Economic Freedom 2005) and World Bank (World Development Indicators)	2004
Highest marginal corporate income tax rate: the highest rate shown on the schedule of tax rates applied to the taxable income of corporations	%	Heritage Foundation (Index of Economic Freedom 2005) and World Bank (World Development Indicators)	2004
Gini coefficient: the extent to which the distribution of income (or, in some cases, consumption expenditure) among individuals or households	index (0 to 100)	WIDER (World Income Inequality Database 2.0a)	Av. 2001–03

Description	Units	Year	Source
within an economy deviates from a perfectly equal distribution. A Gini index of 0 represents perfect equality, while an index of 100 implies perfect inequality.			
Difficulty of hiring workers: (i) whether term contracts can only be used for temporary tasks; (ii) the maximum duration of term contracts; and (iii) the ratio of the mandated minimum wage (or apprentice wage, if available) to the average value-added per working person.	index (0 to 100)	2004	World Bank (The Doing Business Indicators) and Botero et al. 2004
Difficulty of firing workers: eight components: (i) whether redundancy is not grounds for dismissal; (ii) whether the employer needs to notify the trade union or labour ministry for firing one redundant worker; (iii) whether the employer needs to notify the trade union or the labour ministry for group dismissals; (iv) whether the employer needs approval from the trade union or the labour ministry for firing one redundant worker; (v) whether the employer needs approval from the trade union or the labour ministry for group dismissals; (vi) whether the law mandates training or replacement prior to dismissal; (vii) whether priority rules apply for dismissals; and (viii) whether priority rules apply for re-employment.	index (0 to 100)	2004	World Bank (The Doing Business Indicators) and Botero et al. 2004

(Continued)

Table 2.3 (Continued)

Indicator and definition	Scaling	Source of data and methodology	Period
Costs of firing workers: the cost of advance notice requirements, and severance payments and penalties due when firing a worker, expressed in terms of weekly wages.	weeks of wages	World Bank (The Doing Business Indicators) and Botero *et al.* 2004	2004
Rigidity of working hours: five components: (i) whether night work is restricted; (ii) whether weekend work is allowed; (iii) whether the working week consists of five-and-a-half days or more; (iv) whether the working day can extend to 12 hours or more (including overtime); and (v) whether annual paid holidays are less then 22 days.	index (0 to 100)	World Bank (The Doing Business Indicators) and Botero *et al.* 2004	2004
Number of start-up procedures to register a business: all generic procedures that are officially required for an entrepreneur to start an industrial or commercial business, including interactions to obtain necessary licences and permits and complete any required notifications, verifications or inscriptions with relevant authorities.	number of procedures	World Bank (The Doing Business Indicators) and Djankov *et al.* 2002	2004

Description	Units	Year	Source
Time to resolve insolvency: the average time to complete the procedure as estimated by insolvency lawyers.	years	2004	World Bank (The Doing Business Indicators)
Number of procedures to register property: the full sequence of procedures necessary to transfer the property title from the seller to the buyer when a business purchases land and a building in the country's most populous city. Every required procedure is included, whether it is the responsibility of the seller, the buyer, or where it is required to be completed by a third party on their behalf.	number of procedures	2004	World Bank (The Doing Business Indicators)
Stock market relative to banking sector in the financial system: the ratio of market capitalization of listed companies to domestic credit provided by the banking sector. The former is the share price times the number of shares outstanding. The latter includes all credit to various sectors on a gross basis, with the exception of credit to the central government, which is net. The banking sector includes monetary authorities and deposit money banks, as well as other banking institutions where data are available.	%	Av. 2001–03	World Bank (World Development Indicators)

60

Table 2.4   The index of strategic versus market coordination, 2001–4

	Country	GDP per capita (PPP, thousands of USD)	Coordination index	Redistribution	Labour market	Business regulation
Strategic coordination	Belarus	5.4	8.9	1.6	1.5	5.9
	Ukraine	4.8	6.4	−2.5	5.2	3.8
	Slovenia	17.6	6.3	3.0	2.1	1.3
	Croatia	9.9	5.6	1.3	2.9	1.5
	Vietnam	2.2	5.0	−2.1	3.6	3.5
	Bosnia and Herzegovina	5.5	4.8	0.5	1.1	3.2
	Czech Republic	15.0	4.4	2.4	−2.0	4.0
	Uzbekistan	1.6	4.1	−2.8	2.3	4.7
	Romania	6.5	4.0	−2.0	5.0	1.0
	Albania	4.1	0.9	−1.8	−0.6	3.3
	China	4.4	0.9	−0.1	0.6	0.4
	Latvia	9.0	0.6	−1.8	1.5	1.0
	Macedonia	6.3	0.6	−1.9	−0.2	2.7
	Azerbaijan	3.1	0.1	−3.2	0.0	3.4
	Bulgaria	6.9	−0.8	−1.8	−1.8	2.8
	Mongolia	1.6	−1.1	−1.1	−1.0	1.1
	Kyrgyzstan	1.6	−1.1	−2.2	−0.7	1.8
	Poland	10.4	−1.8	−0.6	−1.1	0.0
	Kazakhstan	5.7	−2.3	−1.4	−2.3	1.4
	Georgia	2.2	−2.6	−5.5	0.8	2.0
	Moldova	1.4	−2.8	−3.6	1.5	−0.7
	Slovakia	12.4	−2.8	−0.4	−4.5	2.1
	Hungary	13.4	−3.3	−1.8	0.0	−1.5
	Lithuania	10.1	−3.8	−1.3	0.1	−2.5
	Serbia and Montenegro	9.1	−4.3	−3.7	−2.6	2.1
	Armenia	3.1	−4.7	−3.7	−1.1	0.1
	Estonia	11.9	−5.7	−4.4	0.4	−1.7
	Russia	8.1	−9.6	−4.5	−2.3	−2.8
	Greece	18.1	11.6	1.4	6.5	3.7
	France	26.0	8.0	4.5	3.2	0.2
	Portugal	17.4	6.5	1.1	4.4	1.0
	Israel	19.2	5.3	4.3	0.9	0.1
	Germany	26.2	4.8	2.4	3.3	−0.9
	Turkey	6.1	4.8	−0.7	4.4	1.1
	Spain	20.8	4.7	2.9	4.9	−3.1
	Italy	25.5	4.5	2.5	1.7	0.3
	Austria	28.3	3.8	4.1	0.7	−1.0

(Continued)

Table 2.4   (Continued)

Country	GDP per capita (PPP, thousands of USD)	Coordination index	Redistribution	Labour market	Business regulation
Netherlands	27.8	2.7	5.0	−0.2	−2.1
Sweden	25.0	0.9	5.6	0.0	−4.7
Japan	26.0	−1.5	1.0	−2.6	0.1
Denmark	29.6	−1.6	1.6	−2.9	−0.3
Belgium	26.6	−3.4	3.9	−3.5	−3.9
Norway	35.7	−3.5	2.4	−1.9	−4.0
Ireland	34.3	−4.8	−1.0	−0.9	−3.0
Finland	25.6	−5.4	1.6	0.2	−7.3
United Kingdom	25.3	−5.8	1.4	−2.9	−4.3
Australia	27.4	−6.1	2.0	−3.6	−4.5
Switzerland	29.1	−6.3	−0.4	−3.8	−2.1
New Zealand	20.9	−6.9	1.8	−5.4	−3.2
United States	34.7	−8.3	−1.3	−5.6	−1.4
Canada	28.6	−9.8	−0.6	−5.0	−4.3

Market coordination (arrow from Netherlands down to New Zealand)

References

Amable, B. (2003) *The Diversity of Modern Capitalism* (Oxford: Oxford University Press).

Botero, J., S. Djankov, S., R. La Porta, F. Lopez-de-Silanes and A. Shleifer (2004) 'The Regulation of Labor', *Quarterly Journal of Economics*, 119, 1339–82.

Boyer, R., and J. R. Hollingsworth (1997) 'How and Why do Social Systems of Production Change?' in H. J. Rogers. and R. Boyer (eds), *Contemporary Capitalism: The Embeddedness of Institutions* (Cambridge: Cambridge University Press), 189–95.

Carlin, W. and D. Soskice, (1990) *Macroeconomics and the Wage Bargain* (Oxford: Oxford University Press).

Damijan, J. and M. Knell (2005) 'How Important is Trade and Foreign Ownership in Closing the Technology Gap? Evidence from Estonia and Slovenia', *Review of World Economics (Weltwirtschaftliches Archiv)*, 141, 271–95.

Djankov, S., R. La Porta, F. Lopez-de-Silanes, and A. Shleifer (2002) 'The Regulation of Entry', *Quarterly Journal of Economics*, 117, 1–37.

Djelic, M.-L. (1998) *Exporting the American Model: The Postwar Transformation of European Business* (Oxford: Oxford University Press).

EIRO (2004) *Industrial Relations in the EU, Japan and USA, 2002* (Dublin: European Industrial Relations Observatory).

EIRO (2005) *Changes in National Collective Bargaining Systems Since 1990* (Dublin: European Industrial Relations Observatory).

Eurostat (2005) *Continuing Vocational Training Survey (CVTS2)* (Luxembourg: Eurostat).

Gehrke, C. and M. Knell (1992) 'Transitions from Centrally Planned to Market Economy', in M. Knell and C. Rider (eds), *Socialist Economies in Transition: Appraisals of the Market Mechanism* (Aldershot: Edward Elgar), 43–64.

Hall, P. and D. W. Gingerich (2004) 'Varieties of Capitalism and Institutional Complementarities in the Macroeconomy: An Empirical Analysis', MPIfG Discussion Paper 04/5.

Hall, P. and D. Soskice. (2001) 'An Introduction to the Varieties of Capitalism', in Hall, P. and D. Soskice (eds), *Varieties of Capitalism: The Institutional Foundations of Comparative Advantage* (Oxford: Oxford University Press), 1–68.

Hollingsworth, J. R. and R. Boyer. (1997) 'Coordination of Economic Actors and Social Systems of Production', in H. J. Rogers and R. Boyer (eds), *Contemporary Capitalism: The Embeddedness of Institutions* (Cambridge: Cambridge University Press), 1–47.

Johnson, B.-A. (1992) 'Towards a New Approach to National Systems of Innovation', in B.-A. Lundvall (ed.), *National Systems of Innovation* (London: Pinter), 23–44.

ILO (2005) 'LABORSTA Database' (Geneva: ILO).

Löwe, A. (1976) *The Path of Economic Growth* (Cambridge: Cambridge University Press).

Löwe, A. (1977) *On Economic Knowledge: Toward a Science of Political Economics*, 2nd edn (White Plains: M. E. Sharpe).

North, D. (1990) *Institutions, Institutional Change and Economic Performance* (Cambridge: Cambridge University Press).

OECD (2004) *OECD Employment Outlook 2004* (Paris: OECD).

OECD (2005) *Handbook on Constructing Composite Indicators: Methodology and User Guide*, OECD Statistics Working Paper, STD/DOC(2005)3.

Soskice, D. (1999) 'Divergent Production Regimes: Coordinated and Uncoordinated Market Economies in the 1980s and 1990s', in H. Kitschelt *et al.* (eds), *Continuity and Changes in Contemporary Capitalism* (Cambridge: Cambridge University Press), 101–34.

Part II
Consolidated Market Economies

3
Estonia and Slovenia as Antipodes

*Clemens Buchen**

This chapter provides a comparative analysis of Estonia and Slovenia along the lines of the Varieties of Capitalism framework (Soskice 1999; Hall and Soskice 2001) as introduced in Chapter 1. Both countries have been identified as polar opposites against the backdrop of Varieties of Capitalism (VoC), appearing in Chapter 2 as antipodes regarding their institutional configurations, occupying extreme ends of a spectrum of transition economies according to the degree of non-market coordination. This is corroborated by Magnus Feldmann (2006), who analyses the industrial relations of both countries and comes to the conclusion that Estonia and Slovenia can be seen as the incarnations of a liberal and coordinated market economy.

This chapter takes up these results and attempts to confirm them point by point. This will be carried out in two ways: first, the study of industrial relations will be complemented by analysing institutions in the further four determining subsystems of a specific variety of capitalism, namely corporate governance, inter-firm relations, social security and vocational training systems (Hall and Soskice 2001; Estevez-Abe *et al.* 2001); secondly, the chapter will attempt to illuminate a further implication of the VoC literature, which is the concept of comparative institutional advantages. There, it is argued that specific systems, by means of institutional complementarities among subsystems, lead to distinct incentives to invest in different degrees of asset specificity. This, in turn, opens up institutional comparative advantages in different economic sectors according to different innovation patterns. From this it follows that firms and workers in coordinated market economies (CME) are relatively better at producing goods and services which entail incremental innovation. In liberal market economies (LME) the comparative advantage lies within sectors which largely rely on radical innovation. This helps to explain the economic

structures of countries, which can be traced back to institutional complementarities. Hence, the qualitative analysis of possible institutional
complementarities in Estonia and Slovenia will by complemented by
studying emerging comparative institutional advantages. This will be done
using both contributions to the trade balance and patterns of foreign direct
investment into both countries in terms of their sectoral and geographical
distributions.

Estonia and Slovenia provide excellent cases for comparison for the VoC
framework. Not only do they show divergent institutional frameworks,
but both countries also display similarly good macroeconomic outcomes.
This statement is crucial, because one central tenet of VoC is that it predicts
equally good macroeconomic performance for countries of different
variants of capitalist coordination (Hall and Soskice 2001: 20–1; Amable
2003: 213–24).

Estonia and Slovenia as LME and CME

Estonia and Slovenia have performed very well in the transition process,
being above the average of transition countries regarding growth and
unemployment figures.

Figure 3.1 shows that particularly Slovenia quickly managed to regain
pre-transition GDP levels: the former output level was restored as early
as 1997. In Estonia this process took longer: the previous level could not
be achieved until 2003. From 1997 onwards both countries are above the
average of the transition countries as a whole. Comparing with both
the more relevant group of the new EU member states and three candidate
countries Bulgaria, Croatia and Romania, the picture is similar, albeit less
clear in the Estonian case: Estonia manages to catch up with the rest only
in 2001.

Unemployment figures again show very good results for Estonia and
Slovenia in comparison with other EU members and candidates. From the
mid 1990s until 2003 both countries had average unemployment below
the average EU and candidate countries – 10 per cent for Estonia, 7 per cent
for Slovenia – compared with 12 per cent for the EU and candidate countries. This assessment can be corroborated by looking at competitiveness
figures issued by the World Economic Forum: its 2004 report (Porter *et al.*
2004) ranks both Estonia and Slovenia highest of all transition economies
under study in the WEF's *Growth Competitiveness Index* and *Business Competitiveness Index*. Thus, it is safe to say that the two countries are above-
average performers among CEECs (Central and East European countries).

At the same time, Estonia and Slovenia are associated with opposing
approaches to the transition process: while Estonia is commonly seen as

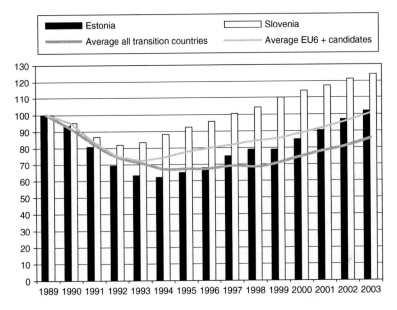

Figure 3.1 Real GDP (1989 = 100) in Estonia and Slovenia compared with other transition countries
Notes: The EU6 refers to the remaining Central and Eastern European EU member states. The candidate countries are Romania, Bulgaria and Croatia.
Sources: EBRD (2002 and 2004), figures for 2003 based on growth estimates.

a very radical and fast ('big bang') reformer (cf. Smith 2001), Slovenia's way of reforms can be described as more gradual and slow (cf. Mencinger 2004). Accordingly, both countries are good transition reformers with apparently diametrically opposed approaches and outcomes.

VoC covers analysis of institutions in five subsystems; industrial relations, corporate governance, inter-firm relations, social security systems and vocational training, which I examine with respect to Estonia and Slovenia. The analysis emphasizes current institutional settings in both countries. Initial institutional conditions and legacies are mentioned only in passing. The goal of linking systemic institutional outcomes to origins seems promising, but goes beyond the scope of this chapter.

Industrial relations

Trade unions, employers and wage bargaining

Industrial relations in socialism were fundamentally different from what is traditionally known in Western economies. Trade unions were perceived as part of the regime, and usually not rooted on firm levels. From this it follows that the reputation of unions was generally bad,[1] so that a drop in membership after the dismantling of the system was inevitable (Boeri and Terrell 2002). Correspondingly, membership figures in both Estonia and Slovenia dropped sharply, in Estonia from 93 per cent of workers unionized in 1990 to 14 per cent in 2000, and in Slovenia from 69 per cent in 1989 to 40 per cent in 2001. However, Slovenian figures are the highest of all CEECs (Ladó 2002).

In Estonia there are two umbrella organizations which represent several smaller unions. These are the Confederation of Estonian Trade Unions (Eesti Ametiühingute Keskliit, EAKL), the successor from the Soviet period with twenty-six affiliated unions representing a total of about 58,000 members, and the Estonian Employees' Unions' Confederation (Teenistujate Ametiliitude Keskorganisatsioon, TALO), with eleven affiliated unions and 40,000 members. Apart from these, the Farmers' Union has about 9,600 members. On the employers' side the Estonian Employers' Confederation (Eesti Tööandjate Keskliit, ETTK) represents a mere 4 per cent of firms (Feldmann 2006). There are both tripartite and bipartite agreements. The former include the state, unions and employers and mainly deal with minimum wages and overall working conditions. Bipartite collective wage agreements are not very far-reaching: in the year 2003 eleven out of thirty-seven unions concluded an agreement, meaning that 28 per cent of workers were covered by a collective agreement. Agreements at the firm level are the most common. The Ministry of Social Affairs encourages social partners to reach bilateral agreements, but at the same time explicitly underlines their voluntary character (Philips and Eamets 2003a).

In Slovenia, there are six umbrella associations. The leading role is played by the successor organization from communist times, the Association of Free Trade Unions (Zveza Svobodnich Sindikatov Slovenije, ZSSS) which represents about half of the organized workforce. This figure has remained stable throughout the 1990s. A further seventeen independent unions exist. The most influential employers' organization is the Slovenian Chamber of Commerce, to which membership is compulsory (Stanojević 2000). Also, a law from the final years of Yugoslav federalism concerning wage-bargaining legislation makes agreements between unions and employers compulsory. This, together with compulsory membership in the Chamber of Commerce, creates a situation in which almost 100 per cent of the workforce is covered by up to three collective agreements. A new law under debate in parliament in 2005 would most certainly reduce this high figure, because compulsory agreements are against the guidelines of both the ILO and the EU (Skledar 2005).

Apart from the large importance of collective wage bargaining, other institutions point to a strong corporatist culture in Slovenia. The National Council exists as a second parliamentary chamber composed of regional delegates and representatives from different interest groups, including employers, employees, farmers and others. Although the Council's formal power remains rather small, it fulfils a supervisory function and counterbalances the party representation in the National Assembly. Furthermore, there is an Economic-Social Council as a tripartite body with growing influence on setting standards with respect to economic and social policies (Lukšič 2003).

To sum up, while in Slovenia we find a corporatist culture with strong employers' associations and unions with far-reaching wage agreements, in Estonia the opposite is true: neither employers nor workers are formally organized. Additionally, the large majority of wages are set at the firm level. Complementarily to this, there is considerable workers' participation in the Slovenian case at the firm level.

Worker participation

In Estonia, the first experimental reform measures were taken in the second half of the 1980s. Workers' councils were founded in a number of firms. Following independence these projects rapidly lost significance. As the independence movement became the dominant issue, councils split along ethnic lines of Estonians and ethnic Russians. 'Soviet experiments' were discredited and eventually dropped (Wielgohs 2001) so that workers' councils, or any other form of codetermination, played no further significant role (Feldmann 2006).

In contrast, Slovenian workers' councils have considerable influence, a fact that can be traced back to peculiarities of the Yugoslav system of self-management which led to greater autonomy for firms and increased worker involvement in their decision-making processes. In 1993 the system was transformed into one of councils modelled on the example of German *Betriebsräte*. Works councils in Slovenia are very important entities for unions, rooting their power at the firm level (Stanojević 2001). Today, works councils exist in the majority of firms (Stanojević 2003: 288).

This brief overview of industrial relations in both countries has shown that in this sphere Estonia and Slovenia can be regarded as polar opposites, as antipodes. While in Estonia we find firm-level wage setting, accompanied by weak unions and employers organizations, wage bargaining in Slovenia is conducted industry-wide and both unions and employers are strongly cohesive. This is in line with the institutional complementarities postulated by VoC.

Corporate governance

The creation of private property is the most fundamental challenge former communist states are facing on their journey from socialism to capitalism. Apart from new companies emerging after liberalization measures, privatization has had a decisive impact on the formation of a new ownership structure of former state-owned companies and thereby on corporate governance. In the following we look at the resulting ownership structure, the way management is organized and stakeholders are represented, and at market capitalization figures.

Ownership structure

Estonian privatization can be characterized by two distinct phases. While in the first phase privatization clearly favoured insiders, the second was dominated by direct sales with equal treatment of foreigners. Starting with reform measures during the Gorbachev era, a considerable number of small private firms and cooperatives were established. Later, 'leasing' of firms was introduced, and from October 1990 onwards it was possible to sell off 20 per cent of a firm to employees. Following the introduction of the Estonian kroon in 1992 a small privatization scheme was established, which was modelled on the East German *Treuhandanstalt*. This meant a step away from initial employee-favouring forms of privatization. During this second phase small privatization proceeded rapidly, so that all small enterprises subject to privatization were sold by 1994. For large privatization, experts from the *Treuhand* were hired to advise a newly founded agency. Equal treatment of foreign investors was thereby secured (Mygind 1997: 40–4). The method of direct sales during the second, and larger, wave of privatization led to high ownership concentration: on average the largest shareholder in Estonia holds 56.2 per cent of shares, while the second and third largest are relatively small, holding 9 per cent and 4 per cent respectively (Berglöf and Pajuste 2003). While the beginning of privatization fostered the formation of employee ownership, throughout the 1990s the numbers of employee-controlled companies continuously decreased. Another direct consequence of privatization is a strong foreign ownership of about 25 per cent of shares (Kalmi 2003).

In Slovenia the Law on Ownership Transformation of 1992 laid the legislative basis for privatization. During the course of privatization vouchers were issued with value equivalent to 40 per cent of GDP. In the privatization process 40 per cent of the capital of a firm had to be transferred to three state-controlled funds (SCFs), 20 per cent to employees, while for the remaining 40 per cent there were two options: they could be sold either to employees or directly to the public. The majority of firms chose the internal method by allocating this remaining share to insiders. Hence, in Slovenia a mixed scheme of voucher and management and employee buy-outs was carried out, whereby the latter was insider-biased in practice. The actual method of privatization can be seen as a political compromise between left-wing parties favouring insider buy-outs and right-wing parties supporting a voucher scheme (Šušteršič 2004: 403). Privatization Investment Funds (PIFs) were founded to exert active control. The ownership structure of firms listed on the Ljubljana Stock Exchange at the end of 2000 still reflected the privatization method: 25 per cent of firms were held by PIFs or their successors, 16 per cent by insiders, the same amount by SCFs, and 15 per cent by firms. Twelve per cent of shares were held by small investors. On average the largest owner controlled 32 per cent of shares, with 15 per cent and 11 per cent for the second and third largest investor. The average coalition voting block of the three largest owners in over 70 per cent of firms amounted to 62 per cent. This figure is close to Austrian and German percentages (Gregorič 2003: 33ff). In this relatively dense corporate network, with considerable cross-ownership, the central role is played by various state funds.

It is widely held that initial privatization methods were planned considering both political acceptability and speed of transformation. Therefore, it can be expected that initial ownership structures will be changing during transformation when 'true' owners with an economic interest acquire shares of companies. Thus, further insight is gained by also considering changes in ownership.

In Estonia the proportion of employee-controlled firms fell from 17.2 per cent to 5.7 per cent between the end of the privatization process and 2001, including both privatized and new companies (Jones and Mygind 2005). Additionally, the percentage of domestic investors controlling firms fell more modestly from about 31.5 per cent to 25 per cent. Manager-owned firms spread continuously over the years, from 24 per cent to 34 per cent. Foreign control remained fairly unchanged at about 25 per cent (Kalmi 2003: 1222).

In Slovenia SCFs on aggregate decreased their stakes by about half in the 1998–2002 period. Shares of domestic firms more than tripled. Shares held by PIFs, banks, managers and minority holders remained unchanged, while foreign stakes doubled, coming from a very low level. The number of firms in which insiders constitute the dominant group dropped from 50 per cent of firms in 1998 to about 18 per cent in 2002, while the overall aggregate ownership stakes of insiders remained fairly high, at 26.8 and 26.2 per cent, in 2001 and 2002. The number of firms with SCFs as dominant holders remained unchanged. Cases where domestic firms act as dominant owners of other firms increased from 11 per cent to 33 per cent (Damijan *et al.* 2004). Here we can observe a consolidation process: SCFs seem to concentrate on firms where they have a dominant position, while domestic non-financial companies increase their voting power. Insiders are slowly withdrawing from enterprise control, but also seem to consolidate. It is interesting to note that the ownership share of insiders, managers excluded, in Slovenia has a statistically significant positive effect on management decision power (Prašnikar and Gregorič 2002).

Organization of management

In 1995 the new Commercial Code brought far-reaching changes for Estonian enterprises. A two-tier board structure was introduced, based on the German model with a management board and supervisory board (Gerndorf *et al.* 1999). Slovenia also adopted a two-tier board structure, following legislation in 1993 (Bohinc and Bainbridge 1999).

The Estonian Commercial Code does not define the composition of the supervisory board in detail. Representation of workers and other interested groups is not compulsory and generally does not occur (Gerndorf *et al.* 1999: 13). Shareholders holding more than 50 per cent of shares have the right to appoint the supervisory board unilaterally.

In Slovenia, workers participate in both supervisory boards and management boards. In companies employing more than 1,000 workers, half of the supervisory board consists of workers' representatives, whereas in firms with more than 500 employees, at least one third of the supervisory board is appointed by workers, except for financial institutions. Moreover, one representative, the 'workers' director', can be part of the management board. Workers and the firm agree on a contract of participation rights, which includes an obligation on management to provide information and conditions for consultation, codetermination and workers' veto rights on personnel decisions (Prašnikar and Gregorič 2002: 274 ff). Pahor *et al.* (2004) study the composition of supervisory boards in a representative sample of companies. In about 22 per cent employees take up more than half of the seats. Representatives of state funds are present in about one third of companies.

Market capitalization

The Estonian stock market is considerably larger than the Slovenian, equivalent to 41.7 per cent of GDP in 2003 as compared to 14.6 per cent in Slovenia. Moreover, the Estonian stock market capitalization is the highest of all eight CEECs within, or set to join, the European Union. However, the Estonian value is still much smaller than corresponding values for typical LMEs, such as the UK and the USA. Also, the turnover ratio, meaning the value of shares actually traded, is much lower in Estonia (see Table A.5 in the Statistical Appendix and EBRD 2004). Comparing our results with practice prevailing in the UK, an LME, and Germany, a CME, we observe the following picture in Table 3.1.

Two observations catch the eye: first of all the striking similarities between Slovenia and Germany regarding management organization and representation of stakeholders clearly confirms the view of Slovenia as a CME. In both areas legislation was modelled on the German example. However, the ownership structure shows the legacies of post-socialist reforms, with shares held by insiders and state-controlled funds. Banks do not play any significant role in corporate governance, apart from influence exerted through bank-owned PIFs (Gregorič 2003). Taken together, this is clearly a deviation from Western CME-type corporate governance coordination. With regard to state influence, Pahor *et al.* (2004) examine

Table 3.1 Comparison of basic corporate governance features of Estonia and Slovenia with the UK and Germany

LME		CME	
Estonia	*UK*	*Slovenia*	*Germany*
Ownership structure			
Very strong largest voting block; considerable foreign ownership, declining insider ownership	Small largest voting block; overall dispersed	Relatively large voting blocks (large coalitions); considerable insider ownership (employee and managerial)	Large voting blocks (large coalitions)
Management			
Two-tier board structure with management and supervisory board	One-tier management board	Two-tier board structure with management and supervisory board	Two-tier board structure with management and supervisory board
Representation of stakeholders			
Voluntary	Voluntary	Workers' and other interest groups' representatives on supervisory board	Workers' and other interest groups' representatives on supervisory board

emerging company networks with regard to ownership and control patterns, looking at seats on supervisory boards. They come to the conclusion that direct state influence in the economy remains within the two types of state-run funds. Stated differently, in order to eradicate state control entirely, dissolution of these funds would suffice.

The second observation is not that straightforward. The Estonian picture seems highly inconsistent with VoC. On the one hand Estonia has the biggest capital market among CEECs and representation of stakeholders is voluntary. This does not go well with ownership concentration and the German-type two-tier board structure. However, looking at practice, we discover deviations from the stakeholder model. Gerndorf *et al.* (1999) report that in daily practice supervisory boards are often circumvented when it comes to decision making.[2] They are perceived as overly bureaucratic. Moreover, the high concentration of ownership allows circumvention of the system by careful choice of members of the supervisory board.

Generally speaking, the introduction of a market-based system of corporate governance from the beginning of the transition process does not seem feasible. Berglöf and Bolton (2002) ascribe this to weak and not credible protection of small shareholders, a lack of experts in firms and banking, costly information gathering, and a comparably risky business environment. Additionally, Djankov and Murrell (2002) find that when it comes to enterprise restructuring, concentrated ownership delivers better results than dispersed ownership. Hence, there are good reasons why a pure shareholder model of corporate governance cannot evolve early after the change of system. Also, in the Estonian case, the chosen privatization method could not lead to dispersed shares of companies.

The divergence in methods of dealing with insiders in the Estonian and Slovenian case is remarkable. In Estonia the initial conditions of privatization, favouring insiders, were replaced with a model of direct sales to outsiders, but the bias in favour of insiders in Slovenia lasted throughout the whole process. Accordingly, as already mentioned above, employee ownership dropped sharply in Estonia over time. In Slovenia figures also decreased, but seem to consolidate on a higher level. If we assume that employee ownership can be an incentive to acquire firm-specific skills (Blair 1999), the comparison of Estonia and Slovenia as opposites implies potential transitional institutional complementarities. In this case employee owners could be a functional equivalent (Crouch *et al.* 2005: 375) to an efficient banking system in a post-communist CME. As seen above, the Slovenian banking sector is not in a position to grant 'patient capital' to companies, whose managers cannot credibly commit themselves to retain the workforce in economic downturns. Then, the equivalent incentive for workers to acquire firm-specific human capital can be ownership of shares in the company and the accompanying responsibilities. Accordingly, in Slovenia a far larger portion of firms was, and still is, in the hands of employees, while in Estonia the initial preferential treatment of employees was abandoned. Prašnikar and Gregorič (2002) report that insider ownership does not necessarily lead to 'employeeism' (Nuti 1997) in Slovenia, while in the Estonian case one can speak in parts at least of the degeneration of employee ownership (Kalmi 2003). However, one has to bear in mind that this complementary institution can be efficient as a 'transitional institution' (Qian 2003), but it could vanish as the economy matures.

In sum, while in Slovenia we find a stakeholder approach to corporate governance with insiders and state influence, analysis of the Estonian case reveals a somewhat imperfect stakeholder approach to corporate governance. Stated differently, the Estonian model seems to be neither a pure shareholder nor a perfect stakeholder approach.

Inter-firm relations

Due to strong state control, in socialist countries comparable kinds of intercompany relations did not exist. R&D was centrally conducted by planning authorities, which also decided in which sectors which technology for which production should be used (Kornai 1992). Moreover, no kind of horizontal informational flow fitted into the logic of the whole system (Ericson 1991).

After removal of the planning system firms had to find ways to cooperate. In Estonia, no significant attempts to cooperate 'beyond the market' were made; following VoC this would be neither necessary nor possible, due to the lack of encompassing business organizations. When it comes to CMEs, Goodin (2003: 208–12) remarks that trust is a precondition for the building of committed cooperation between firms. As many firms had to build up completely new relationships with new business partners following the breakdown of firms and markets in CEECs, it is not surprising that in Slovenia trust is as yet not well developed[3] (Czaban *et al.* 2003). Nevertheless, an institutional infrastructure enabling cooperation is provided by the strong presence of chambers and business associations.

Social security systems

Before turning to the contemporary situation in both countries under study, it is useful first to depict peculiarities within this system during socialist rule. In socialism the state fulfilled a paternalistic function. It gave a job guarantee for every citizen, and losing one's job rarely happened.

Therefore, employment protection (EP) was very high in socialism. Firms were also involved in other welfare activities by providing kindergartens, health care or vacation facilities. On the other hand, unemployment protection (UP) was low for citizens, who were not part of the workforce, apart from subsidies on rents and basic food (Götting 1998: 57–88). Thus, the task for transitional economies was to change labour legislation to more market-based rules and to institutionalize a system of UP.

Employment protection

To compare LMEs and CMEs, Estevez-Abe *et al.* (2001) calculate an index consisting of two OECD indexes, employment protection legislation (EPL), which captures the restrictiveness of individual hiring-and-firing rules for regular employments, and collective dismissals protection. As a third indicator they construct an index of company-based protection (see Table 3.2 for explanations). With the help of these three indexes, an

Table 3.2   Employment protection in the UK, Estonia, Germany and Slovenia

	Employment protection legislation (EPL by OECD, regular employment)	*Collective dismissals protection (OECD)*	*Company-based protection[a]*	*Index of employment protection[b]*
UK	0.8	2.9	1	0.18
Estonia	3.1	4.1	1	0.44
Germany	2.8	3.1	3	0.59
Slovenia	2.9 (3.4)[c]	4.9 (4.8)	3 (3)	0.67 (0.71)

Notes:[a] Based on the following criteria: (a) presence of employee-elected bodies with a significant role in manpower decisions; (b) existence of strong external unions with some monitoring and sanctioning capacity; and (c) use of employee-sharing practices such as job-sharing or job-rotation. Where at least two criteria are met, a '3' is assigned, and a '1' where none is present. A '2' is assigned for mixed cases (Estevez-Abe *et al.* 2001: 166). Due to the existence of workers' councils and strong unions we assigned a '3' for the Slovenian case, the absence of both in Estonia allows a value of '1'. To our knowledge job-rotation or the like is not practised in the transition world, and furthermore it does not seem very likely in a state of transition.
[b] Weighted average of columns 1–3, after each indicator has been standardized to vary between 0 and 1. The weights are 5/9, 2/9 and 2/9, as in Estevez-Abe *et al.* (2001). However, values for the USA and Germany differ from Estevez-Abe *et al.* (2001), because they use the highest value of the sample as a reference value when standardizing the EPL-index. To be able to compare the indexes with the CEEC ones, here EPL is standardized for the scale of the OECD, which takes values between 0 and 6. This does not change the ranking of values.
[c] Values in brackets refer to the pre-2003 Labour Code.
Sources: based on Estevez-Abe *et al.* (2001: table 4.1); OECD (1999); Riboud *et al.* (2002).

overall index of employment protection is calculated as a weighted average. In Table 3.2 we calculate this index for Estonia and Slovenia, using figures for EPL and collective dismissals protection legislation estimated by Riboud *et al.* (2002). We then compare it with results for the USA (LME) and Germany (CME). For Slovenia two figures are given to capture changes associated with a new Labour Code that came into force on 1 January 2003. The similarity between Slovenia and Germany is striking. The higher overall value of 0.67 can be put down almost exclusively to a higher collective dismissals protection in Slovenia. With respect to EPL values, Slovenia can be grouped together with Germany, Austria or the Netherlands (OECD 1999). In Estonia the EPL Index is still higher than in Germany, the archetypal CME. A new Labour Code discussed in Parliament in 2005 can be expected to lead to a lower value of EPL (Philips and Eamets 2003b; 2004).

A comparison of the EPL index for groups of CMEs, LMEs and transition economies shows Estonia, Slovenia and the Czech Republic to have greater protection legislation than Germany, the highest of the CMEs. Poland and Hungary were lower than France, but very much higher than the typical LME (Ireland, Great Britain and USA). Overall employment protection in transition economies is higher than in both typical LMEs and CMEs. One can still find legacies from the communist past in this area. The Slovenian figure, which captures the EPL after reforms, fits very well among the first group of CMEs. However, the Estonian index sits uneasily among the second cluster of LMEs. As stated above, new legislation will most probably bring this value in line with typical LME-values.

Unemployment protection

To measure different degrees of UP, Estevez-Abe *et al.* (2001: 167–9) make use of net replacement rates, meaning unemployment benefits as the percentage of previous income, net of taxes. Furthermore, the share of GDP paid in unemployment benefits as a percentage of the share of unemployed in the total population is considered. As a third measure they construct an index which expresses the discretion an unemployed person has in rejecting a job offer without losing eligibility for benefits. As in the case of EP, an overall index of UP is calculated from these three indicators. For lack of exactly corresponding data, we content ourselves with indicators from which analogous conclusions can be drawn. These are gross replacement rates, the share of GDP paid in unemployment benefits as a percentage of the share of unemployment in the total labour

Table 3.3   Unemployment protection in the UK, Estonia, Germany and Slovenia, end of 1990s

	Gross replacement rate, %[a]	Share of GDP paid in unemployment benefits per percentage point of unemployment rates[b]	Maximum duration of unemployment benefits, in months
UK	36	0.17	12
Estonia	40[c]	0.02	12
Germany	61	0.39	32
Slovenia	63	0.22	24

Notes: [a] Unemployment benefits as percentage of previous income.
[b] Share of unemployed in total labour force.
[c] Estimation for 2003 by Vodopivec *et al.* (2003); 50 per cent in the first 100 days of unemployment period.
Sources: Riboud *et al.* (2002); Vodopivec *et al.* (2003).

force, and the maximum duration of unemployment benefits. These figures are presented in Table 3.3.

The Slovenian replacement rate constitutes, with the exception of Hungary, the highest of the studied transitional economies (Riboud *et al.* 2002). It is well in line with the German rate. In addition, its expenditures are the highest, although lower than in Germany. This is most probably also conditioned by strained budgets in most transition countries. In Estonia new legislation came into force in 2003. Before that the replacement rate was 10 per cent (!) of average income. Vodopivec *et al.* (2003) estimate a rate of 40 per cent of previous income (50 per cent in the first 100 days) for the new law. Still, it seems that it is too early to evaluate the new legislation, because of continuing discussions about further reform (Leetmaa 2003). That means that the value for unemployment benefits (2 per cent) might also be an underestimate.

All this goes to show that both countries, coming from similar points of departure, went in opposite directions. Slovenia built up a CME-like system with a generous replacement rate, relatively high overall expenditures, and a long maximum duration of payments. Estonia stuck to a policy of very low replacement rates and expenditures similar to LMEs throughout the 1990s, only to raise them a little above the value for the UK. The duration of benefits is the same as in the UK.

Vocational training

The area of vocational training is a key element for VoC, because here appropriate skills are formed for distinct innovation strategies. In socialism vocational training was roughly the same in all CEECs: large state-controlled firms cooperated with state-run technical schools. This led, very similarly to Germany, to firm-specific and industry-specific skill formation. Along with the collapse of many firms with the shock of system change schools lost the opportunity to train students appropriately (Roberts 2001: 317–20). Thus, a new way of vocational training eventually had to be found.

In Estonia the inherited Soviet-style training scheme was retained until 1998. In June the Law on Vocational Education Institutions (Kutseoppeastuse seadus) was enacted as the outcome of several amendments to previous legislation. The curricula of high schools, meaning secondary general schools, and vocational schools were brought closer to each other by splitting vocational education into a secondary and a higher education branch. The division into training connected to the different sectors was abolished. The explicit goal was to prepare apprentices for more general tasks which could be applied more broadly. This meant a fundamental change of the system of education and vocational training, and at the same time a shift towards an emphasis on general skills (OECD 2001, ch. 4).

In contrast, in Slovenia, the struggling old system was put on a new basis by introducing a dual system of apprenticeships, very much like the German one. Apprentices are trained in both firms and vocational schools, thereby acquiring both firm-specific and industry-specific skills, the latter ensured by a common standardization and mutual recognition of qualifications. A similar system had existed previously in Slovenia, but was abolished at the beginning of the 1980s. As reintroduced, the dual system is expected to become the dominant form of vocational education (Geržina *et al.* 2000: 51).

Emerging comparative institutional advantages

Beyond a classification of countries as LMEs or CMEs, VoC goes further to argue that the institutional configurations based on institutional complementarities can serve to explain economic structures. Although in their basic introduction to the concept, Hall and Soskice (2001) only tentatively touch on that topic, the underlying thought is far-reaching for internal economic structures, foreign direct investment and trade. The sectoral representation should be highest in those economic activities in which countries have a comparative institutional advantage. Hence, one should be able to observe specific trade patterns according to comparative institutional advantages of nations. More recently, due to ongoing liberalization of capital flows, institutional configurations may lead to an 'institutional arbitrage', in the sense that companies shift production to those countries which serve their institutional needs better, particularly regarding modes of innovation: 'companies may locate ... activities in coordinated market economies in order to secure access to the quality control, skill levels, and capacities for incremental innovation that their institutional frameworks offer' (Hall and Soskice 2001: 57). The reverse is true for activities which rely on radical innovations: here firms use greater openness on a global scale to move activities to liberal market economies. A clear-cut empirical investigation into the issue of comparative institutional advantages is still to come (cf. Taylor 2004).

In the present case of Estonia and Slovenia a first examination of trade patterns and foreign direct investment according to the identified economic systems will shed light on comparative institutional advantages.

Sectoral contributions to the trade balance

The contribution of specific sectors to the trade of nations is a first measure to identify possible comparative advantages. Freudenberg and Lemoine (1999) use trade data for Central and Eastern Europe for the period from 1993 to 1996. They apply an index developed by Lafay (1992) for the sectoral contribution to the trade balance. The index takes a negative value for comparative disadvantage and a positive for an advantage in a specific sector.[4] Their overall assessment of the specialization of transition economies in their trade with the EU reveals that comparative advantages can be predominantly found in resource- and/or labour-intensive industries, such as wood or textiles. This is mostly due to huge wage differentials to Western economies. However, the authors also identify the beginning of a trend towards 'despecialization' in these sectors. A detailed analysis of Estonia and Slovenia in this period reveals the following patterns. Estonia shows comparative advantages in areas such as wood, coke and textiles and comparative disadvantages in manufacturing sectors such as optics, motor vehicles or machinery and equipment increased in the period from 1993 to 1996. Slovenia also shows comparative advantages in similar sectors, such as wearing apparel and wood. Apart from that, it proves to make a comparatively large contribution to the trade balance in electrical machinery. In more advanced manufacturing sectors, such as motor vehicles and chemicals, the comparative disadvantage in the beginning of the period significantly decreased, especially in the motor vehicles sector. Also, a shift towards specialization, indicated by a move from a negative value of the index in 1993 to a positive one in 1996, occurred in machinery.

To get further insights into the development of comparative advantages in both countries over the course of transition the Lafay Index has been calculated for 2000–3 using SITC Revision 3 data from the UN COMTRADE database.[5] It can be assumed that this reveals a clearer picture of comparative advantages in both countries as the catch-up process has carried on. To obtain a first impression in Figure 3.2, a selection of those sectors is shown in which one country has a comparative advantage in those manufacturing sectors where the other enjoys a comparative disadvantage, and vice versa. What interests us most are manufacturing sectors to asses the shift from labour- and resource-intensive to more advanced industries.

The analysis of trade patterns of both countries according to trade figures in the SITC classification has potential drawbacks. As these data do not include services, potential comparative institutional advantages of LMEs may not be revealed. In fact, the analysis seems to be suited best to analysing CMEs, which reveal comparative institutional advantage in manufacturing sectors captured by international trade data. However, some conclusions still can be drawn from the analysis of Lafay-Indexes of Estonia and Slovenia. First of all, from Figure 3.2 it follows that Slovenian trade figures reveal a comparative advantage in typical CME-sectors, such as road vehicles, electric machinery and rubber manufacturing. In these sectors Estonia has a comparative disadvantage. Second, the trend predicted by Freudenberg and Lemoine (1999) in Slovenia can be confirmed.

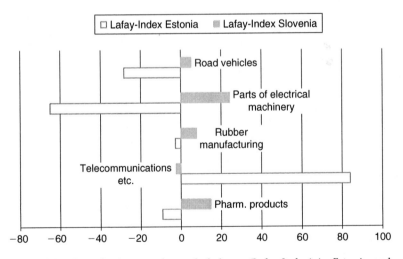

Figure 3.2 Contributions to the trade balance (Lafay-Index) in Estonia and Slovenia, average 2000–2003
Source: UN COMTRADE Database, SITC Revision 3, two-digit levels.

The top category of chemicals (SITC 5) reveals a positive index in 2003. The case of motor vehicles is most revealing in this respect. Until 1996 this figure was negative, but from 2000 at least it shows positive figures. This points to a deep structural change in the economy. The third observation refers to the Estonian case where the telecommunications sector reveals a strong comparative advantage.

Not only can contributions to the trade balance point to comparative institutional advantage of countries, but also movements of foreign direct investments. As argued above, firms should locate their activities, or parts of them, in those institutional settings which fit them best. At the same time, activities in trade and foreign direct investment are interrelated, as large sectoral inflows of foreign direct investment impact on trade performances. Consequently, in a next step patterns of FDI in Estonia and Slovenia will be analysed.

Patterns of foreign direct investment

Foreign direct investment flows in CEECs are quite concentrated. The bulk of investments went to Central and Eastern Europe and the Baltic states, while the CIS and south-eastern Europe received a much smaller part. Regarding determinants of foreign direct investment, Kinoshita and Campos (2003) find in a study of twenty-five transition countries that, when controlling for 'traditional' determinants of foreign direct investment such as labour costs, quality of labour, natural resources, infrastructure, proximity to the home country and macroeconomic factors, the most important drivers for FDI are agglomeration effects and institutions. Institutions are measured as the quality of bureaucracy and the rule of law. From a VoC perspective one can argue now that apart from the quality of institutions the *type* of institutions comprising a capitalist system also should be important for FDI. Different institutional settings with different comparative institutional advantages should attract different kinds of industries. A rigorous quantitative analysis of this claim goes beyond the scope of this chapter. However, a look at patterns of foreign direct investment for the country studies of Estonia and Slovenia gives first insights into the validity of this proposition.

Sectoral breakdowns of FDI in Estonia and Slovenia suffer from difficulties with comparability of data. The Bank of Estonia does not provide more detailed data under the top class in ISIC Revision 1 classification due to confidentiality issues. Slovenian figures are more detailed, but not all sections are provided, for the same reason. This leaves us with a rather rough picture of foreign direct investment stock in both countries in Table 3.4.

Table 3.4 Foreign direct investment stocks per selected activities as shares in total stocks, 2004

Sector, ISIC Revision 1	Estonia	Slovenia
Manufacturing (D)	16.7	45.6
Wholesale and retail trade (G)	10.0	13.6
Transport, storage and communication (I)	5.3	4.5
Financial intermediation (J)	31.5	19.0
Real estate, renting and business services (K)	22.7	11.7

Sources: Bank of Estonia and Bank of Slovenia.

The figures in Table 3.4 elucidate the importance of FDI for different sectors of both economies. It can be seen that the manufacturing sector is the largest absorber of FDI in Slovenia. Within this, pharmaceuticals is the largest branch, corresponding to the trade figures above. On the other hand, manufacturing plays a subordinate role for Estonia. There, financial intermediation investments have a dominant position, followed by a growing stock of activities connected with real estate, renting and other business activities. Unsatisfactory data notwithstanding, a few conclusions can be drawn from these figures. First, manufacturing investors prefer Slovenia over Estonia. In fact, when comparing manufacturing stocks for all eight new EU members in 2000, Slovenia scores the highest values of the share of manufacturing in total stocks together with the Czech Republic (UNCTAD, various years). Secondly, investment in Estonia predominantly goes into sectors with a stronger service character, such as financial intermediation and real estate.

Geographical origin serves as another indicator of emerging structures. From a VoC perspective we would expect firms to shift activities where institutional settings and the prevailing variety of capitalism suits best. However, a few qualifications have to be taken into consideration. In the case of transition economies one must be careful, because large wage differentials were and still are drivers for investment in the region. In this case, firms also shift activities, which match institutional settings of both home and host country due to cost advantages. Also the distance of the country of origin plays a major role. The most important countries of origin of direct investment stocks for Estonia were Sweden and Finland, and for Slovenia, Austria and Germany.

Both cases show the strong influence of geographical proximity of home countries of FDI. For Estonia these are Sweden and Finland, for Slovenia Austria and to a certain extent Italy and Croatia. In the Estonian case large figures of FDI from the Nordic countries reflect the origins of large companies, such as Ericsson or Nokia, and the importance of trade in the telecommunications sector. Högselius (2005) reports that telecommunications traditionally played a prominent role in Estonia even before independence. While in the beginning of the 1990s companies investing in this sector primarily regarded the country as a low-cost production site, now innovative and service-related telecommunications industries are also starting to grow in importance.

On the whole, European CMEs are the dominant investors in both countries. However, the role of the USA is particularly telling, because here considerations of geographical distance are the same throughout Eastern Europe. When comparing FDI stocks from the US as a share of GDP in 2002 for all eight new EU members, Estonia reveals the highest share of all (UNCTAD, various years). The fact that Estonia is most important for American investors can be explained by its variety of capitalist system, because firms seeking cost advantages find similar institutions like in their home country.

Conclusion

The preceding discussion has shown that Estonia and Slovenia can be seen as polar opposites regarding their capitalist systems. At the same time, both countries show a high degree of complementary institutions. The Slovenian case very much resembles coordinated market economies like Germany or Austria: it reveals corporatist-like labour relations with a large degree of wage-bargaining coverage and codetermination. Complementarily to this, unemployment and employment protection are high. The vocational training system is capable of providing firm-specific and industry-specific skills. In Estonia, however, industrial relations are characterized by a dominance of firm-level relations and a poorly organized workforce. Employment protection is high, but there is evidence that this is a legacy from Soviet times and is likely to be reduced. The vocational training system has been reshaped towards general education of the workforce.

However, in the area of corporate governance deviations from the VoC framework occur in both countries. On the one hand, the Estonian system cannot be described as a shareholder model as one would expect for an LME. Enterprise legislation is organized as in a stakeholder model, but it is circumvented in practice. More importantly, the comparatively small stock market cannot provide the same function as in an advanced LMEs. The possibility of a functional equivalent, which could provide similar disciplining measures as a stock market, provides opportunities for future research.

On the other hand, in Slovenia the influence of investment funds, partly state-owned, and employee ownership of companies, have been identified as deviant from representative CMEs. It has been argued that this could be a functional equivalent in the absence of proficient banks providing patient capital. Then, the fact that workers partly own their company can be seen as a transitional institutional complementarity. Thereby incentives to invest in a high degree of asset specificity can be established. One has to be cautious with this claim, because the efficiency criterion connected to the notion of institutional complementarities requires a thorough proof in order to be distinguished from mere clustering of institutions. As employee ownership is common to other transition economies as well, a comparative study could illuminate this claim further in future research.

All in all, while the present analysis did answer the question of what kind of capitalism is emerging in the two countries under study, many more questions have been raised. For instance, the divergent experience in the reformation of vocational training systems in both countries is remarkable. Coming from more or less the same starting points, the two moved into opposite directions. While Estonia accentuated a more general education perspective in its vocational training system, Slovenia aimed at firmly institutionalizing a scheme which is able to provide companies with apprentices endowed with a mix of firm-specific and industry-specific skills. This discrepancy makes a suitable case for studying the much debated issue of possible influences of institutional complementarities on the emergence of institutions (Crouch *et al.* 2005). Also, when studying emerging comparative institutional advantages of Eastern European countries it seems desirable to go beyond the illustrative data employed here and conduct a thorough analysis of a wider country sample.

Notes

*I would like to thank the participants of two conferences in Cambridge and Paisley for comments on earlier drafts, especially both editors of this volume. In addition, the chapter has greatly benefited from comments by Joachim Ahrens, Masahiko Aoki, Olaf Labitzke, Sang-Min Park and Carsten Renner. Most of all I am indebted to Frank Bönker and Hans-Jürgen Wagener for constant fruitful discussions and encouragement.

1. Polish *Solidarność* being an exception.
2. In this case one should not assume this to be an institution, because it is not perceived as one by actors (Aoki 2001: 13). However, in this case anecdotal

evidence is reported and hence, thorough empirical evaluation, would be needed to clarify matters.

3. However, more recent data is needed to assess this more accurately, for Czaban *et al.* (2003) report research conducted in the first half of the 1990s.

4. This Lafay-indicator is defined as: $L_I = [(X_I - M_I) \div Y] - [[X_I + M_I \div X_T + M_T]X_T - M_T \div Y]$ where subscript I denotes specific industries under study and T refers to total trade volumes, for exports X and imports M. Y stands for the country's GDP. The first term of the indicator measures the trade balance for a single industry weighted with GDP. The second term attempts to eliminate variations caused by business cycles. It expresses a theoretical trade balance for the case that all industries contribute according to their share in total trade. Thus, a positive L for a given industry indicates that it contributes comparatively more than the 'expected' share. This is also the case for a trade deficit, which is smaller than expected. For $L_I > 0$ a given industry therefore exhibits a comparative advantage, and for $L_I < 0$ an industry reveals a comparative disadvantage (Lafay 1992).

5. Freudenberg and Lemoine (1999) use data according to the NACE classification system.

References

Amable, B. (2003) *The Diversity of Modern Capitalism* (Oxford: Oxford University Press).

Aoki, M. (2001) *Toward a Comparative Institutional Analysis* (Cambridge, MA: MIT Press).

Berglöf, E. and P. Bolton (2002) 'The Great Divide and Beyond: Financial Architecture in Transition', *Journal of Economic Perspectives*, 16, 77–100.

Berglöf, E. and A. Pajuste (2003) 'Emerging Owners, Eclipsing Markets? Corporate Governance in Transition', in P. Cornelius and B. Kogut (eds), *Corporate Governance and Capital Flows in a Global Economy* (Oxford: Oxford University Press), 267–303.

Blair, M. (1999) 'Firm-Specific Human Capital and the Theory of the Firm', in M. Blair and M. Roe (eds), *Employees and Corporate Governance* (Washington, DC: Brookings Institutions Press), 58–90.

Boeri, T. and K. Terrell (2002) 'Institutional Determinants of Labor Reallocation in Transition', *Journal of Economic Perspectives*, 16, 51–76.

Bohinc, R. and S.M. Bainbridge (1999) 'Corporate Governance in Post-Privatized Slovenia', *American Journal of Comparative Law*, 49, 49–77.

Crouch, C., W. Streeck, R. Boyer, B. Amable, P.A. Hall and G. Jackson (2005) 'Dialogue on Institutional Complementarity and Political Economy', *Socio-Economic Review*, 3, 359–81.

Czaban, L., M. Hocevar, M. Jaklic, and R. Whitley (2003) 'Path Dependence and Contractual Relations: Contrasting State Socialist Legacies and Inter-firm Cooperation in Hungary and Slovenia', *Organization Studies*, 24, 7–28.

Damijan, J.P., A. Gregorič, and J. Prašnikar (2004) *Ownership Concentration and Firm Performance in Slovenia*, Leuven, LICOS Discussion Paper, No.142. (Katholieke Universiteit Leuven).

Djankov, S, and P. Murrell (2002) 'Enterprise Restructuring in Transition: A Quantitative Survey', *Journal of Economic Literature*, 40, 739–92.

EBRD (2002) *Transition Report 2002: Agriculture and Rural Transition* (London: European Bank for Reconstruction and Development).

EBRD (2004) *Transition Report 2004: Infrastructure* (London: European Bank for Reconstruction and Development).

Ericson, R.E. (1991) 'The Classical Soviet-Type Economy: Nature of the System and Implications for Reform', *Journal of Economic Perspectives*, 5, 11–27.

Estevez-Abe, M., T. Iversen, D. Soskice, (2001) 'Social Protection and the Formation of Skills: A Reinterpretation of the Welfare Sate', in P.A. Hall and D. Soskice (eds), *Varieties of Capitalism: The Institutional Foundations of Comparative Advantage* (Oxford: Oxford University Press), 145–83.

Feldmann, M. (2006) 'Emerging Varieties of Capitalism in Transition Countries: The Case of Wage Bargaining in Estonia and Slovenia', *Comparative Political Studies*, forthcoming.

Freudenberg, M. and F. Lemoine (1999) *Central and Eastern European Countries in the International Division of Labour in Europe*, CEPII Working Paper, No.99-05. (Centre d'études prospectives et d'informations internationales).

Gerndorf, K., T. Elenurm and E. Terk (1999) *Corporate Governance in Estonia* (Vilnius: OECD Seminar Paper).

Geržina, S., P. Vranješ and M. Cek (2000) *Modernisation of Vocational Education and Training in Slovenia 1999 – Final Report* (Ljubljana: National VET Observatory Slovenia).

Götting, U. (1998) *Transformation der Wohlfahrtsstaaten in Mittel- und Osteuropa – eine Zwischenbilanz* (Opladen: Leske + Budrich).

Goodin, R.E. (2003) 'Choose Your Capitalism?', *Comparative European Politics*, 1, 203–13.

Gregorič, A. (2003) *Corporate Governance in Slovenia: An International Perspective*, Doctoral dissertation, University of Ljubljana.

Hall, P.A. and D. Soskice (2001) 'An Introduction to the Varieties of Capitalism', in P.A. Hall and D. Soskice (eds), *Varieties of Capitalism: The Institutional Foundations of Comparative Advantage* (Oxford: Oxford University Press), 1–68.

Högselius, P. (2005) *The Dynamics of Innovation in Eastern Europe: Lessons from Estonia* (Cheltenham: Edward Elgar).

Jones, D.C. and N. Mygind (2005) 'Corporate Governance Cycles during Transition: Theory and Evidence from the Baltics', in I. Filatotchev and M. Wright (eds), *The Life Cycle of Corporate Governance* (Cheltenham: Edward Elgar), 253–86.

Kalmi, P. (2003) 'The Rise and Fall of Employee Ownership in Estonia. 1987–2001', *Europe-Asia Studies*, 55, 1213–39.

Kinoshita, Y. and N.F. Campos (2003) *Why Does FDI Go where it Goes? New Evidence from the Transition Economies*, William Davidson Institute Working Paper, No.573. (Ann Arbour, MI: University of Michigan).

Kornai, J. (1992) *The Socialist System: The Political Economy of Communism* (Oxford: Clarendon Press).

Ladó, Mária (2002) 'Industrial Relations in the Candidate Countries', *European Industrial Relations Observatory* <www.eiro.eurofound.ie>.

Lafay, G. (1992) 'The Measurement of Revealed Comparative Advantages', in M.G. Dagenais and P.A. Muet (eds), *International Trade Modelling* (London: Chapman and Hill), 209–34.

Leetmaa, R. (2003) *Discussions about the Unemployment Insurance System* (Tallinn: PRAXIS, Center for Policy Studies).

Lukšič, I. (2003) 'Corporatism Packaged in Pluralist Ideology: The Case of Slovenia', *Communist and Post-Communist Studies*, 36, 509–25.

Mencinger, J. (2004) 'Transition to a National and Market Economy: A Gradualist Approach', in M. Mrak, M. Rojec and C. Silva-Jáuregui (eds), *Slovenia: From Yugoslavia to the European Union* (Washington, DC: The World Bank), 67–82.

Mygind, N. (1997) 'A Comparative Analysis of the Economic Transition in the Baltic Countries – Barriers, Strategies, Perspectives', in T. Haavisto (ed.), *The Transition to a Market Economy: Transformation and Reform in the Baltic States* (Cheltenham: Edward Elgar), 17–65.

Nuti, M. (1997) 'Employeeism: Corporate Governance and Employee Share Ownership in Transition Economies', in M. Bléjer and M. Skreb (eds), *Macroeconomic Stabilization in Transition Economies* (Cambridge: Cambridge University Press), 126–54.

OECD (1999) *Employment Outlook 1999* (Paris: OECD).

OECD (2001) *Reviews for National Policies for Education: Estonia* (Paris: OECD).

Pahor, M., J. Prašnikar and A. Ferligoj (2004) 'Building a Corporate Network in a Transition Economy: The Case of Slovenia', *Post-Communist Economies*, 16, 307–31.

Philips, K. and R. Eamets (2003a) 'Collective Bargaining Examined', *European Industrial Relations Observatory* <www.eiro.eurofound.ie>.

Philips, K. and R. Eamets (2003b) 'Social Partners Discuss New Employment Contracts Act', *European Industrial Relations Observatory* <www.eiro.eurofound.ie>.

Philips, K. and R. Eamets (2004) 'Government Presents Labour and Social Policy Plans', *European Industrial Relations Observatory* <www.eiro.eurofound.ie>.

Porter, M.E., K. Schwab, X. Sala-i-Martin and A. Lopez-Claros (2004) *Global Competitiveness Report 2004–2005* (Basingstoke: Palgrave Macmillan).

Prašnikar, J. and A. Gregorič (2002) 'The Influence of Workers' Participation on the Power of Management in Transitional Countries: The Case of Slovenia', *Annals of Public and Cooperative Economics*, 73, 269–97.

Qian, Y. (2003) 'How Reform Worked in China?', in D. Rodrik (ed.), *In Search of Prosperity: Analytical Narratives on Economic Growth* (Princeton, NJ: Princeton University Press), 297–333.

Riboud, M., C. Sánchez-Páramo and C. Silva-Jáuregui (2002) *Does Eurosclerosis Matter? Institutional Reform and Labor Market Performance in Central and Eastern European Countries in the 1990s*, Social Protection Discussion Paper 202 (Washington, DC: World Bank).

Roberts, K. (2001) 'The New East European Model of Education, Training and Youth Employment', *Journal of Education and Work*, 14, 315–28.

Skledar, S. (2005) 'Draft Law on Collective Agreements Still under Discussion', *European Industrial Relations Observatory* <www.eiro.eurofound.ie>.

Smith, D. (2001) *Estonia: Independence and European Integration* (London: Routledge).

Soskice, D. (1999) 'Divergent Production Regimes: Coordinated and Uncoordinated Market Economies in the 1980s and 1990s', in K. Herbert, P. Lange., G. Marks and J.D. Stephens (eds), *Continuity and Change in Contemporary Capitalism* (Cambridge: Cambridge University Press), 101–34.

Stanojević, M. (2000) 'Slovenian Trade Unions – The Birth of Labour Organizations in Post-Communism', *Journal of Social Sciences Studies*, 16, 87–100.

Stanojević, M. (2001) 'Industrial Relations in 'Post-Communism': Workplace Cooperation in Hungary and Slovenia', *Journal for East European Management Studies*, 6, 400–20.

Stanojević, M. (2003) 'Workers' Power in Transition Economies: The Cases of Serbia and Slovenia', *European Journal of Industrial Relations*, 9, 283–301.

Šušteršič, J. (2004) 'Political Economy of Slovenia's Transition', in M. Mrak, M. Rojec and C. Silva-Jáuregui (eds), *Slovenia: From Yugoslavia to the European Union* (Washington, DC: World Bank), 399–411.

Taylor, M.Z. (2004) 'Empirical Evidence Against Varieties of Capitalism's Theory of Technological Innovation', *International Organization*, 58, 601–31.

UNCTAD, *World Investment Directory* <www.unctad.org/wid>.

Vodopivec, M., A. Wörgötter and D. Raju (2003) *Unemployment Benefit Systems in Central and Eastern Europe: A Review of the 1990s*, Social Protection Discussion Paper, 310, (Washington, DC: World Bank).

Wielgohs, J. (2001) 'Coping with Privatization and Employment Decline: Three Short Stories of Success', in J. Beyer, J. Wielgohs and H. Wiesenthal (eds), *Successful Transition: Political Factors of Socio-Economic Progress in Postsocialist Countries* (Baden-Baden: Nomos), 153–75.

4
Eastern Germany's Incorporation into the Federal Republic

Rudi Schmidt

The complete set of social and economic institutions, norms and values of the West German system of coordinated market economy ('Soziale Marktwirtschaft') was transferred to Eastern Germany. This denied the former GDR the opportunity to develop home-grown economic institutions like other Central and Eastern European states. With persistent high unemployment of 20 per cent, despite huge financial transfers from West to East, it is an open question whether this transition process will prove successful. This chapter investigates whether the highly developed West German system of market economy was suitable for transfer to a former socialist economy, or whether the actors involved (managers and entrepreneurs) failed in applying the new institutions. Generally, actors play a key role in handling new rules and norms within a given structural framework. The special case of the GDR indicates how managers were shaped by the conditions prevailing in state-run industry and how this influenced their ability to master the problems of the new economic system in which they found themselves after 1989. Furthermore, the huge problems of the Eastern German economy weaken the economic strength of Western Germany. They undermine the 'Rhine Model' and reinforce the shift towards its neo-liberal Anglo-Saxon counterpart.

Economic outcomes fifteen years after German unification

In 1990, an atmosphere of ambivalence prevailed in Europe. While great joy was felt in the East-Central European states released from Soviet tutelage, the feelings of Western Europeans ranged from uncertainty to fear about the emerging new concentration of power in the centre of Europe. Many, particularly François Mitterrand and Margaret Thatcher, feared that the union of the third and, supposedly, tenth largest industrial nations represented a concentration of power destabilizing to the European equilibrium, with all the political problems this would entail, which were projected from past to future in linear fashion. Very few possessed sufficient knowledge of the true condition of the GDR. In practice, the burdens of unification placed a very considerable strain on the efficiency of the German state and economy and will do so for at least a generation.

In 2005, in the fifteenth year of a unified Germany, 4 per cent of GDP was transferred annually from West to East. In absolute numbers, this comes to €130 bn annually and, since unification (1991–2004), a total of €1,300 mn gross or €1,000 mn net, offset against return flows of tax (Ragnitz 2004: 289; Steinitz 2005: 9). This financial aid was overwhelmingly financed through loans. A small portion only was drawn from tax revenue or contributions to redistributive systems of social insurance. The mountain of debts that the Federal Republic piled up was, to a significant degree, the result of these costs of unification. A good third to half, depending on the method of calculation, of the almost €1,500 mn of public debt has been attributed to the costs of German unity (Bach and Vesper 2000: 219).

Despite this enormous financial transfer, the two halves of the state are marked by significant economic disparities. The most explosive is the high unemployment in Eastern Germany: almost one in five was without work there in 2003 (18.5 per cent), compared with 8.5 per cent in Western Germany (Lebenslagen 2005: 153). Other data are also overwhelmingly negative. Eastern German industry contracted dramatically in the wake of the breaking up and privatization of the large combines to become structurally dominated by small and medium-sized firms (SMEs). The resulting disadvantages were made worse by specific weaknesses, some of which were proving chronic: a negligible share of research and development, weak bargaining power in the marketplace, more suppliers than final producers, less added value and productivity (for structural reasons only two-thirds that of Western Germany). Its share of exports of around 24.5 per cent was significantly lower than in Western Germany, where the figure was 39.5 per cent (in 2003, Lebenslagen 2005: 153). Eastern German firms are on an insecure footing in Western Germany too. A mere 2 per cent of the products sold by German businesses in Western Germany come from Eastern Germany. In Eastern Germany itself, only 54 per cent of products sold by German firms come from Eastern Germany (Bellmann *et al.* 2005: 67).

Wages in the Eastern German economy as a whole were around three quarters the Western German level; the figure for industry was 69 per cent (Bellmann *et al.* 2005: 74). Only industrial unit labour costs attained the

Western German level and were in fact somewhat less expensive. Property prices were of course also lower in the East as a result of lower incomes and lower demand. Since 1990 2.4 m Eastern Germans have moved to the Western half of the country, and the migratory balance remained negative. In 2004, building land in Eastern Germany cost an average of €47 per m^2, as opposed to €123 in the West (*Frankfurter Allgemeine Zeitung* 5.8.05). Eastern Germans naturally had fewer assets (40 per cent of the Western German average, see Lebenslagen 2005: 86) and were therefore more heavily dependent on employment and transfer income from the West. 'Every third Euro spent in the East was generated elsewhere' (*Süddeutsche Zeitung* 25.8.05).

It is hardly surprising that transfers on such a scale, most of which were spent on consumption rather than investment, hit everyday social welfare services in the Western German local authority areas and *Länder*, which also have to pay such financial contributions. The OECD calculated that two-thirds of Germany's poor economic growth could be put down to the burden of German unity (*Süddeutsche Zeitung* 25.8.05). These problems were exacerbated by weak economic growth rate of only 0.5 to 1 per cent on average in recent years, by mass unemployment and stagnant state tax income. This growing public poverty contrasts with the enormous profits of German firms with an international presence, profits they explain as shareholder value-driven, while failing to help reduce unemployment.

However, the massive transfer payments were not inducing a self-sustaining upturn in the East, as many still hoped in 1990, but were stabilizing the economy at the level of the late 1990s. Manufacturing industry in Eastern Germany as a whole was growing disproportionately, even in comparison with Western Germany, but from a lower starting point, to which it had sunk following the unprecedented deindustrialization sparked off by the privatization of the East German combine-based economy. Eastern Germany's economic balance sheet was particularly blotted by the sustained decline of the construction industry after its massive tax-induced ascent until 1997, and by stagnation in the service sector. The civil service was also under pressure because it continued to employ a disproportionately large number of workers, a legacy of the GDR.

Because all the major centres of economic decision-making, particularly company headquarters, also lie in the West, as do the major research and development hubs, Eastern Germany may even be described as a dependence economy, or as an example of peripheral capitalism. There are only a few economic hubs in Eastern Germany, such as Jena, Dresden or Leipzig, with sufficient innate innovative potential to generate autonomous growth. The regional halo effect remains very limited, and the cluster effects minor. These existing key industrial areas cannot therefore be expected to remedy poor Eastern German growth rates, even in the medium term.

To put it in a nutshell: expectations of the rapid consolidation of the Eastern German economy and prosperity on a par with Western Germany remain unfulfilled fifteen years after unification. The critical debate on the factors responsible for this stresses above all the failure to appraise accurately the economy of the GDR and a flawed integration policy. This false assessment was due partly to the deceptive statistics produced by the GDR and partly to the deluded if calculated optimism of politicians in both East and West in 1990. The flawed integration policy can be put down to the central economic idea of the conservative-liberal government of the day, which had a fundamental faith in the autonomy of the market and did not care for industrial policy. It took this approach despite the fact that history has produced no examples of structurally deficient countries being successfully integrated into the world market without protectionist and compensatory intervention by the state in the economy.[1]

The two worlds of the Eastern German manager

As soon as the social revolution in Eastern Europe began and it became apparent that capitalism and democracy would soon reign triumphant, questions were asked about the future shape of these societies now shifting away from the old system towards Western models. Furthermore, how would this development affect the varying types of market economy? The discourse of transformation, informed by modernization theory, was thus fused with the debate on the Varieties of Capitalism initiated earlier, providing it with additional stimulus.

Since the late 1990s, social scientists have attempted to define the two main forms of contemporary capitalism – the Anglo-Saxon neo-liberal market model and the European welfare state model, particularly on the continent – as competing models. This debate, labelled 'varieties of capitalism' or 'divergent capitalism', tends to evoke three scenarios.

The first, advocated particularly by Streeck (1997), assumes that the German model will largely converge with the Anglo-American neo-liberal market model. Its ideological hegemony, together with the United States' profound influence on global economic structures and financial systems (Dore 2000), place a great deal of pressure on others to adapt. This scenario is underpinned by the notion that economic activity and organization are subject to a global isomorphism, as expounded in the sociological variant of new institutionalism, Meyer (Meyer *et al.* 1994) being the key commentator here.

The second scenario implicitly takes the hegemony of the Anglo-American market model for granted but does not go on to assume that this will inevitably be the undoing of the German system. Instead, on this view, the neo-liberal model will be emphasized with increasing vigour (Sorge 1996). This, it is claimed, is due to specialization of product markets, which opens up opportunities for German firms in sectors featuring high quality and technological standards. German firms would supposedly have good prospects of holding their own in such sectors long-term.

The third scenario, as advocated notably by Whitley (1999) and Ferner and Varul (1999), assumes that the German system will incrementally adapt to the Anglo-American market model. Core elements of the German model, however, would be retained.

If the first scenario applies at all, it does so only in the case of major German firms quoted on the stock exchange. Even then, the influence of employees' codetermination, strongest of course in major firms, places notable restrictions upon the Anglo-Saxon model (see Zugehör 2003). The other two scenarios are more subtle empirically and thus more probable, but all are wrong to assume that the differences between German firms are more or less irrelevant to the diffusion of the Anglo-American market model. Germany is characterized by a dichotomy between a small sector consisting almost entirely of large companies quoted on the stock exchange and a large sector made up of privately owned SMEs. East Germany provides particularly clear evidence of this. In what follows we shall see that the outcome of social transformation depends not only on an appropriate institutional framework, but also on the actors operating within it. New institutions do not work, when there is a lack of actors using them in the right way. That was the crucial point at the beginning of transformation in Germany in 1990.

In terms of function and aims of action, managers in firms in planned and market economies differ as follows. There are differences with respect to autonomy of action and role ascription (function within the firm). Production in the market economy involves competing to satisfy the needs of sanction-laden individual or anonymous mass customers. In the planned economy, weakly sanctioned supplier monopolies distribute their products either to anonymous mass consumers, who have no effective interaction with the producers, or to individual industrial clients: interaction here is on a *do, ut des* basis (barter transactions). This means that the manager in the planned economy acted mainly in relation to the firm.

In my opinion, the main difference between Eastern and Western managers when state socialism collapsed was the former's perspectival limitation to matters internal to the firm, as opposed to the latter's double focus on firm and market. This was highly consequential for the first few years of privatization and explains, to this day, some of the differences between Eastern and Western German managers. The fact that post-communist managers were imbued over many years with the praxis characteristic of combines within a planned economy does not explain, however, their entire dispositional structure and modes of action within the market economy. It is also crucial to take into account the specific set of circumstances in which they came to assume functions of leadership in firms. It was generally easier for managers in flourishing sectors or those with good future prospects to demonstrate their capabilities in industries such as textiles and clothing, carbon-based chemicals, home electronics, ceramics and classical optics, than it was for those unable to hold their own against global competition. Decisions to invest in some sectors were made almost exclusively by Western owners, for example in the motor vehicle industry, steel and chemicals. Limited decision-making autonomy in such firms contrasted with the autonomy of the formally free owners created by management buy-outs. Yet the new Eastern owners of hived-off businesses were in fact often subject to far greater restrictions than the Eastern German co-managers working alongside or under their Western German colleagues in the branches of Western German corporations. They were under the guardianship of the banks and development fund providers (*Fördergesellschaften*), to whom they had to legitimize their developmental plans. Their weak market position, meanwhile, led to external dependencies, which frequently constrained their scope for decision making more strictly than that of Eastern managers in the dependent branch offices of Western firms.

Only gradually did Eastern German managers attain sufficient scope for independent action to allow one to speak of self-defined conditions of action and thus to ascribe to them more clearly the consequences of their actions. In this sense, the firm's developmental history and the associated economic order are also important in appraising management behaviour. The privatization phase in the first half of the 1990s was thus quite distinct from the period of consolidation in the late 1990s. It became apparent that the successful Eastern German managers tended to be those who expanded their focus to include 'outer' factors as quickly as possible, supplementing the internal perspective with an external focus on the market and customers. Having new products and the ability to deliver them reliably and at a reasonable price was merely one essential for success.

Opening up the market and persuading new customers to buy from one's firm, which of course generally means ousting a competitor, is a quite different, far more difficult task (see Gergs 2002). The fact that companies run by such managers now account for a significant portion of Eastern German economic growth is an encouraging development in the former GDR's long process of transformation and adaptation (see Behr and Schmidt 2005).

Consequences for the varieties of capitalism debate

However, these successes in Eastern German manufacturing are insufficient to make up for weaknesses in other economic sectors, such as the civil service, construction and the service sector. The growth and prosperity gap between Western and Eastern Germany is highly unlikely to be reduced in the foreseeable future. This is due in part to the mistakes of the past, and in part to new errors. The latter can be viewed, to some degree, as a reaction to the former.

The mistakes of the past, as they were the starting errors, include above all the flawed policies of the then government on economic transformation and integration. The rapid and total transfer of Western norms and institutions would have enjoyed the speedy acceptance of the public only if it had been economically successful to the degree expected. As this was not, and clearly could not have been, the case, the public mood changed. It was not only the political framing of the transferred norms and institutions which lost legitimacy, but these things themselves. This was and continues to be palpable in numerous societal domains. People in Eastern Germany are generally less willing to participate and civil society is less developed. This can be seen in the low level of involvement in political parties, voluntary activities (it is, for example, difficult to find mayors in small municipalities), trade unions and other intermediary organizations, as well as in the lack of willingness to start one's own business.[2] This partly attentist, partly reserved attitude has made the process of integration even more difficult. Eastern Germans thus exhibited a psychological reserve *vis-à-vis* the new institutions. In addition, an insufficient number of advisors from the West were made available to help transform the East as quickly as possible.

The rapid privatization policy pursued by the German privatization agency, which saw the selling of 15,000 businesses in five years, of which just under 10,000 were industrial firms, overstretched the market for businesses. Willingness to sell and proceeds sank. Many firms could not be sold and were liquidated in the glutted markets. To make matters worse, economic crisis struck from 1990 to 1992 and the mechanical engineering industry in Germany suffered a structural crisis that lasted until 1993. Many Western German businesses were therefore far from keen on expanding their production capacity by taking over Eastern German firms. The number of jobs in industry in the East thus fell by two-thirds within a few years. An over-industrialized country was turned into an under-industrialized one. This meant, among other things, that only a small number of business-related service sector firms, particularly adept at adding value, became established in Eastern Germany. Most politicians failed to grasp that this skewed economic structure would prove a persistent structural deficit and significantly hinder economic growth. It also gave rise to new problems. Because of the steady migration of young workers and the low birth rate in Eastern Germany, there may in a few years' time be too few workers to ensure the economic success of Eastern German firms.

The problems afflicting Eastern Germany have become so severe and chronic that they are having a knock-on effect on the economic and social situation of Western Germany, as indicated above. They also have long-term consequences, of a potentially serious nature, within the contemporary context of global competition. The vast majority of the fiscal transfer of around 4 per cent of GDP, made necessary by Eastern Germany's inability to add sufficient economic value, is spent on consumption and thus contributes, at least indirectly, to Western Germany's inability to invest sufficiently. The debt burden imposed by unification and massive financial transfers has hindered much necessary investment in infrastructure, basic research and the education system. In 2006, the budget deficit was more than 3 per cent for the fourth year running, thus failing to meet the criteria of the EU's Stability and Growth Pact. There is thus little scope to strengthen domestic demand; the necessary growth stimuli are thin on the ground. This predicament, and the high level of unemployment of 9–10 per cent, increase employers' pressure on the government and the unions to intensify deregulation, that is, to diminish workers' rights, collective bargaining agreements and codetermination (Schmidt *et al.* 2003). They are receiving massive support from foreign investors in this pursuit.

On the whole, it took the key actors in economic transformation, particularly managers of firms, longer than originally hoped to adjust to the logic of the new economic system and develop a successful strategy for their businesses. This was also initially made more difficult by a widespread scepticism among Western business partners about whether their firms would consistently be able to make good on their promises (in terms of quality, service, maintenance, delivery of spare parts and the like), if they had existed in this new form for a mere two or three years. They also had to hold their ground in Germany, one of the most competitive markets in the world, and found it difficult to access foreign markets for want of sociocultural and linguistic competence (see Internationalisation 2002).

In their fundamental economic, social and political tendencies, Eastern German managers have largely followed the Western German example. For the international comparative debate on Varieties of Capitalism, this means that post-communist Eastern German society has not seen the rise of a new variant of the capitalist market economy, but a formal, not a real, copy of the Western German model in which the institutions did not work as expected. Apart from those mentioned above, there are, however, additional notable differences.

We have already looked at structural deficits. While they can be viewed as conditions of economic and social action and societal tendencies which might change, there is little prospect of them being brought into line with Western German realities in the foreseeable future. It is therefore highly likely that these deficits will be reflected long-term in the consciousness of the people.[3] The differences between East and West in party structure and voting preferences are significant: this applies to other areas of political life as well. In the economic subsystem surveyed here the differences are equally striking. Alongside differences in the structure of industrial sectors and production (a smaller proportion of high-tech industries, fewer final producers), and regional structures (fewer areas of high industrial concentration such as the Ruhr, Stuttgart and Munich and their surrounding areas, and thus fewer cluster effects), the two parts of the country differ above all in the structure of their firms. In Eastern Germany there are merely a few major companies and almost no company headquarters. Small and medium-sized firms determine the industrial structure even more than in Western Germany. This has consequences on several levels.

In contrast with the situation in France, the UK or the Netherlands, the vast majority of independent small and medium-sized firms in Germany are partnerships. They rarely take the form of a public limited company. This means that entrepreneurs dominate within the firm, while appointed managers are in the minority. Further, this means that these firms, because they are not quoted on the stock exchange, are less dependent on the capital market and tend to obtain their capital through bank loans. The liberalization and globalization of the financial markets, which constitute the central gateway enabling the Anglo-Saxon concept of shareholder value to take effect, have thus far gained little ground in the stakeholder society of German small and medium-sized firms. 'Marketization plus financialization' (Dore 2000: 3) does have indirect consequences for firms independent of the stock exchanges. This is a result of the changed rules governing the granting of credit and bank refinancing, and the ratings and accounting regulations, which these require, changes which are part and parcel of re-regulation by the Bank for International Settlements in Basle. The consequences of this will, however, only take on force in the long term and may be left to one side here (for details see Schmidt 2004; 2005). All of this applies equally to the small and medium-sized firms in Eastern and Western Germany.

The differences between the two parts of the country lie in the indirect structural effects which arise from this. While in Western Germany the policies of the industrial and employers' associations are in part determined by major companies, and strongly by the car industry in the metal-processing and metal-working industries, in Eastern Germany the entrepreneurs of small and medium-sized firms are among others of their own ilk in their associations. Major firms remain pillars of the system of collective industry-specific norms on working conditions and wages. While in Western Germany, however, the decades-long tradition of workers' codetermination and collective industry-specific norms have induced normative seepage into small and medium-sized businesses usually averse to standardization, this corporative disciplining pressure was absent in Eastern Germany (Artus 2001; Schroeder 2000). In 1990–1 all firms administered by the German privatization agency joined the employers' associations in line with a decree by the agency and were thus bound by agreements with trade unions and established works councils. This collective commitment to certain norms, however, was seriously eroded after privatization and is now far weaker than in Western Germany.[4] A similar gap exists in the works councils. Newly established firms tend in principle not to join the employees' association. The SMEs among them, moreover, do not usually establish a works council. Deviation from collective norms, however, almost always means weakening these norms (Hinke *et al.* 2002, Schmidt *et al.* 2003).[5]

In effect, this has caused wages and working conditions in Eastern Germany to fall below sectoral standards, which were relatively low in the first place. The collectively agreed wage in Eastern Germany has thus ceased to be the standard wage and instead is now the maximum wage. This is in line with a dual process of adaptation to the pressure of competition from Western Germany and the East-Central European states within the context of globalization and EU integration. In Western Germany, too, collectively agreed wages have sunk from their former status as minimum wage to that of standard wage.

The pressure to deregulate the economy and make it more flexible intensified from the 1990s in both Western and Eastern Germany. In this context, commentators have frequently tended to conclude, on the basis of the tendency towards 'self-regulation' of pay and conditions, that Eastern Germany has functioned as an experimental area and pioneer. Its suitability for this role, however, is overstated (for a recent treatment, see Brinkmann 2003). The Eastern German economy has the status of an economic dependency in relation to Western Germany. In Western German companies, industrial standards and business principles are increasingly being formulated in light of international competition, chiefly with reference to the USA and Asia, and now Eastern Europe as well. Eastern Germany plays a fairly minor role in such considerations, for example when firms have to decide where best to locate their Eastern German subsidiaries. Attempts by employers to implement a coordinated policy of de-standardization are doomed from the outset because the Eastern German employers' associations strictly insist upon their independence from their Western German counterparts and defend their cost advantages. This was apparent in the failed strike in the Eastern German metals industry in 2003 (Schmidt 2003a). Western German companies' published relocation plans also refer far more frequently to the countries of Central Europe than to Eastern Germany.

Since Eastern German companies are unwilling to give up the competitive advantage they enjoy as a result of lower wages and longer working hours, there will be no levelling down of Western German labour costs to Eastern German levels in the foreseeable future. That is, if labour costs fall in the West, they tend to do so in the East as well.

The economist concerned with shareholder value will find, as he compares Eastern and Western Germany, that the former ticks a few of the boxes on her checklist left blank by the latter. Employees' codetermination and standardization of pay agreements are weaker and labour costs lower. Despite this, Eastern Germany is not an attractive place for international financial capital: Eastern German companies are for the most part too small and tend not to be joint-stock companies. If they are, they are rarely quoted on the stock exchange. As a rule, highly speculative modern financial capital, such as private equity funds and hedge funds, does not found new companies. It has an exploitative, or at best supportive, relationship with industrial capital. Its rigorous shareholder focus has a levelling effect in acquired companies. Eastern Germany lacks the kind of firms that might be subject to such an approach. Fears that Eastern German firms might be 'Americanized' through a process of dual modernization have thus proved unfounded (Gergs and Schmidt 2002; Martens *et al.* 2003).

Eastern Germany, however, is indirectly implicated in the process of neo-liberal marketization occurring in Western Germany. There are two reasons for this. First, no positive forces defending or further developing the socially inclusive 'Rhine model' of (Western) German capitalism (what Hall and Soskice (2001) refer to as the 'coordinated market economy') are coming from this economic dependency. Second, the massive financial transfers have weakened the state's capacity to take effective action. Transfers from West to East by the state and by the social security and health insurance systems constitute, alongside negative demographic trends and the high level of unemployment in Germany, a key factor underpinning the state's inability to invest more and the fiscal weakness of systems of social insurance. The redistributive, solidarity-based German social system is being turned, bit by bit, into one reliant on financial capital and individual responsibility, that is, one which increases the burden on the lower classes. At present, such financing merely plays a supplementary role. Institutional capital investors will thus become more important in Germany in future. Such investors are not only on the lookout for investment opportunities, they obtain them by applying economic and political pressure. From the only perspective relevant to these investors, that of profit maximization, stakeholder interests and workers' rights are obstacles, to be removed if at all possible.

The case of Eastern Germany has demonstrated that the latter are not subject to direct pressure to achieve shareholder value. It is possible, however, that liberalized capital markets will influence SMEs indirectly. The extent to which this will affect corporate governance, management style, working conditions and SMEs' relationship to capital markets is as yet uncertain.

Notes

1. In the wake of the privatization of the East German combines, many firms were liquidated and entire branches of industry threatened to disappear. At times, therefore, the federal government deviated from this principle in order, for instance, to safeguard the traditional Halle–Bitterfeld–Leuna triangle as a key location for the industrial production of chemicals. The shift from carbon-based chemicals to petrochemicals required enormous investment, which the major Western German chemical firms were unwilling to provide. Elf Aquitaine was finally persuaded by billions of Euros in subsidies to take on the task.
2. There is also a difference in the proportions political parties can recruit members: 2.5 per cent of the population in Western Germany, but only 1.3 per cent in Eastern Germany (Niedermayer 2005: 386).
3. The mental difference between Western and Eastern Germans has been a frequent subject of sociological studies. The differing consciousness of Eastern

Germans is presented partly as a legacy of GDR society, and partly as a response to the failed policies aimed at bringing the East into line with the West, which were perceived as discriminatory. The latter approach is favoured by Eastern German authors, the former by their Western German counterparts. The (Eastern German) cultural sociologist Wolfgang Engler is an example of an author who refers to both perspectives (Engler 1999; 2004).

4. This is the case even if the structural effect of firm size is factored out. According to a representative survey carried out by the *Institut für Soziologie* in Jena, in the Eastern German metals industry in 2001 a mere 23 per cent of firms with more than fifty employees were party to collective bargaining agreements, compared to just under half of Western German firms (Hinke *et al.* 2002). In 2003 the ratio for the economy as whole and all firms was 21 per cent: 43 per cent. If one excludes the civil service, as highly organized in Eastern Germany as in the West, the figure for manufacturing is just 14 per cent.

5. On the development and praxis of Eastern German labour relations in general see Bergmann 1996, Schroeder 2000, Artus 2001, and Schmidt 2003b.

References

Artus, I. (2001) *Krise des deutschen Tarifsystems: Die Erosion des Flächentarifvertrags in Ost und West* (Wiesbaden: Westdeutscher Verlag).

Bach, S. and D. Vesper (2000) 'Finanzpolitik und Wiedervereinigung – Bilanz nach 10 Jahren', *Vierteljahreshefte zur Wirtschaftsforschung*, 69, 194–224.

Bellmann, L., V. Dahms and J. Wahse (2005) *IAB-Betriebspanel Ost – Ergebnisse der neunten Welle 2004 – Teil III* (Nuremberg: IAB).

Behr, M. and R. Schmidt (eds) (2005) *Aufbau Ost – Betriebliche und überbetriebliche Erfolgsfaktoren im verarbeitenden Gewerbe Ostdeutschlands* (Jena: Jenaer Beiträge zur Soziologie).

Bergmann, J. (1996) 'Industrielle Beziehungen in Ostdeutschland: Transferierte Institutionen im Deindustrialisierungsprozeß', in B. Lutz, H. M. Nickel, R. Schmidt and A. Sorge (eds), *Arbeit, Arbeitsmarkt und Betriebe* (KSPW Berichte Bd.1) (Opladen: Westdeutscher Verlag), 257–94.

Brinkmann, U. (2003) 'Die Labormaus des Westens: Ostdeutschland als Vorwegnahme des neuen Produktionsmodells', in K. Dörre and B. Röttger (eds), *Das neue Marktregime* (Hamburg: VSA), 270–88.

Dore, R. (2000) *Stock Market Capitalism: Welfare Capitalism. Japan and Germany versus the Anglo-Saxons* (Oxford: Oxford University Press).

Engler, W. (1999) *Die Ostdeutschen: Kunde von einem verlorenen Land* (Berlin: Aufbau).

Engler, W. (2004) *Die Ostdeutschen als Avantgarde* (Berlin: Aufbau).

Ferner, A. and M. Z. Varul (1999) *The German Way: German Multinationals and Human Resource Management* (London: Anglo-German Foundation for Study of Industrial Society).

Gergs, H. (2002) *Manager und Märkte: Eine soziologische Untersuchung der Markterschließungslogiken im ostdeutschen Management* (Munich and Mehring: Hampp).

Gergs, H.-J. and R. Schmidt (2002) 'Generationswechsel im Management ost- und westdeutscher Unternehmen. Kommt es zu einer Amerikanisierung des deutschen

Managementmodells?' *Kölner Zeitschrift für Soziologie und Sozialpsychologie*, 54, 553–78.

Hall, P. A. and D. Soskice (eds) (2001) *Varieties of Capitalism: The Institutional Foundations of Comparative Advantage* (Oxford: Oxford University Press).

Hinke, R., S. Röbenack and R. Schmidt (2002) *Diesseits und jenseits des Tarifvertrages: Die Gestaltung der Lohn- und Leistungsbedingungen in der ostdeutschen Metall- und Elektroindustrie* (Berlin: Otto Brenner Stiftung).

Internationalisation of European Small and Medium-Sized Enterprises (SMEs) (2002) unpublished report of the EU project National Corporate Cultures and International Competitiveness Strategies – the Challenge of Globalisation for European SMEs, coordinated by Institut für Soziologie, Friedrich Schiller-Universität Jena.

Lebenslagen in Deutschland: Der 2. Armuts- und Reichtumsbericht der Bundesregierung (2005) (Berlin, unpublished paper) <http://www.sozialpolitikaktuell.de/docs/Lebenslagen per cent20in per cent20Deutschland_EndBericht.pdf>.

Martens, B., M. Michailow and R. Schmidt (eds) (2003) *Managementkulturen im Umbruch* (Jena: Mitteilungen des SFB 580, Heft 10).

Meyer, J.W., J. Boli and G. M. Thomas (1994) 'Ontology and Rationalization in the Western Cultural Account', in R.W. Scott and J. W. Meyer (eds), *Institutional Environments and Organizations, Structural Complexity and Individualism* (Thousand Oaks: Sage), 9–27.

Niedermayer, O. (2005) 'Parteimitgliedschaften im Jahre 2004', *Zeitschrift für Parlamentsfragen* 36, 382–9.

Ragnitz, J. (2004) 'Transferleistungen für die neuen Länder – eine Begriffsbestimmung', *Wirtschaft im Wandel*, 10, 288–9.

Schmidt, R. (2003a) 'Der gescheiterte Streik in der ostdeutschen Metallindustrie', *PROKLA*, 33, 493–509.

Schmidt, R. (2003b) 'The Rebuilding of Industrial Relations in Eastern Germany', in W. Müller-Jentsch, H. Weitbrecht (eds), *The Changing Contours of German Industrial Relations* (Munich/Mehring: Hampp), 81–102.

Schmidt, R., S. Röbenack and R. Hinke (2003) 'Prekarisierung des kollektiven Tarifsystems am Beispiel der ostdeutschen Metallindustrie', *Industrielle Beziehungen*, 10, 220–49.

Schmidt, R. (2004) 'Convergence of Divergences: The Changing Legal Frameworks, Free Market Ideology and Corporate Reorganisation in German Enterprises', in S. Munshi and B. P. Abraham (eds), *Good Governance, Democratic Societies and Globalisation* (London: Sage), 342–59.

Schmidt, R. (ed.) (2005) *Reorganisation unter Marktzwang: Finanzierung kleiner und mittlerer Unternehmen nach Basel II* (Jena: Jenaer Beiträge zur Soziologie, Heft 15).

Schroeder, W. (2000) *Das Modell Deutschland auf dem Prüfstand: Zur Entwicklung der industriellen Beziehungen in Ostdeutschland (1990–2000)* (Wiesbaden: Westdeutscher Verlag).

Sorge, A. (1996) 'Societal Effects in Cross-National Organization Studies: Conceptualizing Diversity in Actors and Systems', in R. Whitley and P.H. Kristensen (eds), *The Changing European Firm: Limits to Convergence* (London: Routledge), 67–86.

Steinitz, R. (2005) *Die Entwicklung der öffentlichen Schulden in Deutschland – Faktoren und Wirkungen* (Berlin: Leibniz Online I <www.ls-journal.de>).

Streeck, W. (1997) 'German Capitalism: Does it Exist? Can it Survive?', in C. Crouch and W. Streeck (eds), *Political Economy of Modern Capitalism* (London: Sage), 33–54.

Whitley, R. (1999) *Divergent Capitalism: The Social Structuring and Change of Business Systems* (Oxford: Oxford University Press).

Zugehör, R.(2003) *Die Zukunft des rheinischen Kapitalismus: Unternehmen zwischen Kapitalmarkt und Mitbestimmung* (Opladen: Leske & Budrich).

5
The Czech Republic: From 'Czech' Capitalism to 'European' Capitalism*

Martin Myant

This contribution aims to set the development of Czech capitalism against the frameworks developed by Hall and Soskice and Amable. The conclusion is that, although the general approach of looking for different kinds of capitalism is extremely fruitful, it is neither possible nor helpful to try to classify the Czech experience within an established model. The nature and significance of the relationships between business, labour relations and social and welfare policies are not the same as in the advanced and mature market economies studied by the above authors. There are three central areas in which their established frameworks need to be modified.

The first area relates to the nature of capitalism in a post-communist society. It had to start as a capitalism without capitalists and also without capital. In the Czech example the first of these problems was resolved, at first, through privatization. That, however, created a particular kind of wealthy individual. It did not create the basis for Schumpeter's vision (1943: 83) of entrepreneurs who could develop productive forces with new products, new methods of production or opening up of new markets. It rather created individuals who could find means to concentrate into their own hands the wealth that had been created under a previous economic system. These were the dominant themes for the business sphere.

The second area requiring modification relates to the complementarity of features within a variety of capitalism. In the established views a particular form of business organization makes sense alongside methods of wage setting, employment relationships and possibly also social service provision. There is therefore reluctance to accept the possibility of hybrid forms (Amable 2003: 56). In the Czech Republic elements could coexist that seemed to belong within different ideal types. A 'liberal-market' approach appeared dominant in some areas and a 'social-democratic' approach in others. This is fully intelligible when set in the context of the political conflicts and compromises of the time. Advocates of different versions of capitalism effectively ceded power to each other in different spheres. Nor does this seem to have been particularly important in determining the economy's competitiveness. That depended overwhelmingly on developments in the business sphere alone.

The third area for modification relates to the permanence of a variety of capitalism. Established accounts point to institutional complementarities as sources of systemic stability. There is strong inertia opposing major changes, irrespective of changes in governments. There is resistance to some changes in the Czech Republic, but it largely reflects continuing support for substantial social provision rather than inertia associated with institutional complementarities. More generally, Czech experience was one of systemic change, as was inevitable when a form of capitalism was initially created.

Indeed, the argument here is that there was a further substantial change from the late 1990s. An initial attempt to create 'Czech capitalism' ended in failure and was followed by movement to a 'European capitalism'. These terms do not represent an attempt to create still more ideal types: these are descriptions rather than analytical categories. Moreover, neither fits easily into established 'varieties'. The big difference between the two was in the business sphere which was stabilized by foreign ownership and inward investment, providing the economy with a competitive position in certain branches of industry. This did affect labour relations, but it had no direct effect on social policy areas. It was the conditions associated with EU accession that led to pressures for cost reductions there.

Ideas and their backers

There was broad consensus in 1990 that the communist period had been a complete failure and that Czechoslovakia should become a modern, democratic society with a market economy, essentially similar to the existing mature market economies. It was generally assumed that this would involve dismantling central authority and giving greater autonomy to lower levels and that principle was applied throughout much of economic and social life. However, the detailed forms that emerged reflected a complex interaction of ideas and interests. The important elements for creating 'Czech' capitalism can be summarized around four overlapping lines of thought (cf. Myant 2003b: esp. chs 1 and 2).

First came neo-classical or neo-liberal economics in a very pure and abstract form. The most prominent advocate was Václav Klaus, Czech Prime Minister from 1992 to 1997, who set the aim of a 'market economy without adjectives'. Any consideration of different forms of capitalism was condemned as a compromise with socialism. This clearly could not be seen as an ideology for a capitalist class – there were, at first, no capitalists – but support for an unregulated free market had an obvious appeal to individuals keen to make a quick fortune. The approach also had a much wider appeal as one apparently based on modern academic thinking that pointed to the clearest and most uncompromising rejection of the communist past.

The second line of thought – vaguer and more widely shared when expressed in the most general terms – was an assumption that Czechoslovakia, and subsequently the Czech Republic, belonged in the mainstream European tradition. It was compared with, and examples sought from, neighbouring Western European countries, leading to some tensions with the neo-liberal approach. Pride in a European heritage was also associated with an exaggerated view of the country's economic strength and of the standing of its leading industrial enterprises. This helped to justify an aim, supported by Klaus, of privatizing into domestic ownership and creating capitalist structures to match those of larger Western European countries. There were doubts from some prominent figures (Žák 1999) and some big enterprises were sold into foreign ownership, such as the Škoda car manufacturer bought by Volkswagen in 1991.

The third line of thought was a 'social-democratic' approach. There would be a market economy, but it would be one that recognized social interests. This was broadly accepted, at least when stated in such general terms, by all apart from the firmest proponents of the free market. The coexistence of this with the apparently very different neo-liberal approach raises difficult questions about the nature of Klaus's political thinking (cf. Orenstein 2001). The varieties of capitalism literature provide a framework for resolving the apparent dilemma. The two approaches could coexist largely because of a divergence in perceptions of the 'hierarchy of institutions' (Amable 2003: 11). To Klaus and his allies, private ownership would ultimately determine all else. Other issues, such as labour relations or welfare systems, would fall into line once private owners could enforce discipline on businesses. For some others, such as trade unions, social protection was the primary concern and they did not see this as threatened by privatization (Myant 1993a). Different social and political actors could therefore pursue distinct agendas without worrying too much about apparent inconsistencies when set against ideal types of capitalism.

The fourth line of thought was a faith in the 'legal' state, a point worth emphasizing as a contrast with countries further East. Political power and business were to be separated. Institutions were to be protected by law and parts of the public sphere, such as a central bank, were to take on distinct roles and responsibilities. This separation and formalization of powers and responsibilities was supported by commitment to the country's European traditions, possibly by an established role for the legal system during the communist period and also by the fact of a plurality of political forces preventing any single one from gaining absolute dominance. However, it often clashed with the chaotic, informal and personalized nature of relationships, reflected in frequent reports of corruption that left the Czech Republic alongside Greece and Slovakia in 47th place in Transparency International's Corruption Perceptions Index in 2005. The evolution of a legal state, although not formally opposed by any significant force, was therefore also a contested terrain.

Privatization

No political or philosophical trend was able to impose its 'model' of capitalism. The initiative in economic policy making was taken by the neoliberal trend which advocated voucher privatization, but had to accept compromises with other conceptions and interests and was itself soon looking for means to reduce the effects of the resulting, highly dispersed ownership (for details and discussion, see Myant 1993; Myant 2003b; Pollert 1999: 100–3; Schütte 2000; and Takla 1999). Participation was very high with 77 per cent and 74 per cent of the adult population taking part in the two waves that were started in 1992. However, by 1997 only 48 per cent of the assets set for privatization had been exchanged for vouchers, 13 per cent were disposed of by various forms of free transfer, 12 per cent had been sold – some to foreign companies – and 27 per cent were still with the state awaiting disposal (calculated from ČSÚ 1998: 543).

Even in enterprises partly privatized by the voucher method, the government increasingly favoured allotting a large shareholding to managers who came forward with promises to save major enterprises that were on the brink of financial collapse as a result of past debts and falling demand for exports to traditional markets in the old Soviet bloc. Thus fear of bankruptcies, job losses, social catastrophe and possible political instability led to more active involvement in seeking solutions for ailing enterprises, rather than just leaving everything to new private owners. The solution was not based simply on state subsidies to maintain social peace. Instead, the government, starting from Prime Minister Klaus, became actively involved in promoting the managers that they believed could bring success to the country's traditional enterprises.

Behind this 'entrepreneurial' privatization lay an unspoken vision of how capitalism should work which was not, despite some of the rhetoric surrounding voucher privatization, based on the accepted LME model of shareholders disciplining management. It was built instead around individual entrepreneurs, strong-willed, egotistical and autocratic men, directing and inspiring enterprises, reminiscent of Schumpeter's version of an early stage of capitalist development. Nor did business associations play the coordinating role referred to by Hall and Soskice (2001: 25–6): they were often one more arena in which egos could clash. There was minimal cross-ownership and, under conditions of poor payments discipline, cooperation between enterprises was only secure when one actually owned another. The emerging model, then, was one of isolated capitalists satisfactorily coordinated neither by formal linkages nor by a liberal market (Myant 2000). Their business plans varied from the unrealistically ambitious to absurd pipe dreams.

Support from government was vital for these new entrepreneurs, but was rarely unanimous. The fact of political pluralism, with three parties represented in Klaus's coalition government in the new Czech Republic and media capable of reporting uncomfortable facts, ruled out too close a linkage between business and political power. Entrepreneurs frequently made secret donations to political parties, but often received no favours after the privatization decision. Indeed, relations could be rather acrimonious as the entrepreneurs sought further financial support from a government that, despite being dragged on occasion into some involvement in enterprise restructuring (McDermott 2002: ch. 4), thought firms should be able to stand on their own feet. In fact, they continued to face serious financial difficulties, largely reflecting their inability to find a means to compete in the new, open environment. For a time, however, the fact of rapid privatization gave the Czech Republic excellent international standing. This was a measurable indicator of economic transformation. There were some sobering voices, but the new breed of entrepreneurs also won praise abroad. *The Economist* (18 February 1995) described one of the most important cases of entrepreneurial privatization, the giant Škoda-Plzeň heavy engineering combine, as 'one of the most promising attempts to create a post-communist industrial group'. There was little real substance behind this.

The third wave

Voucher privatization, when set against the beliefs of its founders, suffered from a fundamental contradiction. It would very rapidly create private owners, but they would be dispersed individuals, not the 'concrete owners' promised in the government's propaganda booklet (Federální ministerstvo financí 1991: 3) who, it was believed, would turn up to shareholders' meetings and hold managements to account. Instead, advocates of the voucher method reassured themselves with hopes that a rapid process of concentration would follow, putting 'entrepreneurs' in control. One initial help was the emergence of investment funds set up by enterprising individuals, companies and, above all, banks, into which individuals invested their voucher points. This still left substantial dispersion, with 294 funds formed for the first wave alone, although from the start they controlled 70 per cent of the voucher points to be exchanged for shares (Myant 2003b: 119).

The process of concentration that followed came to be known as the 'third wave'. Individuals were selling their shares: probably only about 5 per cent of the population held shares in 2005 (V. Lavička and M. Čepický, *Hospodářské noviny*, 5 August 2005). Fund managements were selling too, often for their own personal gain. The key to the concentration of ownership was a deliberately lax legal environment, making it easy to buy and sell shares and to ignore the interests of minority shareholders. Even the controls available under existing laws were not applied rigorously. The kind of capitalist who could gain was one involved in speculating and share dealing. The ultimate buyers, once a majority of a company's shares had been accumulated in one set of hands, were often the companies' managements, seeking security against hostile takeover. Finance came either from bending the rules to use the resources of the parent company or from bank loans. They could thereby secure their positions as capitalists, but they had little remaining scope to finance productive investment.

Klaus gave tacit backing to the most ambitious practitioners of the 'third wave', Motoinvest, a small stock-broking company that set out in the autumn of 1995 to use bank credits to buy up shares in individual hands *en masse* so as to establish a vast financial empire. However, even support from within the government was not enough when Motoinvest threatened to take control of the biggest investment fund of the country's biggest bank. Its activities were brought to an end by the central bank, probably under pressure from established banks, on the legal pretext that it had transgressed banking regulations. The leading figure in Motoinvest saw his 'mistake' in 'interpreting entrepreneurship as no more than trade' and in not taking care to act 'politically' and to avoid treading on too many toes (P. Tykač, *Právo*, 31 July 1997). This, plus a number of scandals in the mid 1990s, pushed governments towards a gradual tightening of company law and regulation of the capital market. In the meantime, Motoinvest was required to sell its shares to big banks, albeit at very favourable prices, thereby helping the latter to enjoy a temporary period of great importance.

Banks

Initial ideas on economic reform made no mention of banks or of any special role they might be asked to play. The implicit assumption from the neo-liberal camp was that the market would resolve all questions. Leading bankers, on the other hand, sought to follow examples from Western Europe. A number of completely new banks emerged, but their managements were either corrupt or incompetent and they had largely disappeared by the end of the decade. The sector was dominated by four big banks inherited from reforms at the end of the communist period and given state help to enable them to operate in a market environment. Three were partially privatized in the first voucher wave. They had resources as household deposits grew from 33 per cent of GDP in 1991 to 42 per cent in 1997 as this form of saving was preferred to the riskier and less intelligible share ownership. However, each pursued a different strategy, partly under government pressure and partly reflecting the preferences of their own managements. There was thus no general 'model' of Czech banking (Myant 2003a).

In a time of rapid economic transformation, a cautiously sensible bank would be very reluctant to give credits to new, or substantially changed, enterprises. In a state-led version of capitalism, finance could have been directed towards specific sectors or activities. In the Czech version there was a more generalized pressure – including public criticisms of banks for cautiously assessing risks and asking for collateral for loans – ensuring that banks gave credits to new small businesses, to enterprises facing financial difficulties, to entrepreneurs seeking loans for privatization and to all sorts of businesses aiming to buy shares. Bribery was probably endemic, but for larger loans banks sought collateral and that was most readily available in the form of shares. They were therefore happier to finance acquisitions than productive investment. There were a number of substantial investment projects in the 1990s, leading to an investment to GDP ratio that peaked at almost 32 per cent in 1995 but, with a very few exceptions, they were undertaken only by foreign or state-owned firms.

Some authors have presented evidence of banks playing a significant role in corporate governance, leading to greater efficiency in the enterprises they could influence (e.g. Schütte 2000), but they were more frequently passive owners, often concerned only with quick financial gains from share dealing (Myant 2003b: esp. ch. 9; Pollert 1999: 100–3; Coffee 1996). Others gave banks a central role in taking the Czech economy 'from public ownership to public ownership in five years' (Mertlík 1995). Banks were, at the time this argument was popular, formally under state domination. They, either directly or through investment funds, owned much of the new private sector. Ultimate control was therefore back with the state, leading to labels of 'state capitalism' or 'bank socialism' (e.g. Mlčoch 1999) and this could be used to explain the continuing inefficiency and slow restructuring of Czech enterprises.

Neither of these approaches satisfactorily explains the role of banks in the Czech transformation. It was also very different from that of banks in CMEs which can use dense networks and intimate knowledge of companies, built from long-term relationships, to provide creditors with confidence (Hall and Soskice 2001: 22–3). The necessary preconditions for such a role did not exist. There were some discussions in general terms of banks playing a similar role to those in Germany's, or even Czechoslovakia's, more distant past, but the nature of the emerging relationship was actually very different.

Banks were pressed to become involved neither as supporters of inefficiency and high employment, nor as long-term partners concerned with productive investment, although the outcome appeared closer to the first of these. They were to play the role of facilitators of privatization, concentration of ownership and the emergence of new enterprises; precisely the changes that advocates of neo-classical economic theory saw as preconditions for greater efficiency. However, far from ensuring the soundness of the emerging model, they were in this case crucial to the development of a fundamentally unsound version of capitalism. The most extreme case was the IPB (Investiční a poštovní banka) which, after a controversial privatization in 1994, was closely linked to part of the government via personal contacts and advisers to Klaus on its Supervisory Board. It was praised from government circles as being the 'most flexible' of the banks (R. Češka, *Hospodářské noviny*, 27 June 1996) and went the furthest in substituting personal contacts and mutual favours for serious assessments of business risks. Its ownership structure came to include enterprises that it financed, both by loans and by the purchase of shares, and they in turn were able to build up business empires, often helping the government's privatization aims by buying enterprises with no serious prospects.

Three of the four big banks lent unsoundly, leading to estimates that up to one third of credits, equivalent to almost 20 per cent of GDP in 1997, could probably never be repaid. Although reluctant to admit the depth of their problems, the banks gradually narrowed the range of enterprises to which they would lend. Granting of new credits to troubled Czech enterprises largely ended from 1997. The volume of bank credit as a percentage of GDP fell from 63.9 per cent in 1997 to 39.0 per cent in 2002. The catastrophic effects on businesses in turn led to a drop in share prices, stimulating further caution among banks for which shares had provided important collateral. The key elements of Czech capitalism quickly unravelled, leaving major enterprises paralysed, unable to secure credits even for working capital. Wages were owed to an estimated 53,000 employees (*Hospodářské noviny*, 13 April 2000). Late 1998 saw growing fears of the kind of economic chaos felt to belong further East. The solution required a new form of capitalism.

Indeed, this was already coexisting with 'Czech' capitalism. Firms that had passed into foreign ownership were generally prospering. From the mid 1990s, they became the most dynamic part of the economy with the motor-vehicle industry the leading force. There were also a number of financially sound state-owned or partially privatized firms, such as utilities, that were able to borrow from foreign banks and were therefore largely unaffected by the problems in other parts of the economy.

Social-democratic elements

The neo-liberal project, leading into the failed structures of Czech capitalism, was accompanied by what appear as 'social-democratic' elements. These were given formal support across quite a wide political spectrum, often around general support of the successful West German slogan of a 'social market economy', and from a mass trade union movement, inherited largely intact in terms of membership from the communist past. It sought, as part of its transformation, the creation of a tripartite structure, in line with ILO practice and experience across much of Western Europe. This was accepted in early 1990 by government ministers who were sympathetic to seeking social consensus rather than the neo-liberal concern to exclude interest representation from the political process (Pollert 1999: 141–6; Myant, Slocock and Smith 2000).

There were some very effective demonstrations of labour discontent in 1991, aimed against wage cuts and possible job losses (Myant 1993: 217–18). They served to warn of the need to avoid causing too much social pain and to keep trade union organizations on board through what has been characterized as 'pre-emptive' corporatism (Wiesenthal 1996). This facilitated agreement on much of a new labour code, giving considerable continued protection to employees and a framework for trade union representation and collective bargaining. The most likely advocates of substantial deregulation of the labour market saw privatization as the decisive step towards a market system and avoided unnecessary conflict on this front.

It can be added that unions had little to say either on privatization in general or on projects for individual enterprises. They confessed to a lack of expertise and were also constrained by the need to carve out a role that would not risk accusations of defending elements of the communist past. For them, too, the model was Western Europe, but the form of transition to a market economy was somebody else's business. However, they were a potential danger to managers who themselves felt insecure, not least in view of previous Communist Party membership, and were seeking to 're-engineer' themselves as modern capitalist managers (Soulsby and Clark 1996). Part of the means to this end was good relations with employees' representatives. A willingness to concede to reasonably modest wage demands from unions that were themselves confused about their new role ensured a steady rise in real wages after 1991. Despite the presence of often highly autocratic managers, there were practically no strikes in enterprises privatized into Czech ownership.

Collective bargaining appeared similar to German practice which, in the Hall and Soskice account (2001: 25), may help protect against the danger of poaching skilled workers, thereby providing a necessary condition for investment by firms in employees' training. The similarity is not a complete coincidence – unions did press for adoption of that Western European practice – but the quoted cause was of little importance. Training was not a central concern at the time. The system inherited from the communist past suffered from a sharp drop in funding amid disputes between enterprises and the government over who should take responsibility, although many enterprises feared a skill shortage as qualified workers sought better pay in alternative occupations or abroad (Pollert 1999: 200). More important considerations were the desire not to offend trade unions and the lack of any sophisticated conception of human resources strategy (Soulsby and Clark 1998). Managements, as indicated, had one overriding concern – to gain and keep control over their enterprises.

Gradually, as they became more confident, they did push back the scope of collective bargaining. A prominent issue was the extent and significance of 'higher-level' agreements covering large numbers of enterprises. Many managements resented these as a restriction on their autonomy. The law gave the government power to extend these to cover non-signatories. Figures for 2003 showed 23 per cent of employees covered by sectoral agreements signed by affiliates of the main union confederation of which a fifth were covered by extensions (*Sondy*, 2003, No. 34). This represented an approximate halving of the scope of this kind of bargaining compared with 1994, some of the decline being due to disaffiliation of some unions. Agreements usually included a figure for the 'average nominal wage' and often further details on permitted pay scales. Agreements were less common in public services where wages were formally set by the government, albeit under clear union pressure.

The importance of this for changes in the pattern of income distribution are difficult to follow because of the weakness of statistics in the early transformation period when widening dispersion was driven primarily by sharp increases for a small group at the top: this would not have been influenced by collective bargaining. Industrial relations practices may have been a factor holding in check growth in inequality. A continuing gradual differentiation largely reflected dispersion across the middle of the range – the coefficient of variation increased from 61.9 to 73.2 from 1998 to 2001 while the relationship between the highest and lowest deciles remained unchanged (ČSÚ 2004) – which is consistent with a declining influence for collective bargaining. Pay increases for individual branches were also very similar in the mid 1990s, but gradually dispersed as Czech capitalism broke down, economic difficulties restricted the financial resources in troubled sectors and foreign-owned firms could comfortably afford to pay above any 'going rate'.

Health and pensions

Changes in social services and social policy were led in part by examples from Western Europe, often following 'social-democratic' thinking, and in part by the input of those with the most immediate interests. Sometimes this led to an agenda of substantial reform and sometimes to an agenda for minimal changes from the communist past (cf. Ringold 1999). Health and pensions illustrate the different possibilities.

Changes in health care were led by members of the medical profession, a group with high status and good international contacts. The system that emerged from 1992 was based on greater autonomy for lower levels and the provision of primary care by independent professionals on a fee-for-service basis with payment coming from an insurance fund (Vepřek *et al.* 2002). Following the typical Western European practice thereby satisfied the agenda of the most powerful provider group and that of a population used to a broadly free health service.

In line with free-market thinking, the government believed in the power of competition and allowed the emergence of twenty-seven new insurance companies. These threatened no established interests and the state insurance fund redistributed resources to ensure adequate cover for every-one. Nevertheless, several of these new companies were soon facing finan-cial difficulties: they had jumped quickly on the marketization bandwagon, investing in excessive overheads while underestimating the payments they would have to make. By 2001 only nine were left (Vepřek *et al.* 2002: 23). More generally, the new system, alongside the new scope for import-ing medical technology, led to an escalation in health spending, rising by 32 per cent in 1993, and employees still demanded higher pay. The medical profession was the most militant and one group of doctors even staged a strike in October 1996. The crisis was serious enough to encour-age Klaus to intervene. He apologized for the half-hearted nature of pre-vious reforms, which he attributed to his own involvement in other issues back in 1992. He proposed a move towards the system used in Singapore, in which patients had limited funds available from the state which they could supplement from their own sources. This would have clashed with the Czech, and European, tradition of effectively free health treatment. It met strong opposition and was soon quietly dropped. The following years saw successive proposals for further reform, but steps towards greater financial contributions from patients or privatization of more of the service were blocked as long as Social Democrats dominated the government.

Pensions proved an area of more open conflict (Rueschemeyer and Wolchik 1999: 133). There was no powerful provider group to set an agenda and any significant reforms were bound to arouse fears among much of the population. The communist system had been generous, allowing retire-ment at 60 for men and 53–57 for women, depending on the number of children. Proposals for raising the retirement age were developed through 1993 and approved by the government in October 1994. Funding was still to come from the state budget. This, then, was not a move towards a market-based system. Such an option might have been available earl-ier, by transferring shares into pension funds, but that had been effect-ively ruled out by mass voucher privatization.

Trade unions were able to mobilize opposition, including a 15-minute 'warning' strike on 21 December 1994 in which they claimed participa-tion from about one tenth of the working population. They won back-ing from much of the political spectrum, but the original proposal was passed with minor amendments in June 1995. Nevertheless, their protests marked the limits to a hardening of social policy. The 'European' prin-ciple of finding a consensus was pushing the country towards a very slow departure from the communist past. The retirement ages for men and women were still only rising to 62 and 57–61 in 2006.

Klaus followed up with a determined attempt to put an end to the tripartite structures which were giving trade unions a formal right to expect to be consulted on major decisions. He was only partially successful: he was held in check by his coalition partners. This, plus subsequent threats posed by industrial unrest, led in 1997 to a full reinstatement of the original tripartite structure (Myant, Slocock and Smith 2000).

The end of Czech capitalism

'Czech' capitalism was a failure in economic terms, but its demise depended on political decisions. Economic difficulties, in terms of budget and current account deficits, led to criticism from the IMF and to the imposition of two packages of budget cuts in April and May 1997. International confidence in the economy fell and a sudden withdrawal of short-term credits led the central bank to accept a devaluation and subsequent floating of the currency. Klaus's government fell in November 1997, following revelations over secret donations to his party from beneficiaries of entrepreneurial privatization, to be followed by an interim administration and then a minority Social Democrat government after elections in June 1998.

The Social Democrats came with a programme which included a state role in helping to revive industry and restore economic growth, but the realities of the situation soon led to changes. By the autumn of 1998 a major bank was in such deep difficulty that the central bank could shortly be obliged to revoke its licence. The solution was to take over bad debts, re-establish majority control, and sell as quickly as possible to a large foreign bank. The same method was followed for two further big banks. Initial promises to revive industrial enterprises were also soon modified amid *ad hoc* measures to keep production going. The policy soon shifted, as with the banks, to removing the existing owners and managers and selling enterprises to successful foreign companies as soon as possible. By a variety of means, the business empires that had dominated the scene in the mid 1990s disappeared or suffered massive reductions in size (Myant 2003b: ch. 10). Attempts to find foreign owners to match the success of Volkswagen's takeover of the Škoda car manufacturer proved fruitless.

In social policy the government was initially generous. Public sector pay increased and pension reform was delayed. However, generosity was constrained by the annual need for the minority government to pass a budget while the deficit was gradually increasing. It passed 3 per cent of GDP in 2000 and continued rising. The 'costs of transformation' – the term used for the cost to the state budget of the burden of debt left from failed banks and enterprises – rose to a peak of 2.8 per cent of GDP in 2002.

In many respects, the issues confronting Czech policy makers could appear familiar across much of Europe. Indeed, by 2004 it seemed that 'Czech' capitalism had been replaced by a 'European' capitalism characterized also by a growing dominance of foreign-owned firms with a share in industrial output rising from 14.4 per cent in 1997 to 48.6 per cent in 2003 and a 70 per cent share of industrial exports. Thus the problem of creating capitalists was overcome by importing them in the form of branches of established multinational companies. They were attracted by the country's location in Central Europe, by its reasonably experienced labour force with wage levels comfortably below the Western European average, by government policies for providing financial incentives and the appropriate infrastructure and by the assured markets with impending EU membership. Banks too came under largely Western European ownership, breaking any special links to Czech-owned enterprises.

Trade union membership continued its gradual decline, from almost all employees in 1989 to probably little over the EU average of 26 per cent by 2005, largely because of lower membership in the expanding sectors of the economy. The managements of multinational companies, with their own human resources strategies, could adopt a different approach towards bargaining to that of the earlier Czech employers. Not all even recognized trade unions. This was a period of higher unemployment, rising to over 10 per cent by 2003, and there were frequent reports of employers, particularly in retailing, ignoring established labour law on pay and conditions. Nevertheless, foreign firms often chose to be generous. It is noteworthy that pay in the transport equipment branch increased from 95 per cent of the industrial average in 1991 to 114 per cent in 2003, indicating the gradual impact of the progressive domination by foreign ownership. Thus the wage-setting mechanisms established under 'Czech' capitalism, and supported by laws and established practices, were weakened under 'European' capitalism, leading to the greater dispersion referred to above. The change towards foreign ownership was shifting the labour market in the LME direction. However, the Social Democrat-dominated governments continued to support a legal framework that gave substantial protection to employees and rights to trade unions and welcomed discussion of major policy issues through tripartite structures.

The moves towards EU accession set standards for, and constraints on, many important areas of economic policy. Forms of state aid to business were restricted by European competition rules, leaving little alternative to selling off the privatization failures to foreign companies. The budget deficit was restricted by the rules for joining the common European currency. This, particularly when combined with strong pressure for keeping tax levels in check from much of the political spectrum, set limits to state spending in the social sphere. The resulting cost-cutting pressures gave new life to neo-liberal thinking in social policy. More immediately, they imposed constraints on those areas of policy that depended directly on state spending. The average pension relative to the average wage dropped from 47.0 per cent in 1993 to 45.3 per cent in 1997 when Klaus's government fell. It rose marginally in 1998 but dropped to 40.6 per cent in 2004. Behind this lay a more fundamental lack of consensus over the future shape of the pension system with one possibility being a free-market system with a small, flat-rate, universal pension supplemented by private schemes. Social Democrats in government argued for a state system, following much of Western European practice, but no agreement had been reached by 2006.

What kind of capitalism?

The characteristics of capitalism in the Czech Republic are set out under the headings of 'Czech' and 'European' capitalism in Table 5.1. This does not follow exactly either the Amable or the Hall and Soskice frameworks partly because priority is given to government aims and partly because consideration of the business sphere requires a recognition that managements had interests distinct from those of the enterprises in which they were formally employed. The outcomes, both before and after 1998, embodied elements that belong within different Varieties of Capitalism. Complementarities can be identified, but they are different from those found in established approaches and are frequently not linked to enhancing competitiveness.

Indeed, capitalism in the Czech Republic lacked the stability provided by complementary features that can support each other. Instead, it was undergoing substantial transformation, driven primarily by political ideologies and social interests. An interpretation of the nature and development of the system therefore logically begins with the aims of the key political actors. They had a vision of the kind of capitalism they wanted but, as Table 5.1 indicates, a number of different actors were involved. Once their interests and activities are unravelled, the differences from both a CME and an LME become clear. The outcome was an unsound system that failed in the mid 1990s.

This left a legacy of caution on the part of the public towards share purchases and on the part of banks towards generosity in granting credits. The failure thereby created further barriers to autonomous development based on private, domestically owned firms. Any thoughts of replacing

Table 5.1   Characteristics of Czech and 'European' capitalism

	Czech capitalism, 1992–7	*European capitalism, from 1998*
Government aims	Priority to privatization and favouring charismatic new business leaders	Guided by conditions for EU membership; attract inward investment; maintain 'European social model'
Business	Dominated by big, Czech-owned firms; minimal coordination between them	Dominated by subsidiaries of multinational companies and smaller Czech-owned firms
Management aims	To gain full control over their company and to build a business empire	Role as part of international operation Managements in Czech-owned firms are more realistic and less ambitious than in previous period
Business links to banks	Need for finance for privatization and further acquisitions; banks willing to lend unsoundly under government pressure	Inward investors not dependent on Czech-based banks; Czech-owned enterprises also have limited chance of substantial credits
Business relationship to stock market	Arena of frantic trading as managements try to consolidate and expand control	Little relevance to foreign-owned companies and little chance for Czech-owned companies to raise finance by new share issues
Industrial relations	Managements avoid conflict with trade unions and accept much of the latter's conception for collective bargaining	Collective bargaining less relevant to both foreign- and Czech-owned firms; trade unions in decline; Widening wage dispersion
Training	Ignored and declining	Foreign-owned firms generally able to train existing labour force to level they require
Labour law	Government and managements avoid major challenges to labour and allow role for trade unions in labour law	Social Democratic government sympathetic to maintaining employee protection; not a major concern for inward investors
Social welfare	Irrelevant to companies and secondary to government, but widespread public concern	Area of political conflict, reflecting renewed confidence of neo-liberal trend and constraints imposed by EU on budget

that version with a state-led form of capitalism also stood little chance, irrespective of whether it could have been successful, in view of the extent of consensus against such an option. Even thoughts of a greater role for the state in restructuring and reviving individual enterprises were ruled out by the EU's competition rules and EU accession was accepted by the post-1997 governments as the cornerstone of economic policy. The outcome is summarized in the second column of Table 5.1. The striking feature is the declining importance of links between banks and the stock market and enterprises. The degree of internationalization again makes it impossible to classify the Czech Republic as either a CME or an LME. It has much in common with some other, smaller, EU members.

However, the notion of complementarity does gain significance in relation to wages and industrial relations. At first the political context was important too. Evolution under 'Czech capitalism' depended partly on the strength of social-democratic thinking, partly on the heritage of an earlier legal framework that gave strong employee protection and partly on the weakness and fears of enterprise managements who had no desire for confrontation with organized labour. Thus a particular labour market regime matched with a particular set of management, as well as government, aims. This, however, had nothing to do with improving or maintaining economic competitiveness.

The principal change after 1997, reflecting a stabilization of Czech managements and, above all, growing importance of foreign firms, was to make collective bargaining less relevant to employers. This time, then, there was a lack of complementarity between management aims and thinking of a Social Democrat government. There was little open conflict between the two, but rather a gradual evolution towards practices more appropriate to an LME. The political opposition was more vocal, taking a standard neo-liberal position against Social Democrat-dominated governments which continued to favour laws supporting employee protection and trade union rights, in line with one of the approaches common in the EU. Industrial relations and labour laws consistent with the social-democratic approach would therefore not appear to have been deeply entrenched and could change with a change in government.

Social welfare, the final row in Table 5.1, was characterized by a different set of interests and constraints. Enterprise managements were not directly concerned with this area. Much of the population was very concerned. This set limits on changes in the LME direction. However, the crucial distinguishing feature of this sphere is that governments need to spend and are therefore constrained by pressures from the state budget. That was exacerbated by costs from the failure of the earlier economic transformation and, above all, by the need to comply with agreements reached within the EU as preparation for joining the European Monetary System. This was also an arena of political conflict, but it was one in which the social-democratic vision was on the defensive. The outcome of that conflict, as in the second sphere referred to above, need not make much difference to short-term economic competitiveness. That continued to depend on inward investment by multinational companies. Thus capitalism in the Czech Republic was yet to take a definitive form. The period of 'Czech' capitalism represented an attempt from political leaders to create a system based on large, Czech-owned companies. The characterization of 'European' capitalism appears appropriate for the development after 1998 when the central government aim was EU accession and the dominant change in the business sphere was foreign ownership, often by European companies or by others targeting the European market. However, there was still no settled outcome. Indeed, the European element relates as much to the areas of conflict, which match the conflicts over labour and social policies throughout the EU.

Note

*Part of the research for this chapter was supported by a three-week visit to Prague in September 2004 through the British Academy's academic exchange programme.

References

Amable, B. (2003) *The Diversity of Modern Capitalism* (Oxford: Oxford University Press).

Coffee, J. C. Jr (1996) 'Institutional Investors in Transitional Economies: Lessons from the Czech Experience', in R. Frydman, C. Gray and A. Rapaczynski (eds), *Corporate Governance in Central Europe and Russia*, vol. 1 (Budapest, London and New York: Central European University Press), 111–86.

ČSÚ (Czech Statistical Office) (1998) *Statistická ročenka České republiky 1998* (Prague: Scientia).

ČSÚ (Czech Statistical Office) (2004) *Vývoj mezd v letech 1993–2003* <http://www.czso.cz> (accessed 26 May 2005).

Federální ministerstvo financí (1991) *Kuponová privatizace Informační příručka* (Prague).

Hall, P. and D. Soskice (2001) (eds) *Varieties of Capitalism: The Institutional Foundations of Comparative Advantage* (Oxford: Oxford University Press).

McDermott, G. (2002) *Embedded Politics: Industrial Networks and Institutional Change in Postcommunism* (Ann Arbor, MI: Michigan University Press).

Mertlík, P. (1995) 'Czech Privatization: from Public Ownership to Public Ownership in Five Years?' *Prague Economic Papers*, 4, 321–36.

Mlčoch, L. (1999) 'Jaký model pro český kapitalismus?', in M. Potůček (ed.), *Česká společnost na konci tisíciletí* (Prague: Karolinum).

Myant, M. (1993) *Transforming Socialist Economies: The Case of Poland and Czechoslovakia* (Aldershot: Edward Elgar).

Myant, M. (2000) 'Employers' Interest Representation in the Czech Republic', *Journal of Communist Studies and Transition Politics*, 16, 1–20.

Myant, M. (2003a) 'Czech Banking in Comparative Perspective', *Prague Economic Papers*, 12, 131–44.

Myant, M. (2003b) *The Rise and Fall of Czech Capitalism: Economic Development in the Czech Republic since 1989* (Cheltenham, UK and Northampton, MA: Edward Elgar).

Myant, M. and S. Smith (1999) 'Czech Trade Unions in Comparative Perspective', *European Journal of Industrial Relations*, 5, 265–85.

Myant, M., B. Slocock and S. Smith (2000) 'Tripartism in the Czech and Slovak Republics', *Europe-Asia Studies*, 52, 723–39.

Orenstein, M. (2001) *Out of the Red: Building Capitalism and Democracy in Postcommunist Europe* (Ann Arbor, MI: University of Michigan Press).

Pollert, A. (1999) *Transformation at Work in the New Market Economies of Central Eastern Europe* (London: Sage Publications).

Ringold, D. (1999) 'Social Policy in Postcommunist Europe', in L. Cook, M. Orenstein and M. Rueschemeyer (eds), *Left Parties and Social Policy in Postcommunist Europe* (Boulder, CO: Westview Press), 11–46.

Rueschemeyer, M. and S. Wolchik (1999) 'The Return of Left-Oriented Parties in Eastern Germany and the Czech Republic and their Social Policies', in L. Cook, M. Orenstein and M. Rueschemeyer (eds), *Left Parties and Social Policy in Postcommunist Europe* (Boulder, CO: Westview Press), 109–43.

Schumpeter, J. (1943) *Capitalism, Socialism and Democracy* (London: George Allen & Unwin).

Schütte, C. (2000) *Privatization and Corporate Control in the Czech Republic* (Cheltenham, UK and Northampton, MA: Edward Elgar).

Soulsby, A. and E. Clark (1996) 'The Emergence of Post-Communist Management in the Czech Republic', *Organization Studies*, 17, 227–48.

Soulsby, A. and E. Clark (1998) 'Controlling Personnel: Management and Motive in the Transformation of the Czech Enterprise', *International Journal of Human Resource Management*, 9, 79–98.

Takla, L. (1999) 'Privatization: A Comparative Experiment – Poland, the Czech Republic and Hungary', in C. Helmenstein (ed.), *Capital Markets in Central and Eastern Europe* (Cheltenham, UK and Northampton, MA: Edward Elgar), 318–70.

Vepřek, J., P. Vepřek and J. Janda (2002) *Zpráva o léčení českého zdravotnictví anebo Zdravotnická reforma včera, dnes a zítra* (Prague: Grada Publishing).

Žák, V. (1999) 'Rozhovor s Janem Vrbou', *Listy*, No.6.

Wiesenthal, H. (1996) 'Organized Interests in Contemporary East Central Europe: Theoretical Perspectives and Tentative Hypotheses' in A. Ágh and G. Ilonszki (eds), *Parliaments and Organized Interests: The Second Steps* (Budapest: Hungarian Center for Democracy Studies Foundation), 40–58.

6
Poland and Ukraine: Institutional Structures and Economic Performance

Vlad Mykhnenko

This chapter uses the varieties of capitalism (VoC) approach to outline and conceptualize the major current features of the emerging capitalist systems in two large neighbouring post-communist countries. It follows potential linkages between different institutional forms of post-communist capitalism, examining whether the newly emerged institutional forms of post-communist capitalism function as complementary systemic elements, and changes in the revealed comparative advantage of the Polish and Ukrainian economies. This is then related to the social and macroeconomic performance of the two countries in the last phases of transformation. The chapter relies on primary analysis, based mainly on new international comparative sets of institutional, foreign trade, and macroeconomic performance-related data.

In the path-dependent tradition (see Stark and Bruszt 1998; 2001), I view 'post-communist capitalism' as a generic term, that is, not as one socio-economic formation in transit towards one pure competitive market-based capitalism, but as capitalism in the making after the collapse of state socialism in Eastern Europe. This chapter argues that there are a number of dissimilarities between the institutional frameworks of Polish and Ukrainian capitalisms as well as between them and the major Western examples of modern capitalism. Nevertheless, both appear to be representative cases of what Elena Iankova (2002) has labelled a 'dynamic hybrid' Eastern European capitalism or what Hall and Soskice (2003) have described as 'mixed' or 'weakly-coordinated' market economies (see also Rhodes *et al.* 2005).

Differences in the macroeconomic and social performance of the two economies are highlighted by an application of Bela Balassa's concept of 'revealed comparative advantage' (Balassa 1965; 1989). This indicates differences between the countries in the generation of industrial and trade specialization. It also reveals substantial historical continuity in their competitive advantages. The question of why and how this kind of post-communist capitalism has been constructed in Poland and Ukraine is briefly addressed in the concluding section.

What type of capitalism in Poland and Ukraine?

The main assumption of the theorists working on the VoC theme is that the alleged superiority of liberal market-based economies needs to be qualified. As Amable has argued, it is not only deregulated markets and stock market-based financial systems that can deliver good growth performance (2003: 218). The VoC framework allows one to abandon the constraints imposed by the fundamental assumption of the dominant neo-liberal transition paradigm that, in order to progress and succeed, all post-communist countries must transit towards the singular destination of Anglo-American capitalism. The VoC approach implies that – besides the Anglo-American or rather Anglophone[1] model of competitive liberal capitalism – there are a number of other effective and efficient transformation ends which can be better suited to the inherited and newly constructed institutional complementarities and comparative advantages of the emerging market economies of the post-communist world.

My investigation follows Bruno Amable's (2003) analysis of modern capitalism, concentrating on the following elements of the Polish and Ukrainian political economies; product-market regulation, the wage-labour nexus and labour-market institutions, the financial system and corporate governance, the social protection sector, and the education and knowledge sector. For the comparative analysis of post-communist capitalism in Poland and Ukraine, I adopt the established methodology based on the extensive database compiled by the OECD research staff in the late 1990s and early 2000s. The missing institutional indicators, chiefly for Ukraine, presented in this section are my own calculations, scores, and estimates constructed from primary sources and national data using the respective OECD techniques and methods. The institutional features of the two post-communist political economies are compared against each other and against countries that are found in the literature (see Amable 2003: ch. 5; cf. Hall and Soskice 2001; 2003) to be the most extreme representative cases of five different ideal types of modern capitalism, namely Finland (epitomizing social-democratic economies or the Scandinavian model), Germany (coordinated market economies or the Continental European model), Italy (mixed-market economies or the Mediterranean model[2]), South Korea (coordinated market economies or Asian capitalism), and the United Kingdom (liberal market economies or the Anglophone model).

Product-market competition

The nature, form, and intensity of competition between firms in the markets of goods and services are determined by public regulation. This is the first fundamental institutional domain that is believed to differentiate existing models of capitalism. Nicoletti, Scarpetta and Boylaud (2000) of the OECD have collected and formatted a database of internationally comparable data and provided a multi-stage estimation of indicators of regulation that summarize the extensive information on the regulatory environments characterizing OECD member states (see also Conway, Janod and Nicoletti 2005). They have constructed seventeen detailed indicators to describe the regulatory environment in the product market. They were classified in the three broad regulatory domains of state control over business enterprises, barriers to entrepreneurship, and explicit barriers to international trade and investment.

On the basis of factor analysis matrices and other techniques developed by Nicoletti *et al.* (2000), and using the relevant Ukrainian regulatory policy documents and other legislation, I have compiled a number of detailed and summary indicators of product-market regulation in Ukraine and made the necessary comparative scores. Table 6.1 on page 135 presents the summary indicators of the product-market regulatory framework effective as of 2003–2004 in the three domains mentioned above for Ukraine, Poland, Finland, Germany, Italy, Korea, and the UK.

The data indicate that Polish capitalism is characterized by relatively heavily regulated product markets, government involvement in the economy, a large public sector, a relatively high level of coordination of economic agents through non-market signals, administrative burdens for entrepreneurship, and trade and investment protectionism. On average, the reported degree of product-market regulation in Poland appears to be moderately high or what the OECD (Conway *et al.* 2005) has described as 'relatively restrictive', placing it among the paragons of Amable's 'Mediterranean' and 'Asian' capitalisms or Hall and Soskice's mixed and coordinated market economies (e.g. Greece, Italy, France, Spain, and Korea).

Ukrainian capitalism is also characterized by relatively heavy product-market regulation: the involvement of the state is far-reaching and the formal protection of domestic product markets and administrative burdens and barriers to entrepreneurship are relatively high. On average, the Ukrainian regulatory framework is analogous to the South European model, as exemplified by Italy. Thus, both the Polish and Ukrainian types of formal product-market regulation fit generally into the ('weakly') coordinated or mixed market economy models of Hall and Soskice, or the Mediterranean model of Amable.

The wage-labour nexus and labour market institutions

The second institutional arena to be examined concerns industrial and employment relations and the institutions which govern them. The OECD research staff have developed a comprehensive technique to analyse employment protection legislation, based on fifteen detailed indicators of its strictness (Nicoletti *et al.* 2000; reviewed in OECD 2004: ch. 2). They have grouped these indicators into two broad domains of provisions for workers with regular contracts and of provisions affecting workers with fixed-term contracts or employed through temporary work agencies.

Table 6.1 (p. 135) presents the results of the factor analysis for regulation affecting regular and temporary contracts in Poland, Ukraine, and the five representative countries of major models of modern capitalism. It shows that, in general, in 2003 Poland was characterized by a moderate level of employment protection, analogous to that of social-democratic economies, such as Finland. Ukraine, on the other hand, appears to have much less flexible labour-market regulation, close to the level of employment protection attributed to the Continental and Mediterranean European economies of Germany and Italy and well above all other cases.

The second aspect of the wage–labour nexus that can be compared is industrial relations. The major variables considered here concern wage-bargaining centralization and corporatism, trade union density, practices of national social dialogue and relations between managers and employees evaluated through the collective agreement coverage and the number of industrial disputes, the effectiveness of collective bargaining analysed through the actual degree of wage differentiation in the industry and, finally, the degree of state intervention in labour markets and government commitment to supporting the unemployed.

It appears that the major features of Polish industrial relations are decentralized wage-bargaining and weak coordination, a low level of unionization, and narrow collective agreement coverage. Relations between managers and employees in Poland are non-confrontational, as the small scale of industrial disputes indicates. The moderate level of collective bargaining coverage, well above the actual union membership, signals some involvement by the state in industrial relations. However, the combination of employment protection and decentralized, company-based wage bargaining in Poland resembles very closely the regulated labour markets of Asian capitalism, as exemplified by Korea.

Ukraine's industrial relations are characterized by a high degree of wage-bargaining centralization and extensive coordination, a high level of trade union density, and broad collective agreement coverage. As regards the degree of wage-bargaining coordination, Ukraine's industrial relations have retained strong neo-corporatist features and the country's wage–labour nexus is clearly different from the Anglophone model. Table 6.2 shows that the Ukrainian pattern of capital–labour relations has similarities with both the social-democratic and Continental European models, as indicated by the wide coordination of wage bargaining, non-confrontational relations between managers and employees in the country, and the relatively high collective bargaining coverage.

Yet, with some limitations, the wage–labour nexus in both Poland and Ukraine can be described as 'tripartism' or the 'tripartite coordination' defined by Iankova (2002: 11) as a new post-communist species of institutionalized compromise amongst social actors in the industrial arena. This, she argues, 'developed as a dynamic hybrid characterised by political negotiations (rather than Western Europe's neo-corporatist bargaining over purely social and economic conditions)'. It represents a broad civic arrangement rather than just a coordination of the interests of labour, business and the state and it links actors at various levels. The complexity of post-communist 'tripartism' as a broad, accommodating, and civic arrangement appears to be the main difference between the Polish and Ukrainian labour market institutions and their Western European counterparts. However, these complex, multilevel political structures of 'tripartism' have coexisted with very broad inter-sectoral variance in the degree of centralization and coordination of wage bargaining, wage 'flexibility', limited active employment policy, and a low level of direct state support.

Table 6.1 demonstrates that the extent of state intervention and public commitment in Poland's and Ukraine's labour markets, summarized by the simple average net replacement wage in the early 2000s, has been low and close to the Anglophone liberal market economy model, exemplified by Great Britain. However, 'tripartism' in these two countries has involved relatively high employment protection and consensual industrial relations. In the Ukrainian case of what can be described as 'hard' tripartism, trade unions have benefited from massive membership support and statutory provisions for mandatory collective bargaining coverage concerning regular permanent employees. The Polish case of 'soft' tripartism has been characterized by much weaker trade unions and narrower collective bargaining coverage.

Financial intermediation and corporate governance

Capital markets and corporate control represent the third distinctive institutional domain of modern capitalism. Table 6.2 (p. 137) – summarizes a number of fundamental indicators that are typically used to evaluate the financial intermediation sector. The financial systems of both Poland and Ukraine appear to be underdeveloped. Although the Polish capital market appears to be slightly bigger than the Ukrainian one, the overall size of the financial sector is very small in both countries. The two financial systems are bank-based, elementary, and with low levels of banking concentration.

The observed weaknesses of the Polish and Ukrainian financial markets are accompanied by mediocre corporate governance standards and relatively poor business environment provision. In 1999, 2002 and 2005 the World Bank and the European Bank for Reconstruction and Development conducted three large-scale qualitative surveys of the business environment and enterprise performance in twenty-six post-communist countries. The BEEPS (Business Environment and Enterprise Performance Survey) 2002 survey covered 6,100 firms, including 500 in Poland and 463 in Ukraine (see World Bank 2005a). According to this qualitative assessment of the business environment by both Polish and Ukrainian entrepreneurs, firm managers and other representatives of the business community, taxation, finance, and corruption were the three most significant obstacles to doing business. On the scale from 1 (minor obstacle) to 4 (major obstacle), the average score of the Ukrainian business environment in 2002 was 2.22 while for Poland it was 2.45. Compared with other post-communist countries, Poland's business environment was ranked the second worst (25th position out of 26 countries), between Moldova (24th) and Albania (26th). Ukraine's position was seventh worst (20th), between Bulgaria (19th) and Bosnia and Herzegovina (21st) (author's calculation on the basis of Fries, Lysenko, and Polanec 2003).

In terms of the market for corporate control, evaluated through the importance of foreign direct investment, cross-border takeovers, mergers and acquisitions, by the mid 2000s the Polish financial intermediation sector was relatively more developed than its Ukrainian counterpart. The third section of Table 6.2 indicates that there was more active direct investment, and more merger and acquisition activity by foreign companies in Poland. Ukraine's financial-intermediation sector lagged behind all the comparators used here.

Social protection and the welfare system

The social protection systems of Poland and Ukraine appear closer to established models. A number of typologies have been developed (Amable 2003: 154–60; Ebbinghaus and Manow 2001) and prevailing opinion groups the USA, Australia, Ireland, Canada, Japan and Korea (that is most of the countries of the market-based and Asian capitalism models, except for the UK) within the liberal 'residual welfare' model (or the weak, non-welfare, 'zero-level' model of social protection). The United Kingdom, the Netherlands, Spain and Portugal are said to possess liberal, 'minimal-universal' welfare systems. The welfare systems of the remaining Continental European countries are characterized as the 'conservative corporatist' type of welfare state, in which the remaining Mediterranean countries are regarded as belonging to a slightly less generous 'Latin' subtype. The Nordic countries are said to belong to the 'maximal-universal', social-democratic model of the integral welfare state.

The welfare systems of the two post-communist countries are analysed here by comparing the levels of general government sector outlays and public social expenditure in Poland and Ukraine with the variety of advanced capitalist countries. Table 6.2 indicates that, with almost identical shares of public social spending in Poland's and Ukraine's GDP of about 22.3 per cent between 2002 and 2006, marginally below the UK level, the welfare systems of both countries have drifted towards the 'minimal-universal' system of social protection. However, it is contended that in the case of Poland the welfare state's recent development trajectory was downwards from the 'Latin paternalist' subtype of the conservative Continental European welfare model (as exemplified by Italy), whereas in the Ukrainian system social protection has expanded from the liberal 'residualist' non-welfare model.

This is supported by the analysis of shifts in the degree of government intervention in the two economies. The average shares of general government sector expenditures to GDP in Poland have been relatively large and comparable with the Continental European and Mediterranean examples (cf. Germany and Italy). In turn, under post-communism Ukraine has experienced a drastic reduction in the level of government involvement in the economy to the levels associated with the Anglophone model of liberal market economies. Thus, the surprisingly similar levels of public social spending registered in the two post-communist countries in the 2002–6 period suggest a relative reversal in the two welfare states' developments.

The education sector

The education sector is considered the fifth institutional foundation on which a nation's comparative advantage can be built. Historically, both the Polish and Ukrainian education systems were formed under the influence of the Russian Imperial educational system and the Continental European models of France and Germany (Aventur, Campo and Möbus 1999). Both have high levels of curricula standardization and mainly school-based vocational training and professional education. The major difference between the Soviet Ukrainian educational system and its Central European counterparts, however, was in the lower degree of differentiation between 'general' and 'vocational' programmes in the former. Under post-communism, some of the inherited institutional features of the Polish and Ukrainian systems of training and education have been retained, whereas others have experienced major changes.

Table 6.2 provides a synopsis of several contemporary educational and science indicators for Poland, Ukraine and the chosen comparators. It indicates that Poland's system has been characterized by the emphasis on publicly funded institutions and by relatively short mandatory schooling. Poland's education sector is further characterized by the low importance and weak private funding for R&D activities. Life-long learning and continuing professional training play no major role. Several of the indicators indicate close similarities to the Mediterranean model, as exemplified by Italy. The most distinctive feature of the Polish education system appears to be its very low production of science- and industry-related specialists.

The Ukrainian education system has been characterized by relatively high public expenditure, low enrolment rates and a relatively short period of 'school life', i.e. time spent within the formal education system. As in Poland, life-long learning and continuing professional training are of relatively low importance. The main differences between the two systems have been Ukraine's emphasis on university-level education in contrast to Poland's priority to spending on primary education and the greater role of non-governmental funding for R&D in Ukraine.

Macroeconomic performance

This section follows the impact of these institutional forms on the macroeconomic performance of Poland and Ukraine, focusing on economic growth, investment, and employment between 1995 and 2005, well after the initial exogenous shocks associated with the collapse of state socialism had settled.

As indicated in Figure 6.1 both countries enjoyed broadly positive – albeit unstable – rates of growth in these indicators. However, the data in Tables A.7, A.8 and A.9 in the Statistical Appendix show major differences in the countries' performance in respect to unemployment, the distribution of income, and absolute poverty. Unemployment, measured from

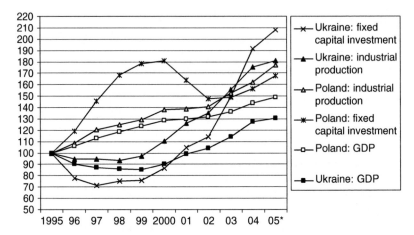

Figure 6.1 Key economic indicators for Poland and Ukraine, 1995 to 2005, as per cent of the 1995 level.
Note: *2005 figure is for the first seven months only.
Sources: Author's calculations on the basis of GUS (various years); Derzhkomstat (various years).

national labour force surveys, increased in both countries, but was only 8.7 per cent in Ukraine compared with 18.9 per cent in Poland in 2005 (GUS 2006d; Derzhkomstat 2006e). Moreover, by 2004, Ukraine returned to a more equitable distribution of income and consumption. The phenomenon of absolute poverty was also tackled better in Ukraine than in Poland or in most of the other post-communist economies.

The VoC approach helps to explain socio-economic peculiarities of the two post-communist economies. The reported differences between Poland's and Ukraine's poverty and income inequality indicators appear to indicate the early positive outcomes of Ukraine's expanding social protection sector *vis-à-vis* Poland's contracting welfare state. The observed difference in unemployment trends support the VoC theoretical assumption that relatively more decentralized and deregulated labour markets are not compatible with regulated product markets and thus should result in higher levels of unemployment (as in the case of Poland) than one would expect in a country with more cocoordinated labour markets and regulated product markets (as in the case of Ukraine).

Revealed comparative advantages

A central prediction of the VoC approach is the existence of a strong link between countries' institutional design and the type of scientific, technological and industrial activities in which they specialize (Hall and Soskice 2001: 36–44; Amable 2003: 197–200). Thus, as Amable's analysis demonstrates (2003: 200–9), the Mediterranean model countries have a strong orientation towards 'traditional' resource-based and low technology industries which appears to complement the relative weakness of their education systems. Similarly, Hall and Soskice link Germany's institutional framework to its comparative advantage in medium technology industries, such as general industrial machinery, transport equipment, metalworking machinery, machine tools, electric household-type appliances, and chemical products (2001: 36–44).

To discover and compare any potential comparative institutional advantages between Poland and Ukraine, this chapter will apply the most typical measurement – Bela Balassa's revealed comparative advantage index (Balassa 1965; 1977; 1989). The revealed comparative advantage (RCA) index compares the export share of a given sector in a country with the export share of that sector in the world market. When the index is unity for a given sector in a given country, the export share of that sector is identical to the average for all countries in the world. When the index is greater than unity, with a range from one to infinity, the country is said to have a relative comparative advantage in that sector. When the index is below one, ranging down to zero, the country is said to have a relative weakness in that sector.

UNCTAD (2006a) provides the three-digit SITC product code of annual exports and imports for over 230 types of products from the total of 67 branches of agriculture, mining and quarrying, manufacturing, and electricity supply. To examine the shifts in RCAs of the two countries under post-communism, whilst minimizing possible ad hoc changes in the national foreign trade structures, I use the average figures for exports for the 2001–2002 period as the end-point of post-communist transformation. To ease understanding of the patterns, the SITC-based data were converted into the International Standard of Industrial Classification data groups.

Table 6.3 (p. 141) contains the RCA indexes for Poland and Ukraine for 2001–2002. It shows that, even after a decade of transition, both countries retained their traditionally strong comparative advantages. It appears that as late as 2002, Poland's major strength was in shipbuilding, whereas Ukraine's key competitive sector was iron and steel. Although the revealed comparative advantages of the two economies may appear to be analogous to those of the less advanced OECD member states, their strongest resemblance is to their pasts under state socialism. The five most competitive Polish manufacturing industries were shipbuilding, furniture, fabricated metals (non-machinery), rubber and plastics, and wearing apparel. In turn, iron and steel, railway vehicles, coke, non-ferrous metals, and wood (non-furniture) were Ukraine's most competitive manufacturing branches. On the other side of the RCA spectrum, the weakest Polish industries in terms of competitiveness were aerospace, pharmaceuticals, medical, precision and optical equipment, and office and computing machinery. The weakest branches of Ukrainian manufacturing were radio, TV and communication equipment, pharmaceuticals, motor vehicles, and office and computing machinery. According to Table 6.3, the major difference between the revealed comparative advantages of the two economies lies in the overall number of competitive manufacturing industries rather than in the nature of their innovative and technological capacities. In 2001–2002, on average, there were almost twice as many internationally competitive Polish as Ukrainian manufacturing industries, which might be attributed to Poland's relatively more developed sector of financial intermediation and the country's large FDI in-flows with potential technology spillovers.

The VoC claims about the institutional foundations of comparative advantage, especially the approach's emphasis on radical innovation – as, for example, in the pharmaceuticals industry – as the attribute of LMEs and incremental innovation – as in heavy engineering – as the attribute of CMEs, have been questioned by a number of authors. Matthew Watson (2003) has argued that it is not different models of capitalism but fundamental features of the social structure of accumulation and the geopolitical division of power which can explain cross-national differences in specialization, trade and comparative advantage. A robust empirical investigation by Mark Z. Taylor has revealed that 'the existing evidence depends heavily on the inclusion of a major outlier, the United States, in the class of liberal market economies' (2004: 625). Moreover, all the most radically innovative countries of the world, including Japan, Canada, the United Kingdom, Israel, and Taiwan, have strong military ties with the USA. Taylor has therefore suggested concentrating more on international relations than on domestic institutions to explain the political economy of comparative rates of innovation. The evidence in this chapter suggests that, in addition, *past* dependence is a crucial factor in explaining comparative advantages of post-communist economies.

Conclusion: post-communist capitalism

The core features of the two forms of post-communist capitalism in Poland and Ukraine are summarized in Table 6.1. It shows that the two political

Table 6.1 Summary features of post-communist capitalism in Poland and Ukraine, early 2000s

Institutional arena	Poland	Ukraine
Product markets	'Relatively restrictive' product-market regulation	'Relatively restrictive' product-market regulation
Wage–labour nexus	'Restrained tripartism'	'Hard tripartism'
Finance	Elementary, small, bank-based system	Underdeveloped, small, bank-based system
Welfare	Contracting conservative 'Latin' welfare state	Expanding liberal 'universalist' welfare state
Education	Weak, 'general skills' public education system	Weak, 'polytechnic skills' public education system

economies share a large number of institutional characteristics, including regulated product markets, the 'tripartite' regulation of the wage–labour nexus, elementary and bank-based financial-intermediation sectors, public education systems, and similarly endowed welfare states.

However, each of the two capitalisms appears to be at a formative stage, characterized, at least at a theoretical level, by a number of complementarities. Although both of the two domestic finance sectors are currently bank-based, which is fairly complementary with the other institutional features of the two post-communist political economies, the financial systems in Poland and Ukraine remain immature and weak in comparison with any of the existing models of modern capitalism. Furthermore, in the case of Poland, the wage–labour nexus, which is based on 'soft' regulation, is not entirely complementary with the overall logic of the national type of regulated capitalism. Competitive labour markets can make structural adjustment less costly if the released labour is quickly absorbed by low-wage, small and medium-sized firms or business start-ups. These are held back in Poland by economic and administrative barriers to entry.

In turn, Ukraine's limited welfare system is, at least theoretically, incompatible with the overall institutional logic of the regulated capitalism model towards which the country has been evolving. A minimal public-funded social protection system does not protect against unemployment and fluid labour markets are therefore necessary. Low protection for specific-skills investment provides incentives for individuals to acquire general skills in order to move from job to job and make retraining easier. All these institutional effects that typically emanate from a minimal social protection system contravene the inner workings of a regulated market economy based upon industry-specific knowledge and skills.

The discussion about the reasons behind the establishment of post-communist capitalism and about domestic political and exogenous factors which have contributed to, and influenced the construction of, such types of capitalism in Poland and Ukraine is undeveloped. However, it has been argued elsewhere that it was Poland's consensual political regime that structured the particular political choices generated in the partisan struggles of post-communism to produce its heavily regulated variant of capitalism. In turn, although Ukraine's chief executive office was occupied by a centre-right figure for a much longer period than in Poland, a large number of built-in veto mechanisms combined with the overall ideological fragmentation in the country have pushed the post-communist political struggles towards more consensual decision-making. As a result, post-communist capitalism in Ukraine, as in Poland, has acquired practically none of the attributes of the Anglophone model and institutional change in the country, and in the region, was directed towards a social compromise formed around the construction of the 'social-market' neo-corporatist model of regulated capitalism (Mykhnenko 2005: ch. 8).

Notwithstanding some unambiguous differences in terms of short- and long-term performance generated by the two economies in the 1990s and early 2000s, the majority of more recent macro- and socio-economic indicators of Poland and Ukraine have been similar. This may be interpreted as the outcome of positive returns on complementary institutions established within the two post-communist political economies. However, no particular linkage has been discovered between the current institutional designs of the two economies and their revealed comparative trade advantages and industrial specializations. It appears that the exclusive focus on the institutional forms of the two national models of production, consumption and distribution, and on their endogenous micro-logic – developed in accordance with the VoC framework – provide only a partial explanation for the trajectories and variations in macroeconomic performance of post-communist countries. It seems that future research should focus less on contemporary national regulatory frameworks and domestic institutions and more on the historical legacies and industrial assets of the state-socialist past and on international relations and global power networks. These have a more immediate effect on the performance of Eastern European economies.

Table 6.2 Major indicators of five core institutional domains in selected economies, late 1990s – early 2000s

	Finland	Germany	Italy	Korea	Poland	UK	Ukraine
Product markets, 2003							
Overall level of regulation, 0–6 from the least to the most restrictive	1.3	1.4	1.9	1.5	2.8	0.9	1.9 (2004)
of which: State control	2.3	2.2	3.2	1.7	3.6	1.7	3.0 (2004)
Barriers to entrepreneurship	1.1	1.6	1.4	1.7	2.3	0.8	1.6 (2004)
Barriers to trade and investment	0.6	0.6	1.1	1.3	2.4	0.4	1.1 (2004)
Labour markets, 1999–2004							
Overall level of employment protection legislation, 0–6 from the least to the most restrictive, 2003	2.12	2.47	2.44	2.00	2.14	1.04	2.50
Levels of collective bargaining, maximum score is 5 divided over three levels, 1999–2001 of which Intersectoral	xxx						x
Sectoral	x	xxxx	xxx	x	x	x	xxx
Company	x	x	xx	xxxx	xxxx	xxxx	x
Union density, 2000 % of employees	76.2	25.0	34.9	11.4	14.7	31.2	67.9 (2003)
Collective bargaining coverage, 2000 % of employees	92.5	68.0	82.5	12.5	42.5	32.5	68.6 (2003)
Days lost due to strikes, 2000–4 average per 1,000 employees	42.52	3.22	137.51	112.65	1.63	28.8	2.64
Wage differentiation within manufacturing (the ratio of (latest available year)	1.86	1.85	n/d	3.29	3.73	2.08	6.64

(Continued)

Table 6.2 (Continued)

		Finland	Germany	Italy	Korea	Poland	UK	Ukraine
the average wage of the highest paid industry to the lowest paid industry, 2003–4								
Initial net replacement rates of unemployed up to 12 months, simple unweighted average for all types of families, forms of employment and level of income,* 2002	% of previous wage	74.3	76.5	60.2	56.4	53.0	48.5	40.9
Finance, 2000–4								
Sum of domestic assets of deposit money banks and market capitalization, 2003	as % of GDP	164.24	181.85	136.27	143.02	54.09	261.56	29.95
Ratio of deposit money bank assets to market capitalization, 2003		0.70	3.92	2.64	1.99	2.53	1.19	3.28
Total private credit, 2003	as % of GDP	61.46	117.39	82.54	119.91	28.13	141.3	19.71
Life and non-life insurance penetration, premium volume, 2003	as % of GDP	8.69	7.08	7.58	9.82	2.99	13.73	3.46
Bank concentration: three largest banks' assets as % of all commercial bank assets, 2003		88.91	63.72	40.52	47.79	41.86	42.68	49.04
Central bank assets, 2003	as % of GDP	0.01	0.21	4.21	1.04	0.43	0.67	7.35
Foreign direct investment cumulative stock	per capita, US$, 2004	10,686.5	4210.2	3803.4	1161.2	1593.1	12,973.6	196.2

139

Mergers and acquisitions, cross-border deals, 2000–4							
as % of GDP, 2003	28.57	16.08	12.34	9.03	26.75	33.86	15.86
Total number of sales per period	362	1179	651	203	406	2826	85
Total value of sales per period, US$ mn	22,380	403,261	65,801	24,865	18,017	391,050	576
Welfare and the state, 2002–6 average							
Public social expenditure, estimate*** as % of GDP	25.56	27.09	24.52	6.60	22.26	23.28	22.34
General government total outlays as % of GDP	50.66	47.70	49.15	26.94	46.04	43.47	39.18
Education, 2002–4, latest year available							
Years of compulsory education	10	13	9	9	9	12	9
Gross enrolment ratio, all levels combined, except pre-primary as % of all people of eligible age**	107.8	88.9	86.8	93.9	90.4	119.0	85.6
School life approximation, all levels combined years	18.3	15.8	15.6	16.0	15.6	21.3	13.4
Continuing learning and training, participation rate, late 1990s early–2000s as % of total workforce	50.4	25.4	25.3	22.0	16.0	50.0	10.0
Public expenditure on education as % of GDP	6.4	4.8	4.7	4.2	5.6	5.3	5.4
as % of total government expenditure	12.7	9.5	10.3	15.5	12.8	11.5	20.3
Educational expenditure by level as % of total educational expenditure:							
pre-primary	5.4	8.4	8.6	1.2	7.9	8.6	11.2
primary	21.6	14.3	25.8	34.0	33.7	23.6	8.8
lower secondary	17.1	30.6	19.5	20.4	17.3	14.8	22.0
upper secondary	23.5	17.9	26.6	23.0	20.6	33.6	9.4
post-secondary non-tertiary	–	2.2	1.0	–	0.9	–	6.0
tertiary	32.5	24.6	18.5	8.1	19.5	20.6	34.0

(Continued)

Table 6.2 (Continued)

		Finland	Germany	Italy	Korea	Poland	UK	Ukraine
	not allocated by level	–	2.1	–	13.3	0.5	–	8.7
Total science and technology graduates	as % of total tertiary graduates	28	26	23	39	12	26	26
Researchers per million inhabitants		7431	3222	1156	2979	1469	2691	1749
Total gross domestic expenditure on R&D (GERD)	as % of GDP	3.46	2.64	1.11	2.91	0.59	1.88	1.18
Government expenditure on GERD	as % of total GERD	26.1	31.9	50.8	23.9	61.1	26.9	37.4

Notes: *Average net replacement rates are calculated as unweighted averages for: (a) earnings levels of 67%, 100% and 150% of average production wage; (b) single-parent households and married couples with one or two working spouses; (c) households with no, one or two children; net replacement rate equals gross personal income received from unemployment and other social benefits after mandatory tax deductions. Ukraine's figure is for 2004 onwards.

** The enrolment ratio is the ratio of enrolled children of the official age for the education level indicated to the total population of that age. Enrolment ratios exceeding 100 per cent reflect discrepancies between these two data sets. A further discrepancy may arise from school pupils repeating a grade who are included in the data set with younger enrolled children of the official age for the same education level.

***Estimate is based on the latest available ratio of general government to public social expenditures and the current levels of general government sector expenditure.

Sources: Beck, Demirgüç-Kunt and Levine (2006); Carley (2002); CMU (2004a, 2004b); Conway, Janod, and Nicoletti (2005); Derzhkomstat (2004); Elmeskov, Martin, and Scarpetta (1998); FEDEE (2005); Halyts'ki Kontrakty (1998); ILO (2006); IMF (2005); Kupets (2004); MLSPU (2005a, 2005b, 2005c); Nicoletti, Scarpetta, and Boylaud (2000); OECD (2006a, 2006b, 2006c, 2006d); Seniv (2004); TUFU (2005); UNCTAD (2006a); UNESCO (2006a, 2006b, 2006c); Visser (2000); VRU (1971, 1991a, 1991b, 1992, 1996, 2000a, 2000b, 2003a, 2003b); World Bank (2004, 2005a, 2005b); and author's own calculations, scores, and estimates.

Table 6.3 Revealed comparative advantage indexes for Poland and Ukraine by manufacturing industry, 2001–2002 average

Poland		Ukraine	
Industry	Index	Industry	Index
Strong comparative advantage (>2.0):		*Strong comparative advantage (>2.0):*	
Ship-building	7.58	Basic iron and steel	13.62
Furniture	2.77	Railway and transport equipment nec	2.63
Fabricated metal products	2.61	Coke, refined petroleum and nuclear fuel	2.43
Rubber and plastics	2.33	Basic precious and non-ferrous metals	2.06
Wearing apparel and fur	2.10	*Comparative advantage (>1.0):*	
Comparative advantage (>1.0):		Wood and cork	1.71
Other non-metallic mineral products	1.96	Wearing apparel and fur	1.35
Paper	1.83	Food and drink	1.27
Wood and cork	1.81	Chemicals	1.16
Basic precious and non-ferrous metals	1.69	*Comparative disadvantage (<1.0):*	
Railway and transport equipment nec	1.48	Rubber and plastics	0.94
Electrical machinery and apparatus	1.46	Leather and footwear	0.85
Basic iron and steel	1.40	Shipbuilding	0.83
Publishing and printing	1.36	Fabricated metal products	0.78
Food and drink	1.27	Machinery and equipment nec	0.75
Machinery and equipment nec	1.17	Paper	0.75
Comparative disadvantage (<1.0):		Tobacco	0.74
Motor vehicles	0.99	Other non-metallic mineral products	0.72
Coke, refined petroleum and nuclear fuel	0.86	Aerospace	0.66
Textiles	0.84	*Strong comparative disadvantage (<0.5):*	
Leather and footwear	0.82	Electrical machinery and apparatus	0.47
Radio, TV and communication equipment and apparatus	0.73	Textiles	0.32
Chemicals	0.69	Medical, precision and optical instruments	0.24
Tobacco	0.50	Publishing and printing	0.22

(Continued)

Table 6.3   (Continued)

Poland		Ukraine	
Industry	*Index*	*Industry*	*Index*
Strong comparative disadvantage (<0.5):		Furniture	0.19
Aerospace	0.21	Radio, TV and communication equipment and apparatus	0.15
Pharmaceuticals	0.21	Pharmaceuticals	0.11
Medical, precision and optical instruments	0.17	Motor vehicles	0.10
Office, accounting and computing machinery	0.13	Office, accounting and computing machinery	0.03

Note: nec – not classified elsewhere; author's conversion of SITC Rev. 2 data into ISIC Rev. 3 data groups.
Source: Author's own compilations and calculations on the basis of UNCTAD (2006a).

Notes

1. Colin Crouch argues that the 'Anglo-Saxon' model 'is in fact used entirely consistently to identify that group of countries where English is the dominant language and the majority population is white-skinned: the UK, Ireland, the USA, Canada, Australia, and New Zealand. The correct, unambiguous term, which precisely identifies this group of countries is "Anglophone", and one wonders why this clear and accurate term is not used instead of the more popular, exotic but highly dubious alternative' (2005: 45).
2. According to Amable's factor analysis, Greece is the most extreme exemplar of Southern European economies (2003: 176–7). However, due to the acute lack of comparable data concerning major institutional indicators of Greece, Italy – the second closest 'paragon' – is used in this chapter as a representative of the Mediterranean model.

References

Amable, B. (2003) *The Diversity of Modern Capitalism* (Oxford: Oxford University Press).
Aventur, F., C. Campo and M. Möbus (1999) 'Factors in the Spread of Continuing Training in the European Community', *Training and Employment*, 35, 1–4.
Balassa, B. (1965) 'Trade Liberalization and "Revealed" Comparative Advantage', *The Manchester School of Economic and Social Studies*, 32, 99–123.
Balassa, B. (1977) 'The Changing Pattern of Comparative Advantage in Manufactured Goods', *Review of Economics and Social Studies*, 45, 327–44.
Balassa, B. (1989) *Comparative Advantage, Trade Policy and Economic Development* (London: Harvester Wheatsheaf).
Beck, T., A. Demirgüç-Kunt and R. Levine (2006) *Financial Structure and Economic Development Database* (Washington, DC: World Bank).

Carley, M. (2002) 'Industrial Relations in the EU Member States and Candidate Countries', *European Industrial Relations Observatory* <www.eiro.eurofound.eu.int>.

CMU (Cabinet of Ministers of Ukraine) (2004a) *Reestratsiia SPD fizychnoi osoby* (Kyiv: CMU) < www.kmu.gov.ua/control/uk/publish/category?cat_id=6133396>.

CMU (Cabinet of Ministers of Ukraine) (2004b) *Reestratsiia SPD iurydychnoi osoby* (Kyiv: CMU) <www.kmu.gov.ua/control/uk/publish/category?cat_id=6133304>.

Conway, P., V. Janod and G. Nicoletti (2005) *Product Market Regulation in OECD Countries: 1998 to 2003*, OECD Economics Department Working Paper, 419 (Paris: OECD).

Crouch, C. (2005) *Capitalist Diversity and Change: Recombinant Governance and Institutional Entrepreneurs* (Oxford: Oxford University Press).

Derzhkomstat (Ukraine State Statistics Committee) (2002 and 2004) *Statystychnyi shchorichnyk Ukraïny* (Kyiv: Tekhnika).

Derzhkomstat (Ukraine State Statistics Committee) (2006a) *Statystychna informatsiia: Natsional'ni rakhunky* (Kyiv: Derzhkomstat) <www.ukrstat.gov.ua/>.

Derzhkomstat (Ukraine State Statistics Committee) (2006b) *Statystychna informatsiia: Promyslovist* (Kyiv: Derzhkomstat) <www.ukrstat.gov.ua/>.

Derzhkomstat (Ukraine State Statistics Committee) (2006c) *Statystychna informatsiia: Investytsii ta budivel'na diial'nist'* (Kyiv: Derzhkomstat) <www.ukrstat.gov.ua/>.

Derzhkomstat (Ukraine State Statistics Committee) (2006d) *Statystychna informatsiia: Ekspres-vypusky* (Kyiv: Derzhkomstat) <www.ukrstat.gov.ua/>.

Derzhkomstat (Ukraine State Statistics Committee) (2006e) *Statystychna informatsiia: Rynok pratsi* (Kyiv: Derzhkomstat) <www.ukrstat.gov.ua/>.

Ebbinghaus, D. and P. Manow (eds) (2001) *Comparing Welfare Capitalism, Social Policy and Political Economy in Europe, Japan and the USA* (London: Routledge).

Elmeskov, J., J.P. Martin, and S. Scarpetta (1998) 'Key Lessons for Labour Market Reforms: Evidence from OECD Countries' Experiences', *Swedish Economic Policy Review*, 5, 205–52.

FEDEE (Federation of European Employers) (2005) *Trade Unions across Europe* (London: FedEE) <www.fedee.com/tradeunions.html>.

Fries, S., T. Lysenko and S. Polanec (2003) *The 2002 Business Environment and Enterprise Performance Survey: Results from a Survey of 6,100 firms* (London: EBRD Working Paper, 84).

GUS (Poland's Central Statistical Office) (2002 and 2004) *Rocznik Statystyczny Rzeczypospolitej Polskiej* (Warsaw: GUS).

GUS (2005) *Mały Rocznik Statystyczny Polski 2005* (Warsaw: GUS).

GUS (2006a) *Informacje Statystyczne. Podstawowe dane: Rachunki narodowe* (Warsaw: GUS) <www.stat.gov.pl/dane_spol-gosp/rachunki_narodowe/index.htm>.

GUS (2006b) *Informacje Statystyczne. Podstawowe dane: Produkcja. Budownictwo. Inwestycje. Środki trwałe* (Warsaw: GUS) <www.stat.gov.pl/dane_spol-gosp/prod_bud_inw/index.htm>.

GUS (2006c) *Informacje Statystyczne. Informacje bieżące Wyniki wstepnę* (Warsaw: GUS) <www.stat.gov.pl/wyniki_wstepne/index.htm>.

GUS (2006d) *Informacje Statystyczne. Podstawowe dane: Praca. Dochody ludnosci* (Warsaw: GUS) <www.stat.gov.pl/dane_spol-gosp/praca_ludność/index.htm>.

Hall, P. A. and D. Soskice (eds) (2001) *Varieties of Capitalism: The Institutional Foundations of Comparative Advantage* (Oxford: Oxford University Press).

Hall, P.A. and D. Soskice (2003) 'Varieties of Capitalism and Institutional Change: A Response to Three Critics,' *Comparative European Politics*, 1, 241–50.

Halyts'ki kontrakty (1998) 'Trudovi vidnosyny: tematychna dobirka. Normatyvni akty, aktual'ni dokumenty', *Halyts'ki Kontrakty: Ukrainian Business Weekly*, 38.

Iankova, E. A. (2002) *Eastern European Capitalism in the Making* (Cambridge: Cambridge University Press).

ILO (International Labour Organization) (2006) *LABORSTA Labour Statistics Database: Yearly Selection* (Geneva: ILO) <http://laborsta.ilo.org>.

IMF (International Monetary Fund) (2005) *Ukraine: IMF Country Report. Statistical Appendix* (Washington, DC: IMF).

Kupets, O. (2004) 'Determinants of Unemployment Duration in Ukraine', Presented at the IER Conference on Labour Market Reforms and Economic Growth in Ukraine: Linkages and Policies, National University 'Kyiv Mohyla Academy', Kyiv, 2–3 March.

MLSPU (Ministry of Labour and Social Policy of Ukraine) (2005a) *General'na uhoda mizh Kabinetom Ministriv Ukrainy, vseukrains'kymy ob'ednanniamy organizatsii robotodavtsiv i pidpryemtsiv ta vseukrains'kymy profspilkamy i profob'ednaniamy na 2004–2005 roky* (Kyiv: MLSPU) <www.mlsp.gov.ua/control/uk/publish/article?art_id=35596&cat_id=34940>.

MLSPU (2005b) *Stan vykonannia kolektyvnykh dohovoriv za vydamy promyslovoi diial'nosti na 1 kvitnia 2005 roku* (Kyiv: MLSPU) <www.mlsp.gov.ua/control/uk/publish/article?art_id=40932&cat_id=34940>.

MLSPU (2005c) *Stan vykonannia kolektyvnykh dohovoriv za vydamy promyslovoi diial'nosti na 1 kvitnia 2005 roku* (Kyiv: MLSPU) <www.mlsp.gov.ua/control/uk/publish/article?art_id=40928&cat_id=34940>.

Mykhnenko, V (2005) *'The Political Economy of Post-Communism: A Comparison of Upper Silesia (Poland) and the Donbas (Ukraine)'*, Ph.D Dissertation, Department of Social and Political Sciences, University of Cambridge <www.policy.hu/mykhnenko/Political_Economy_of_Post-Communism.html>.

Nicoletti, G., S. Scarpetta and O. Boylaud (2000) *Summary Indicators of Product Market Regulation with an Extension to Employment Protection Legislation*, OECD Economics Department Working Paper, 226 (Paris: OECD).

OECD (Organisation for Economic Cooperation and Development) (2004) *Employment Outlook 2004* (Paris: OECD).

OECD (2006a) *Employment Outlook 2005* (Paris: OECD).

OECD (2006b) *The OECD Annual National Accounts Statistics Data Base* (Paris: OECD), <www.oecd.org/topicstatsportal>.

OECD (2006c) *The OECD Labour Statistics Data Base* (Paris: OECD) <www.oecd.org/topicstatsportal>.

OECD (2006d) *The OECD Social and Welfare Statistics Data Base* (Paris: OECD) <www.oecd.org/topicstatsportal>.

Rhodes, M., B. Hancké, and M. Thatcher (2005) 'Institutional Change in Contemporary European Capitalism: Conflict, Contradiction and Complementarities', Paper presented at conference on Institutional Change in Contemporary European Capitalism, London School of Economics and the European University Institute, 3–4 June.

Seniv, A. (2004) *Kolektyvni uhody ta trudovi vidnosyny v Ukraini* (Donetsk: processed private law firm consultation solicited by the author); unpublished.

Stark, D. and L. Bruszt (1998) *Postsocialist Pathways: Transforming Politics and Property in East Central Europe* (Cambridge: Cambridge University Press).

Stark, D. and L. Bruszt (2001) 'One way or multiple paths?: For a Comparative Sociology of East European capitalism', *American Journal of Sociology*, 106, 1129–37.

Taylor, M. Z. (2004) 'Empirical Evidence Against Varieties Capitalism's Theory of Technological Innovation', *International Organization*, 58, 601–31.

TUFU (Trade Unions Federation of Ukraine) (2005) *Vseukrains'ki i regional'ni profspilky u skladi FPU* (Kyiv: TUFU) <http://fpu.org.ua/index.php?id=16>.

UNCTAD (United Nations Conference on Trade and Development) (2006a) *UNCTAD Handbook of Statistics On-line: Database* (New York: United Nations Publications), <www.unctad.org/Templates/Page.asp?intItemID=1890&lang=1>.

UNCTAD (2006b) *Foreign Direct Investment Database* (New York: United Nations Publications) <www.unctad.org/Templates/Page.asp?intItemID=1923& lang=1>.

UNESCO (2006a) *Global Education Digest CD-Rom 2005* (Montreal: UNESCO) <http://stats.uis.unesco.org/ReportFolders/reportfolders.aspx>.

UNESCO (2006b) *Science and Technology: Statistics on Research and Development* (Montreal: UNESCO) <http://stats.uis.unesco.org/ReportFolders/reportfolders.aspx>.

UNESCO (2006c) *Education* (Montreal: UNESCO) <http://stats.uis.unesco.org/ReportFolders/reportfolders.aspx>.

Visser, J. (2000) *Trend in Unionization and Collective Bargaining: International Labour Office Report* (Geneva: ILO).

VRU (Verkhovna Rada of Ukraine) (1971) 'Kodeks zakoniv pro pratsiu Ukrainy', *Vidomosti Verkhovnoi Rady Ukrainy*, 50, Art. 375 <http://zakon.rada.gov.ua/cgi-bin/laws/>.

VRU (1991a) 'Zakon Ukrainy pro hospodars'ki tovarystva', *Vidomosti Verkhovnoi Rady Ukrainy*, 49, Art. 682 <http://zakon.rada.gov.ua/cgi-bin/laws/>.

VRU (1991b) 'Zakon Ukrainy pro pidpryemnytstvo', *Vidomosti Verkhovnoi Rady Ukrainy*, 14, Art. 168 <http://zakon.rada.gov.ua/cgi-bin/laws/>.

VRU (1992) 'Zakon Ukrainy pro inozemni investytsii', *Vidomosti Verkhovnoi Rady Ukrainy*, 26, Art. 357 <http://zakon.rada.gov.ua/cgi-bin/laws/>.

VRU (1996) 'Zakon Ukrainy pro rezhym inozemnogo investuvannia', *Vidomosti Verkhovnoi Rady Ukrainy*, 19, Art. 80 <http://zakon.rada.gov.ua/cgi-bin/laws/>.

VRU (2000a) 'Zakon Ukrainy pro litsenzuvannia pevnykh vydiv hospodars'koi diial'nosti', *Vidomosti Verkhovnoi Rady Ukrainy*, 36, Art. 299 <http://zakon.rada.gov.ua/cgi-bin/laws/>.

VRU (2000b) 'Zakon Ukrainy pro usunennia dyskryminatsii v opodatkuvanni sub-'ektiv pidpryemnyts'koi diial'nosti, stvorenykh z vykorystannia maina ta koshtiv vitchyznianoho pokhodzhennia vid inozemni investytsii', *Vidomosti Verkhovnoi Rady Ukrainy*, 12, Art. 97 <http://zakon.rada.gov.ua/cgi-bin/laws/>.

VRU (2003a) 'Hospodars'kyi kodeks Ukainy', *Vidomosti Verkhovnoi Rady Ukrainy*, 18–22, Art. 144 <http://zakon.rada.gov.ua/cgi-bin/laws/>.

VRU (2003b) 'Zakon Ukrainy pro podatok z dokhodiv fizychnykh osib', *Vidomosti Verkhovnoi Rady Ukrainy*, 37, Art. 308 <http://zakon.rada.gov.ua/cgi-bin/laws/>.

Watson, M. (2003) 'Ricardian Political Economy and the "Varieties of Capitalism" Approach: Specialization, Trade and Comparative Institutional Advantage', *Comparative European Politics*, 1, 227–40.

World Bank (2004) *Doing Business in 2004: Understanding Regulation* (Oxford: Oxford University Press).

World Bank (2005a) *The BEEPS II Interactive Dataset: Enterprise Survey in Transition 2002* (Washington, DC: World Bank).

World Bank (2005b) *Doing Business in 2005: Removing Obstacles to Growth* (Oxford: Oxford University Press).

Part III
Hybrid Economies

7

Russian Political Capitalism and its Environment

*Philip Hanson and Elizabeth Teague**

There are two main arguments in this chapter. First, the indicators putting the Russian economy in the liberal market economy category mask an economic role for the state that is much greater than that in established market economies of any kind. We are not putting forward a normative argument, that Russia *should* become a liberal market economy. What we are saying is that the Varieties of Capitalism approach is not helpful in understanding systemic developments in Russia: it has been developed on the basis of a set of criteria that, when applied to Russia, produce a misleading picture. We believe Russia can be more easily understood as an example of Weberian political capitalism. This might change in time, and Russian economic institutions might eventually be classifiable in ways that fit established capitalist societies.

Our second contention is that there are influences that might, over time, tend to diminish the present dominance of the state, but that they will not easily or quickly do so. We shall dwell particularly on the extent to which Russia's being integrated into the world economy provides feedbacks through international markets that may constrain the economic interventionism of politicians. This issue is touched on, in connexion with other countries, by Lane and by Myant in this volume; Christophe's suggestion that Georgia is embedded in an international shadow economy is a variant on the theme, though one with different implications for the future.

The plan of the chapter is as follows. First we summarize our earlier work characterizing the recent dominance of the state over big business. Then we review, in turn, three factors affecting this state of affairs: state policies, feedbacks to economic policy through international markets, and the changing composition of the Russian business elite. In the conclusion we suggest that Russia does not fit into any of the major 'Varieties of Capitalism'.

Liberal markets and Russian rules of the game

Russia has several of the characteristics of a liberal market economy. That emerges clearly in Knell and Srholec's account in this volume. In particular, and in comparison with fifty other countries, Russia in the early twenty-first century has high-income inequality and low-income tax rates (a flat tax in fact), low employment protection and a high ratio of stock-market capitalization to bank credit. These observations produce scores on 'social cohesion', 'labour market regulation' and 'business regulation' that put Russia in the liberal market-economy category. On the last of these scores, Knell and Srholec note that Russia's 'business regulation' outcome is determined by its high ratio of stock-market capitalization to bank credit (see Chapter 2 and Table A.5 in the Statistical Appendix). This is worth stressing, because Russia's liberal score on business regulation, which would surprise commentators on the Russian business scene, might be characterized as reflecting (a) a stock-market whose relatively high ratio of capitalization to GDP co-exists with low liquidity, that is, a low ratio of turnover to capitalization,[1] and (b) a badly underdeveloped banking system.

If we define a liberal market economy as one whose scores on Hall and Soskice-style indicators place it in that category, then Russia is a liberal market economy. If, on the other hand, we define a liberal market economy more loosely as one that has a competitive market for corporate control, competitive labour and product markets, and state intervention clearly limited by law, then Russia lacks the first and last of these characteristics. We suggest that the second definition of a liberal market economy is more useful. Certainly a state that can destroy and largely renationalize the leading private company (Yukos) in the country's internationally strongest industry (oil) by methods widely deemed to be illegal is not providing what is usually thought of as a liberal environment for business.

One indication of the anomalous mix of institutional characteristics in Russian economic arrangements is that Russia's position in the World Bank rankings for 'Ease of Doing Business' is 79th out of 155 countries (<www.doingbusiness.org/EconomyRankings/>, accessed 3 October 2005), well above Venezuela, China or India and only nine places below Italy, but still a long way behind the leaders. New Zealand tops the list, followed by Singapore, and all the Nordic countries are in the top fourteen. The indicators are measures of the time and cost involved in starting a business, dealing with licences, hiring and firing, registering property and getting credit.

Russia's rankings are all over the place: a respectable 31st on starting a business and 35th on registering property but 143rd on dealing with licences and 148th on getting credit. On hiring and firing the Russian Federation rank is 57th. Two of these rankings bear some relation to Hall and Soskice-style indicators. The ranking on 'hiring and firing' is above the rankings of Germany, France, Sweden, Finland and the Baltics, and just above that of Ireland, but well below those of Denmark, Japan, Botswana or South Africa – not to mention those of the US, UK, Hong Kong or Switzerland. That fits fairly well with a Varieties of Capitalism classification. The abysmal ranking on getting credit shows the anomaly already mentioned: a lousy banking system can easily make a country look 'liberal' on its stock-market capitalization: bank-credit ratio.

A study that probes beneath the surface of such up-and-down scores (Ivanenko 2005) notes that Russian institutions compare moderately well with the average of Brazil, China, India, Indonesia and South Africa on market competition but rather poorly on corporate practices, separation of powers, independence of the judiciary and government efficiency. Ivanenko suggests that the thread connecting these Russian relative weaknesses is mistrust within society as a whole, plus corruption. We suggest that these are important elements in Russia's really existing capitalism, and that they are not captured by the usual Varieties of Capitalism indicators.

In a previous paper we showed that Russian big business has recently become unusually dependent on, and in some respects even subservient to, the state (Hanson and Teague 2005). Our main comparisons, so far as big business–state relations were concerned, were with post-war Japan and Italy. We also compared the general effectiveness of Russian state institutions with those of twenty-one other middle-income countries around the year 2002. We found Russian state 'governance' to be relatively poor, even within that group of countries. So the state appeared to be both dominant and inefficient. We suggested two plausible reasons for the dominance of the state over big business: the salience of natural-resource extracting activities in the Russian economy, and the recent history of legally grey processes of privatization of the underlying assets. Both give the Russian state a great deal of leverage over a large chunk of the private sector.

Properly measured, the oil and gas sector accounts for about 20 per cent of Russian GDP (OECD 2004; Tabata 2006). Its importance in the Russian economy is discussed more fully later on. Petro-states have tended since the 1970s to employ a great deal of state control in their oil and gas sectors. One might therefore argue that geology alone dictates a strong role for the state in the post-communist Russian economy. Popular distaste for the often-corrupt privatizations of the 1990s provides a backing for such a role. This is fair, but we will draw attention to three issues: the abruptness of the change in state–oil industry relations from 2003; the manner in which state influence has been exerted; and the actual and potential spillover effects from an abrupt reintroduction of, in our judgement, somewhat arbitrary state control.

In this chapter we review the influences that might alter the state's present leverage over big business, and make an informal assessment of the prospects of change. It is too early for us to see significant diversification of the economy, reducing its dependence on natural resources; nor has enough time passed to weaken the political legacy of the privatizations of the 1990s. But we can track three kinds of recent development that have a bearing on business–state relations: changes in state policies, notably the Russian authorities' moves to increase state control over the natural-resource sector, where comparisons with some other petro-states are appropriate; the reactions of international markets to those moves; and early signs of changes in the population of Russian big companies. These topics are assessed, in that order, below.

Our concern here is with the process of change in state–business relations. As David Lane argues in Chapter 1, the Hall and Soskice and the Amable classifications of Varieties of Capitalism cover established capitalist countries where institutions have taken shape over long periods of time. We would add that the Central European states are deemed to have imported the whole EU *acquis communautaire* into their own institutional set-ups but even they do not for the most part have structural indicators such as credit to GDP, stock-market capitalization to GDP, or foreign-owned capital stock to GDP that correspond closely to the average figures in Western Europe. Still, it seems reasonable to guess that they are on their way towards one or other recognizable variety of capitalism. For the CIS countries, any such guess would be hazardous. For Russia, in particular, there is a good deal going on that brings Weberian 'political capitalism' to mind: a set-up in which profits are, in part at least, a prerogative of political administration.

The Russian reformer Egor Gaidar considers Russia's long-term choice to be between a 'Western' system and 'Asiatic despotism'. The latter he characterizes as a state of affairs in which 'property is the natural prey and the state is the natural predator' (Gaidar 2003: 5). This is a more colourful term for something akin to Weber's 'political capitalism'. In Gaidar's picture of the options for Russia, the distinction between liberal- and coordinated market economies fades into insignificance. The Gaidar picture may seem too simple and grandiose, but we find it still, sadly, recognizable. Our starting point is that we are dealing with a process of social and institutional development that is more Weberian or Gaidaresque than Soskician.

One last preliminary point: the rules of the economic game look to be rather different in different sectors of the Russian economy: between large and small firms, for example, or between the oil industry and the mobile-phone industry. This is a point to which we shall return in the conclusions. It is almost certainly a consideration that is not unique to Russia.

Changes in Russian state policies towards big business

Since the collapse of communism in the USSR at the end of 1991, the stance of the Russian state towards business has shifted over time. At first, of course, only an embryonic private business sector was in existence. This sector expanded fast with, first, voucher privatization (1992–4) and then (mostly 1994–7, though continuing later) so-called 'cash' privatization. The late 1990s seem, in retrospect, to be the high point of economic, social and political influence for the new Russian tycoons. Evgenii Yasin, former Minister of the Economy and the doyen of Russia's economic liberals, has adapted a chronology, originally proposed by Igor Bunin, to show the changes in state–business relations over time.

In 2003–5 the Russian authorities attacked the privately owned Yukos oil company. By late 2005 the main Yukos production company was in state hands and the largest Yukos shareholder, Mikhail Khodorkovskii, was in a prison camp in Chita *oblast'*. These events damaged business confidence – at least for a time and at least in the Russian oil industry – by increasing uncertainty about property rights in Russia and the rules of the game for Russian business. During this period, the executive branch of the Russian state, made up, at the federal level, of the presidential administration and the government, sent conflicting signals to the business world.

The Kremlin appears intent on asserting control over certain so-called strategic industries – the 'commanding heights' of the Russian economy – by

Table 7.1 The Yasin–Bunin periodization of business–state relations in post-communist Russia

I. 1990–95: Leading role of state, but business increasing in scale and influence.
II. 1995–2000: Oligarchic capitalism.
III. 2000–3: Period of compromise; business forced out of the mass media.
IV. 2003–?: State capitalism: assertion of dominance by the state with the threat of expropriation.

Source: adapted from Yasin (2005a: 185–6).

appointing trusted state officials to positions of authority on their boards. Various explanations have been suggested for this tendency:

• For reasons of national security, the Kremlin seeks to assert state control over strategic industries such as energy, railways and pipelines;
• Foreign ownership is seen as a particular threat;
• Interest groups such as the *siloviki* – former or serving members of the security, intelligence or law enforcement agencies, many of whom have benefited under Putin but who feel they lost out in the privatization process of the 1990s – want to grab their share of Russia's assets;
• Individuals close to Putin are keen to build a nest egg for the period after he leaves power;
• Kremlin officials are seeking cover for personal money-laundering purposes.

These explanations need not be mutually exclusive, though some may appear more likely than others. It should be stressed too that, while these options are commonly attributed to the *siloviki*, they no more form a monolithic bloc than the economic liberals who oppose them. Indeed, the elite in Putin's administration is increasingly factionalized. The structure of the political system encourages this outcome. It is semi-presidential in form. That is, executive power is divided between a president who is head of state, on the one hand, and a prime minister who heads the government, on the other; and both wings play an active role in the day-to-day running of the state (Duverger 1992: 142–9).

The purposes and interests behind the Kremlin's assertion of direct authority over big business in Russia remain a matter of debate. That such authority has been asserted, is clear. Does it amount to a sustainable alteration of the capitalist system that has been evolving in Russia? Russian officials often defend the increased role of the state by arguing that Russia is only following the example of other petro-states, where international oil companies have been excluded or restricted to supporting roles alongside state-owned national oil companies.

Can parallels be drawn with such resource-rich capitalist economies as Norway, Saudi Arabia and Venezuela, for example? Attempts to draw comparisons do not, in fact, prove very fruitful, since the various countries run their national oil companies in such different ways. The Norwegian and Saudi Arabian governments have tended to follow a 'hands-off' policy towards their national oil companies – Statoil, Norsk Hydro and Saudi Aramco – though the 1973 oil crisis did see Saudi Arabia and other members of the Organization of Petroleum Exporting Countries (OPEC) refusing to ship petrol to Western states that had supported Israel in the Yom Kippur War. In Venezuela, by contrast, President Hugo Chávez has invested profits earned by state-owned Petroleos de Venezuela SA in a massive and ambitious programme of poverty reduction. This perhaps bears comparison to the national programmes in education, health care, housing and rural development launched by President Putin in September 2005, also funded by oil revenues, though Putin's projects seem, at first sight, more modest. Similarly, Chavez is courting the support of Venezuela's Latin American neighbours by offering oil at concessionary rates.

The question remains whether national oil companies can in general operate as efficiently or dynamically as privately owned multinationals. So far as Russia is concerned, the track records of state and private oil and gas companies since the early 1990s suggest that a shift back towards state ownership will slow productivity and output growth (see OECD 2004 for a comparison of the production records of private and state oil and gas firms). It is true that state companies such as Gazprom and Rosneft have been encumbered by their historical legacies. Gazprom, for example, is a public utility supplying gas retail as well as an energy-sector company that extracts hydrocarbons and sells some of its output on international markets. One might not expect them to be capable of the levels of efficiency of a private oil company not encumbered in this way. However, what is striking in Russian experience since 1991 is that *improvements* in productivity came almost exclusively in private oil firms.

Feedbacks from international markets

In communist times the Soviet economy was partly insulated from the outside world. An inconvertible currency and state control of trade flows insulated domestic prices from world prices. A deficit in the current account of the balance of payments could be handled without reducing domestic demand, simply by administrative reduction of imports. Domestic budgets and money supply were very little affected by international capital flows: outflows of capital were either state-controlled, as in trade credits to India or Syria, usually in support of arms deliveries, or they were illegal actions by individuals; capital inflows were limited to foreign-bank or state lending in support of exports to the USSR, and, in the last four years of the Soviet Union, to small flows of foreign direct investment into joint ventures; the absence of financial markets in the Soviet Union meant that short-term flows of foreign money into Soviet financial assets were not conceivable.

Now Russia's integration into international markets has installed the following feedbacks to domestic economic policies:

- Russian firms and households can put financial assets offshore, or repatriate them (capital convertibility is already partly in place).
- Russian firms can invest in non-financial assets abroad or at home.
- Foreign investors can create inward investments, or hold back.
- Russian firms can borrow abroad, on markets that will reflect country risk.
- Russian firms can register offshore, and not only in tax havens: several are registered in London.
- Russian firms can issue shares on foreign stock exchanges, limiting the development of domestic share markets.
- Movement of labour can happen, albeit on a limited scale, but
- Russian entrepreneurs can and do move abroad (and some might come back).
- Western senior managers of Russian firms can move abroad (as several did from Yukos).
- Suits brought in Western courts can affect Russian firms or, for example, banks that lend to them, affecting the terms on which they do business.
- Russian firms can and do go global, acquiring foreign firms, as in Severstal's acquisition of Rouge Industries in 2004; the terms on which they can do this are affected by foreign perceptions of Russian country risk and of the extent to which a Russian firm might be perceived as likely to act as an arm of the Russian state.

All of this means that if the Russian state pursues policies that Russian and/or foreign business representatives regard as increasing uncertainty or otherwise adversely affecting business prospects in Russia, there are feedbacks through international markets that are likely to be detrimental, with one qualification noted below, to economic activity levels in Russia. How significant these feedbacks might be, is another matter. They might be modest, and they might be offset by other factors favourable in the short-to-medium term to the Russian economy, such as oil-price rises.

Another question is whether such feedbacks, even if perceptible and more than negligible in size, alter policies. The relevant policy makers may, for example, be willing to trade off some loss of output for a gain in state control of what they consider to be strategic sectors, enhancing what they think of as sovereignty. Here we consider some of the evidence of feedbacks to the 2003–5 increase in Russian state interventionism.

One indicator of business confidence in Russia that is often cited is the private-sector net capital outflow calculated by the Central Bank of Russia.

So far as recent developments are concerned, this indicator gives an ambiguous reading. There was a net outflow of $2.3 bn in 2003, rising to a net outflow of $9.3 bn in 2004 – *prima facie* evidence of a decline in confidence. In 2005, however, a swing back to a net inflow in the third quarter produces a comparatively modest net outflow of $2.7 bn in the first three quarters, with the possibility of a small net inflow in the year as a whole (www.cbr.ru/statistics/credit_statistics/print.asp?file=capital.htm [accessed 11 November 2005]). That shift reflects a substantial year-on-year increase in inward foreign direct investment and in borrowing abroad by Russian companies.

Both of these flows, along with the much smaller inflows of foreign portfolio investment, reflect primarily the confidence of foreign investors – subdued in 2004 (when, it may be noted, the Russian stock market was also very subdued) and early 2005, but apparently recovering from the spring of 2005 onwards. It is, however, our contention that the confidence of Russian business people is of much greater importance. The Russian business world can reasonably be expected to have a keener appreciation of risks and rewards in Russia, especially insofar as those risks and rewards are affected by the behaviour of the Russian state. And important though foreign direct investment may be as a vehicle for new technology and management skills, domestic Russian fixed investment is far larger.

Figure 7.1 is an attempt to capture the behaviour of the Russian corporate, non-bank, sector with respect to cross-border capital flows. It represents components within the net private-sector capital flow, depicted over the period 1998–2005 and representing, approximately, the activities of the corporate sector. The upper, and mostly positive (inflow) series is Russian corporate borrowing abroad. This took off dramatically from 2001. The 2005 figure is preliminary. The lowest, negative series is gross capital flight excluding the net purchase of foreign currencies, on the grounds that the latter represents mainly household behaviour. It is made up of estimates of payments purportedly for imports but for which the commodity inflows did not materialize, plus estimated under-invoicing for exports, plus 'fictitious transactions in securities' – all these being known ways of shifting funds out of Russia – plus total (net) errors and omissions, taken to represent undetected outflows. Both these flows are gross flows – inwards in the case of company borrowing from abroad and outwards in the case of capital flight. Between these two lines on the chart are two series that are net. That is, they are the sum of changes in both assets and liabilities. One is net foreign direct investment (FDI). The other is net foreign portfolio investment (FPI).

It appears that greater state control in the energy sector has one beneficial external effect: foreign banks feel safer lending to the likes of Gazprom

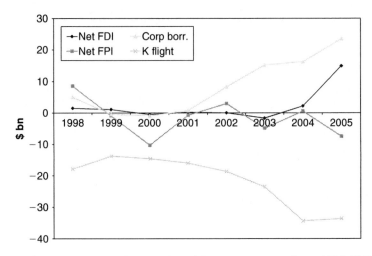

Figure 7.1   Borrowing and saving abroad: Russian corporate flows, 1999–2005
Source: Central Bank of Russia.

than they did, even in 2000–3, to Russian private oil companies. This is partly because Gazprom has great monopoly power, partly because it has state backing, and partly because it is in the process of increasing its size and monopoly power through acquisitions. Gazprom or Rosneft do not have state guarantees behind their borrowing, so they do not have credit ratings as high as those of the Russian state; an enlarged, consolidated Gazprom with the evident backing of the Kremlin is nonetheless an attractive borrower.

Still, negative effects on business confidence generally have probably been quite large. It is clear that economic activity slowed in 2004–5, arguably because business confidence declined as the Yukos affair continued and tax-arrears claims against other firms mounted.

Interpreting such relatively recent developments as clues to the nature of a system is perilous. What we are suggesting is that the state's ability to act in the economy in ways that are not constrained by a rule of law was there before 2003, but was not exploited before, so that there was a prevailing assumption about the informal rules of the game – that the state would not act in this way, and a rule of law might be gradually developed – and this assumption was overturned by the Yukos case and by a new line of policy that emphasized state control.

One complicating factor needs to be considered. The Russian authorities in 2004–5 increased the tax burden on the oil industry. There can be little doubt that the increase in oil taxation has played a part.

However, the Yukos affair, in particular, and large back-tax demands against other companies, seem to have played a substantial role of their own. The sheer volume of commentary on the Yukos case in the Russian media and by investment banks, together with the flattening of the Russian Trading System stock-market index through most of 2004, suggests that state action of this sort came as a surprise to the Russian business community. In other words, it was not merely an example of the sort of risk that everyone had already built into their pricing of assets. One would therefore expect it to have an effect on business confidence and investment levels. Also the slowdown in oil-industry investment began well ahead of the August 2004 increases in export duty, though admittedly there may have been some anticipatory adjustment involved.

Thus the conventional wisdom that both developments have affected investment in the oil industry is probably correct. Looking ahead, however, one would have to say that, of the two developments, the *ad hoc* interventionism exemplified in the Yukos affair is likely to have negative consequences that are less easily rectified. Tax rates can and probably will be eased (OADB 2005), if only by the complicated and corruption-friendly introduction of differentiation of the natural-resource extraction tax according to the state of development of each field. In the longer run, the fact that the state now controls directly some 30 per cent of crude oil output and seems minded to extend that control is likely to render the oil industry as sluggish as state control has already made the gas industry.

The Yukos case and other large back-tax demands have probably therefore made a real difference to Russian business confidence. What we are suggesting is that Russia's enmeshment in international markets, particularly financial markets, makes the negative feedbacks to such interventionist incidents rather quick and clear. If it were possible to imagine a Russian economy dominated by private producers but as insulated from the outside world as the Soviet economy was, then some negative reaction would still have followed an increase in *ad hoc* intervention. But the international linkages described here bring with them both the possibility of Russian entrepreneurs putting their assets, and indeed themselves, outside the country, and of foreign business choosing between Russia and other destinations for investment. This means there are feedbacks that would not operate in a closed economy.

Whether Russian policy makers react to these feedbacks by reconsidering their policies is another matter. President Putin's conciliatory moves suggest that perhaps there has been some such induced rethinking. One might speculate that there has even been some conciliatory action – or refraining from action. There has been no 'second Yukos'; large back-tax demands on other companies have so far been drastically scaled down on appeal or in response to informal negotiation. That suggests that the damage has been acknowledged in the Kremlin, and some damage limitation has been undertaken.

Changes in the composition of Russian business

Is the structure of the Russian economy changing in ways that would alter the dominant position of the state in its dealings with business? In other words, is the economy diversifying away from its dependence on privatized natural-resource sector assets?

The short answer is: so far as big business is concerned, not much. Figure 7.2, based on *Ekspert* magazine's compilation of company sales data in 2004, shows how large a part the natural-resource sector continues to play (for discussion see Gorshankov and Kabalinskii 2005). Russian exports and the dynamics of the Russian economy are still dominated by big companies in the natural-resource sector, working with Soviet-era assets. Those assets have been regrouped into real firms, with marketing, research and finance managed in-house instead of being 'outsourced' to state planning bodies and branch ministries, and with top-management control established, often of vertically integrated businesses (on the importance of these post-Soviet developments and the role of rough-and-ready, often ruthless, methods in achieving them, see Adachi 2006). In addition, a fair

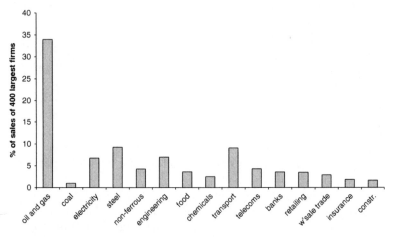

Figure 7.2   Branch composition of sales by the 400 largest firms, 2004
Source: Ekspert, 10 October 2005, 'Ekspert-400'.

amount of post-1998 investment has gone into modernizing and upgrading the basic production assets. Still, this key sector, though modified, remains in substantial measure a Soviet legacy.

This is not to say that these large natural-resource firms dominate employment – they do not – or that they account directly for a large part of economic activity or of economic growth. Tabata (2006) estimates that in 2000–2 the real growth of the oil and gas sector amounted to about one-seventh of real GDP growth.

However, there are indirect effects of the Russian hydrocarbons sector growth through the sector's demand for materials and equipment from other producers and the multiplier effects through income, including state budget income, and spending. There can be little doubt that, when indirect effects are included, a deceleration of the oil industry's growth will have substantial effects on Russian economic growth in general. If a slackening of business confidence affected the metals sector as well, the overall effects would be still greater.

But is the Russian economy showing signs of reducing its dependence on natural-resource sectors that are, as we argue, especially vulnerable to damage by state intervention? The *Ekspert* data on the 400 largest firms (by sales, in 2004) show that the fastest-growing big companies are more of a mixed bag, with retailing and other services prominent among them. There are reported instances of money being channelled out of the natural-resource sector into the services sector – within conglomerates and by reinvesting the proceeds from selling a major stake (Gorshankov and Kabalinskii 2005). But dependence, direct and indirect, on the natural-resource sector is unlikely to be greatly reduced over the next few years.

Russian experience therefore diverges from that of the Central European ex-communist countries and also from many predictions *circa* 1990 about the general character of post-communist growth. It was widely believed that state assets inherited from the old order would be dead weights hampering post-communist growth, and that growth would come above all from new, initially small, firms. That prediction has been supported, broadly speaking, by Central European experience, but not by developments in Russia. The importance of the restructuring of these inherited assets, analysed by Adachi, is considerable; still, the Russian outcome was not widely foreseen.

There is evidence that, belatedly, small-business development has become more substantial. The Center for Economic and Financial Research has been conducting surveys of both new and established small firms across the country to establish whether 2001–3 legislation to reduce bureaucratic burdens in registering new firms, obtaining licences for various lines of activity, and surviving inspections by various state bodies has had an impact on the ground. The evidence is that it has, albeit with highly imperfect implementation of the new rules of the game (www.cefir. ru/index.php?id=32 [accessed 17 February 2006]). The data show that at any rate through 2004 the environment for starting and developing new firms was improving, albeit slowly and unevenly.

Still, the general development of small business lags well behind that in Western or Central Europe – perhaps in part because a significant part of the Russian population lives in sparsely inhabited areas (Kontorovich 2005). Russian capitalism is likely for the foreseeable future to be more heavily biased towards big firms than is usual in other capitalist countries. And within that big-business sector the role of energy and of the state will remain high for some time to come.

Conclusions

The domestic factors that make the Russian state unusually dominant *vis-à-vis* big business, namely the large role of recent and controversial privatizations in creating today's biggest Russian companies and the concentration of successful big companies in the natural-resource sector, are likely to change only slowly. On the other hand, the numerous ways in which the Russian economy is now connected to international markets produce feedbacks that quickly and sharply impose costs on any actions by this powerful state that dent business confidence. Consideration of these costs may limit the exercise of the state's capacity to bully business. Whether such consideration will prevail in the long run is still to be seen. Certainly some pronouncements by leading officials display a fear and distrust of the outside world that would lead them to regard such costs as necessary for the preservation of Russian sovereignty.

There might be longer-term political consequences. Evgenii Yasin (2005a; 2005b) suggests that the authorities' turn towards state control in 2003 has created a cleavage between 'the bureaucracy' and business within the Russian elite that may lead in time to an open political conflict. However, any such open conflict this side of 2008, when Russia's next presidential election is due, looks unlikely. Big business is both subdued by the state and unpopular with the people.

What does a study of Russia contribute to the analysis of varieties of capitalism? We suggest that the original Hall and Soskice approach does not fit Russia because some elements that are common to established capitalist societies, whether 'liberal' or 'coordinated', are not present in Russia, and this allows state direction of economic activity to be applied in ways that are unfamiliar in established capitalist countries. In particular, the judiciary is not – or, more precisely, not reliably – independent of the executive, so that the executive part of the state can act in the economy without legal constraint. A great deal therefore depends on there being a shared understanding of the informal rules of the game. Informal rules matter in all societies, but in Russia their scope is wider and deeper than in established democracies. Up to 2003 the common understanding of these informal rules was that they might well be on a path of convergence with formal rules, which would amount to the development of a rule of law. The state's actions against Yukos, we believe, altered that common perception and left the future course of development more uncertain than it had been.

It can be argued that a low-trust society like Russia can more readily develop the arrangements of a liberal than of a coordinated market economy. It can also be argued that the simple two-way classification of liberal and coordinated market economies misses important differences even between established capitalist countries.

Finally, we are not arguing in some neo-slavophile fashion that Russia is unique. Every country is unique. The present dominance of the state in the Russian economy, and its unpredictability, are features shared with other CIS countries, perhaps with some Balkan countries and with some other middle- or low-income countries that do not have a communist past. Such nations are mostly capitalist, since most economic activity in these countries involves privately owned firms. But they do not lend themselves to systemic classifications that have been devised for what we might call established capitalist countries. Really existing capitalism comes in more than two varieties.

Notes

* Elizabeth Teague writes in a personal capacity and the views expressed here should not be seen as representing those of the British Government. We are grateful to the editors, to other contributors to this volume and to Jean Paul Smith and Jonathan Stern for comments.

1. Turnover data are less readily obtained than capitalization data. It appears that in 2003 market capitalization in Russia was equivalent to 22 per cent of GDP while value of shares traded was equivalent to only 1.4 per cent of GDP. Corresponding figures for Poland were 14 per cent and 4.7 per cent respectively and for the Czech Republic 27 per cent and 9.9 per cent respectively (derived from Lucey and Voronkova 2005: 32).

References

Adachi, Y. (2006) 'Ambiguous Effects of Russian Corporate Governance Abuses of the 1990s', forthcoming in *Post-Soviet Affairs*, 22, 1, 65–89.

Duverger, M. (1992) 'A New Political System Model: Semi-Presidential Government', in Arend Lijphart (ed.), *Parliamentary versus Presidential Government* (Oxford: Oxford University Press).

Gaidar, E. (2003) *State and Evolution: Russia's Search for a Free Market* (Seattle: University of Washington Press).

Gorshankov, D. and D. Kabalinskii (2005) 'Kak nam rasti dal'she?', *Ekspert*, 10 October.

Hanson, P. and E. Teague (2005) 'Big Business and the State in Russia', *Europe–Asia Studies*, 57, 657–80.

Hill, F. (2004) *Energy Empire: Oil, Gas and Russia's Revival* (London: Foreign Policy Centre).

Ivanenko, V. (2005) *Markets and Democracy in Russia* (Helsinki: Bank of Finland) Discussion Papers, No. 16.

Kontorovich, V. (2005) 'Small Business and Putin's Federal Reform', in P. Reddaway and R.W. Orttung (eds), *The Dynamics of Russian Politics: Putin's Reform of Federal-Regional Relations*, Vol. II (Lanham, MD: Rowman & Littlefield), 241–67.

Lucey, B.M. and S. Voronkova (2005) *Russian Equity Market Linkages before and after the 1998 Crisis: Evidence from Time-Varying and Stochastic Cointegration Tests*, Helsinki: BOFIT Discussion Papers No. 12.

OADB (2005) 'RUSSIA: Government reconsiders oil taxes', *Oxford Analytica Daily Brief*, 3 October.

OECD (2004) *Economic Survey of the Russian Federation* (Paris: OECD).

Tabata, S. (2006) 'Observations on the Influence of High Oil Prices on Russia's GDP Growth', *Eurasian Geography and Economics*, 47, forthcoming.

Yasin, E.G. (2005a) *Prizhivetsya li demokratiya v Rossii* (Moscow: Novoe izdatel'stvo).

Yasin, E.G. (2005b) 'Polozhenie rossiiskoi ekonomiki v kontekste proshlogo i budushchego', text of talk delivered at the University of Birmingham European Research Institute, 14 July.

8
Kazakhstan: A State-Led Liberalized Market Economy?

Ken Charman

By 2005, a decade and a half after the foundations of a market economy were first set in place, the extent of capitalism in the Republic of Kazakhstan was evident. Markets had been liberalized for over a decade, the privatization programmes started in the 1990s still continued, there was significant growth in the SME sector, and foreign trade and foreign direct investment were playing a significant and increasingly important role in economic activity. The banking system and financial markets were functioning, and laws to regulate market activity had been passed.

The nature of capitalism in Kazakhstan was less conclusive. Formal rules adopted on corporate governance, inter-firm relations, employment, industrial relations, training and education, the key areas within which firms must coordinate their activities to exploit their core competences, broadly supported the notion that Kazakhstan was already, or was quickly becoming, a liberal market economy, rather than a coordinated market economy in the terminology of Hall and Soskice (2001). However, the prime coordination mechanisms of the classic LME model were missing. Corporate governance was at an early stage, and although new laws to support the role of markets as coordination mechanisms were in place, enforcement was not effective. The stock market played no significant role in private sector development and the level of bank lending was low, although rapidly increasing. Although Kazakhstan was potentially an LME in the making, the long history of authoritarianism and central planning had left a legacy of state dominance not apparent in either traditional LMEs or CMEs.

Key institutions in Kazakhstan, including both the formal and informal 'set of rules' and the governing organizations (Hall and Soskice 2001: 9), were still at a stage of development. While bearing apparent characteristics of an LME, Kazakhstan was carving out a distinct form of 'state-led' capitalism not seen in developed market economies. This chapter suggests that the final outcome is unclear, particularly with respect to the eventual role of the state as regulator of markets, and to its level of direct control over strategic economic sectors. However, a strong state, if able to enforce reformist laws and support high levels of education and health care, could create institutional complementarities that provide this state-led variety of capitalism with a basis for sustainable comparative advantage.

The extent of capitalism

Price liberalization in Kazakhstan started in the early 1990s and was rapid, albeit accompanied by high inflation. The government responded with measures to introduce *inter alia* a sound macroeconomic policy while continuing with price liberalization, the introduction of competition policy, promotion of entrepreneurship, regional policies, development of the housing market and development of foreign economic activity (Kalyuzhnova 1998). Prices for most consumer goods were liberalized by 1994 and exchange rates were moved from fixed to floating in April 1999. The liberalization of foreign trade during the 1990s improved the customs and excise and registration process to assist exporters and importers. Selected customs tariffs to neighbouring countries had been abolished by 1999, the same year the 50 per cent surrender requirement on current account transactions was removed (EBRD 1998; and 2000).

Kazakhstan's liberalization policies had surpassed those of other transition economies, including those of Eastern Europe, leaving no significant quantitative or administrative restrictions on imports or exports and no administered prices within the Consumer Price Index. In 2004 administrative prices still comprised 13 per cent of the CPI in Russia, 17.9 per cent in Hungary, and 10.9 per cent in Czech Republic; the latter two considered leaders in adopting capitalism amongst the former centrally planned economies.

Whilst liberalization had been rapid, development of competition policy had been slower. The EBRD in 2005 gave Kazakhstan an index of only '2' for development of competition policy, against 4.3 for the Czech Republic and Hungary, indicating that, while the institutions to regulate competition in Kazakhstan were broadly in place, it was still not a competitive environment, and state-owned corporations were still dominant. In this respect Kazakhstan was behind other transition countries, having demonstrated little or no progress in competition policy since 1994. This left an important role for the state, either to enforce a regulatory framework, or to provide an alternative basis for coordination of firms' activities.

In 1991, there had been virtually no private sector, and consequently no foreign ownership. The privatization process was started virtually immediately after declaring independence in 1991. Businesses employing less than 200 people were sold at auction for cash. A mass privatization programme based on privatization vouchers was introduced, providing the opportunity for the public to purchase of shares sold through investment funds, created to enable individual investors the opportunity to spread risk. A number of larger state firms were sold through auction or tender (Rysbekov 1995).

According to Kalyuzhnova (1998) only the trade, consumer services and agriculture sectors had been effectively privatized by 1994. By 1995, only 33 per cent of vouchers had been transferred to investment funds: the remainder were unused. The second wave of privatization (1993–5) continued the sale of enterprises, but failed to create an environment within which the private sector could prosper, as an appropriate legal base was not in place. In 1996, five years after declaring independence, the state still accounted for more than half of gross national output and was by far the largest owner of fixed assets, represented mainly in large state-owned enterprises and collective farms.

The third wave of privatization (1996–8) was designed to complete the ownership transfer and create a better environment for the private sector. Steps were taken to ensure that the interests of owners were protected and that the privatization funds could be reinvested through investment funds (Rysbekov 1995). This encouraged a higher proportion of the general public to take part in the mass privatization programme and, by 2001, a total of 170 investment funds had been established in the Republic. The process of privatization continued and, according to the State Agency on Statistics of the Republic of Kazakhstan (ASRK), a total of 2,094 enterprises were privatized during 2004, of which 1,844 enterprises were sold through open auction (ASRK 2005).

However, in 2005 the state retained 100 per cent ownership of fifteen joint-stock companies, each one reporting to a ministry, including natural monopolies and sectors of strategic interest. There also remained a large number of 'state enterprises', which did not issue shares. The total investment by state enterprises in 2004 was KZT 208.5 bn, equivalent to $1.6 bn, representing 16.6 per cent gross fixed capital formation. As Table 8.1 indicates, the oil and gas company KazMunaiGaz was by far the largest investor. The state therefore retained immense influence over the economy and was using it to develop the natural resource sector and, to a lesser extent, transport and communications. Other areas, such as manufacturing and technology development, were receiving far less attention. This

Table 8.1   Investment by selected state-owned joint-stock companies in Kazakhstan, 2004, KZT mn

KazMunaiGaz	125,078
Kazakhstan Temir Zholi (Railways)	29,903
Kazaktelekom	25,495
Kazakh electrical management company	15,269
Kazatomprom (national atomic company)	9,148
Kazakhstan engineering	2,609
Kazpost	705
Kazakhstan food contracting corporation	214
Kazinform (information agency)	53
National technology information company	21
International Airport Astana	15
State national pension fund	–
Total	208,511

Source: Government of Kazakhstan (2004).

had little in common with the state's coordinating role in a CME and the lack of success in implementing a regulatory framework meant that market institutions could not be the coordination mechanism that the classic LME demanded.

However, the 2005 BEEPS Survey (EBRD 2005), jointly carried out by the EBRD and World Bank, indicated that a number of governance requirements were in place in Kazakhstan, including legislation to provide shareholders' rights and access to company information and independent audit. The EBRD noted a legal framework implying high standards of corporate governance, following a law on joint-stock companies in 2003, and accounting and financial reporting rules requiring compliance with international standards (EBRD 2005: 34). Analysis on the basis of the existence of legislation, rather than its enforcement, suggested that Kazakhstan was creating the framework of an LME. The extent of enforcement of that legislation, and of continued state dominance over large enterprises, leaves substantial reservations. It is also clear that Kazakhstan's capitalism was diverging from that of Russia, traditionally regarded as its 'big brother', where large enterprises had been privatized and played an important and influential role *vis-à-vis* the state.

The private sector grew to contribute 65 per cent of GDP in 2004 (EBRD 2005), moving closer to, although still below the level of, developed market economies. The state still dominated the larger enterprise sectors, although only 10 per cent of small businesses were in state hands (ASRK 2005). The annual survey of a proportion of registered small firms carried out by the ASRK shows that the average turnover of small firms had increased 52.6 per cent in real terms between 2000 and 2004. The number of firms with a foreign shareholding had increased 77 per cent from 3,995 in 2001 to 7,070 in 2004. Employment in this group had increased by over one fifth to reach 5 per cent of the total employed workforce. Of these firms, 145 were involved in mining activities, with 18 per cent of the employees in that sector, 846 firms were registered in manufacturing, with 44 per cent of that sector's employees, and 2,829 firms were registered in trade (ASRK 2005). Thus growth in both the SME sector and in foreign-owned firms between 2000 and 2005 had been significant.

Internationalization of the economy

Kazakhstan's exposure to the international economy was biased in terms of both trade and inward investment by its reliance on the natural resources sector, which could absorb high levels of foreign direct investment while providing only low levels of employment. Foreign direct investment accounted for 68 per cent of gross fixed capital formation between 2002 and 2004, while the proportion of employment in foreign affiliates was less than 5 per cent. Similarly, the share of mineral products in exports had risen to 67 per cent in 2004 as oil exports started to come on stream. There were no major growing areas of export revenue apart from oil and gas, and the contribution of high-tech products to export revenue was low. However, the trade surplus generated by exports of hydrocarbons rose from $983 mn in 2001 to $7,791 mn in 2005 (National Bank of Kazakhstan 2005).

The National Fund of the Republic of Kazakhstan, established by Presidential Decree in 2000, was designed to channel the expected huge rise in hydrocarbons revenues into savings for future generations, and to provide a stabilization facility to counter fluctuations in state budget revenues, which were now increasingly subject to world price volatility. The National Fund, managed on behalf of the government by the National Bank of Kazakhstan, was used to purchase low-risk investments in foreign assets. It was funded by official transfers from the Republican (State) budget from a number of sources, including a percentage of revenues from state-owned enterprises in the natural resources sector, revenues of these enterprises in excess of the annual plan, and proceeds from the privatization of state-owned enterprises in the minerals and manufacturing sectors, and from the privatization of land for agricultural use. The President was the Head of the Council on Management of the National Fund (Eurasian Training Centre 2005). According to the National Bank of Kazakhstan (2005) the assets of the National Fund in 2005 amounted to

KZT 828 bn ($6.1 bn), giving the state an immense resource that could be used to influence the direction of economic development.

There was a gradual move away from dependence on trade with Russia, but that country was set to remain the main trading partner due to its size and location, with almost 2,000 miles of common border. After the fall of the Soviet Union, trade between the two countries quickly shifted from barter to a financial payments basis. The share of trade with non-transition economies increased from 58.7 per cent in 1999 to 65.3 per cent in 2004, just behind Russia's figure of 67.5 per cent. The percentage of trade in GDP, at 84.5 per cent, was still lower than the average for transition economies and well below the Czech Republic's 125.4 per cent (EBRD 2005). Again, in all cases, the gradual increase in internationalization of the economy was closely tied to raw-material exports.

Financial intermediation

Domestic credit provided to the private sector by the banking system was equivalent to 26.8 per cent of GDP at the end of 2004 (calculated from ASRK 2005). Although still low by international standards, both short-term and long-term bank lending had risen rapidly since 2002. The sector experiencing the greatest increase in bank lending was trade, dominated by smaller firms and firms with a foreign shareholding, indicating a significant increase in banks' involvement with the private sector. Loans to SMEs increased significantly between 2002 and 2005, with long-term loans in KZT and foreign currency increasing more than 616 per cent and 271 per cent respectively, providing further evidence of the development of trade and structural financing of the private sector.

Pension accruals, also a sign of a move to fully funded pension schemes, increased more than twenty-fold from KZT 23,541 mn ($181 mn) in 1998 to KZT 483,990 mn ($3.7 bn) in 2004, an indication that saving levels were increasing and being channelled through the financial markets. The Kazakhstan economy had significant reserves of cash, and the financial institutions to channel the funds to productive investment were beginning to emerge. In 2003 there were sixteen saving pension funds in the Republic, with only one run by the state, the State Accumulating Pension Fund. Pension fund capital was predominantly invested in corporate and government bonds (Dzhankobaev and Piedra: 2005).

Reforms to support governance of the liberalized economy continued. The 2005 law on securitization provided a basis for significant economic reforms, consolidating the status of the capital markets, and allowing for the establishment of a regional financial centre in Almaty, which had lost its status as capital of Kazakhstan to Astana in 1995. The law allowed the banking system to issue securitized debt, and was heralded as a model for laws in other countries, including Russia, Ukraine and Eastern Europe (Dzhankobaev and Piedra 2005). The banking system in 2005 was expanding, with a capitalization in excess of $1 bn. Several major international banks had been present in Kazakhstan since the mid 1990s, including ABN AMRO, Citibank and HSBC. There was a total of $1 bn in mortgages outstanding, the first results of truly securitized lending. Credit cards were starting to be issued, while car loans and other non-securitized loans were also being offered (Dzhankobaev and Piedra 2005).

Stock-market turnover in Kazakhstan reached KZT 7,995 bn ($58.9 bn) in 2004, roughly five times its 2000 level, having started from zero in 1993 (Kazakhstan Stock Exchange 2004: 7). This growth rate belied an issue. Repo government securities accounted for almost 70 per cent of trade in 2004. These are securities sold with the promise to purchase back within a fixed period of time: they are normally used by governments to effect monetary policy and to influence liquidity levels. Repo corporate securities accounted for another 2 per cent of transactions. Primary flotation of corporate securities accounted for only 3.1 per cent of total turnover. The Kazakhstan Stock Exchange (2004) attributed the growth to continued expansion of financial resources, the inflow of foreign currency from the expansion of exports and the growth of foreign borrowing by Kazakhstani residents.

The capitalization of the stock exchange increased by 62 per cent in dollar terms during 2004, mainly because of a revaluation of share prices rather than the listing of new shares. It is clear that there was a deficit of securities available that could absorb the increase in liquidity. This pointed to the lack of an effective legislative framework and the investment climate being the main barriers to stock-exchange development. If trade in securities was not to become commonplace, Kazakhstan would not fulfil the LME criteria. The main traders on the stock exchange were all banks, using the stock exchange to manage influxes of foreign capital. There was little investment from investment funds or institutional investors.

New laws were introduced in December 2004, signalling the government's intention to increase private investment. Under the law on securities, blocks of state-owned shares in companies could be sold through the stock exchange, signifying a degree of openness to privatization. Corporate governance was improved by new requirements for transparency of company reporting, and the free floating of shares of first-class, meaning fully listed, companies became possible.

Table 8.2 Net foreign direct investment in Kazakhstan and comparator countries, $ mn

	1999	2002	2004
Kazakhstan	1,468	2,164	5,548
Russia	1,102	−72	2,132
Czech Republic	6,234	8,276	3,917
Hungary	3,065	2,590	3,653

Source: EBRD (2005).

However, there was no correlation between the activities of the stock exchange and private sector activity. The investment climate and the lack of developed financial markets and instruments prevented the stock market from driving the allocation of resources, as would befit an LME. Although markets were liberalized and prices were the coordinating mechanism of the SME sector, it appeared that this was not the case in the main strategic sectors, such as hydrocarbons and telecommunications. State-owned firms were still governed by ministries, and competition, especially in utilities, was absent. Thus, again, legal provisions could give a deceptive impression, as Kazakhstan was still significantly different from established types of capitalism.

The weakness of domestic financial intermediation was, as in other post-communist countries, partly compensated by foreign direct investment which was the highest in the CIS. Kazakhstan received over 80 per cent of the total FDI to Central Asia, with cumulative flows reaching $25.9 bn the end of 2003 (EIU 2004). Gross foreign direct investment was $8.4 bn in 2004, up by 83 per cent on the previous year. Of this, consumer goods attracted $268 mn, as against $5.4 bn for mining and quarrying.

The USA was the biggest investor, with foreign direct investment highly geared to the natural resources sector. Even there, however, the state retained a powerful influence. A law of July 2005 on production sharing agreements allowed KazMunaiGaz, the dominant state-run energy corporation, at least a 50 per cent stake in any production sharing agreement in Caspian or Aral Sea energy fields (EBRD 2005). Table 8.2 demonstrates the strong growth in FDI inflows and how Kazakhstan's firm upward trend compares with Russian and Central European results.

Social policy

The main social safety net broke down in the early 1990s as unemployment rose. For most of the 1990s the social safety-net system was underfunded, but the economic growth of the late 1990s and early 2000s created an environment in which the government could restore funding. Social policy was formally incorporated into overall economic policy within a programme for reform and recovery from economic crisis approved in 1994. According to Kalyuzhnova (1998), although this policy addressed social issues, the programme never linked the different aspects of reform. It was economic growth and increasing oil revenues that allowed funding of a social protection policy. However, this amounted to no more than recovery from the underfunded 1990s. Kazakhstan did not catch up with other transition economies, still less advanced capitalist economies.

The labour-force survey figure of 8.4 per cent unemployment in 2004 was around the average for transition economies, comparable to Ukraine and neighbouring Russia. Like many transition economies, Kazakhstan suffered from rising unemployment in the early 1990s. Specific government policies aimed at alleviating the effects of unemployment in the early years of transition were based on protecting jobs in the state sector (Kalyuzhnova 1998: 40), certainly not appropriate policies for an LME. The practice was short-lived. When levels of unemployment fell in the mid 1990s, the cause was not specific government employment protection policy. Growth in employment, particularly after 2001, came from mining, in which there had been considerable investment, manufacturing, construction, transport and communications, and the service sector, including, hotels and restaurants, finance and real estate. There were also significant increases in government, education, health and social work (ASRK 2005: 32).

It can be added that, according to the BEEPS study (EBRD 2005), labour regulation was not identified as a major constraint by the firms questioned. There was no wage regulation outside the government sectors. Kazakhstan was not pursuing the protectionist employment policies that would be expected of a CME.

Expenditure on health and social services also struggled to recover from the collapse of the system to the levels achieved during the Soviet era. Total expenditure on health stood at 3.88 per cent of GDP in 2003 (World Bank 2005a), a level comfortably exceeded by most transition economies. Public expenditure on health in 2004 amounted to 2.37 per cent GDP (calculated from ASRK 2005), a significant increase compared to the previous four years, but still very low by international standards. However, government policies on healthy lifestyles, nutrition, poverty reduction and social payments resulted, by 2005, in Kazakhstan achieving the Millennium Development Goal Targets 1 and 2. The first required a halving, between 1990 and 2015, in the proportion of people with income below the subsistence minimum. Target 2 required a halving in the number of people suffering from hunger (United Nations 2005). Government programmes included one for primary health, started in 1998 with the aim of creating a system that guaranteed the availability and quality of medical services. Further measures were designed to bring state-funded health care to both urban and rural areas and to target particular socio-economic groups. Economic growth after 2000 allowed higher spending so that these programmes could begin to be implemented. Between 2003 and 2005 public health financing doubled and there were plans to increase this to 4 per cent of GDP by 2008, still a low figure in comparison with the Soviet period (United Nations 2005).

Education too was underfunded relative to other countries. Compulsory education, lasting eleven years, was mandatory for everyone under the constitution and under a 1999 law. Stated government policies were aimed at providing high quality and universal access to education, framed within a medium-term programme. However, according to the United Nations (2005), access to secondary education was not universal, due to poor funding, and the quality suffered from the lack of qualified teaching staff, particularly in rural areas. As Table 8.3 indicates, public provision, measured as expenditure per student as a percentage of per capita GDP, was below the average level for a middle-income country at all levels of education. The gap was particularly large at the tertiary level where Kazakhstan's figure was 35 per cent of that for the Czech Republic and under 25 per cent of that for Germany in the period 2002–3 (World Bank 2005a). According to ASRK (2005) public expenditure on education increased from 2.8 per cent of GDP in 2000 to 3.5 per cent of GDP in 2004, still well below that of most developed and former centrally planned economies.

As with health, increasing government revenues allowed funding levels to increase, but this was essentially restoring what had existed before.

Table 8.3 Public expenditure on education per student 2002–3 as a per cent of per capita GDP

	Primary	*Secondary*	*Tertiary*
Kazakhstan	8.1	12.7	10.2
Czech Republic	11.8	21.6	29.0
Middle-income average	11.6	13.8	37.4
United Kingdom	15.1	16.2	23.2
Germany	16.9	21.8	41.2

Source: World Bank (2005a).

Given the Soviet tradition of emphasizing the importance of education, further increase could be expected in this sector. However, the trend has been towards providing a 'general education' without precise targeting, for example with students funded to study abroad. In this respect, the state occupies the role that would be expected in an LME.

Two factors that contributed to the continued low level of public expenditure on education and health were the regional disparities in economic growth, and the structure of central and regional government expenditure. The rapid growth in GDP since 2000 driven by the exploitation of oil reserves led to fiscal surpluses, which were managed by central government, resulted in significant reserves set aside in the National Fund, discussed in this chapter. The growth was concentrated in the oil-rich regions of Western Kazakhstan and the cities of Astana and Almaty. The result was a wide disparity in per capita net revenues between regions. For both education and health care, expenditure was concentrated at the *Oblast* (regional) or *Rayon* (district) level, requiring a transfer of funds from central government to the regions. More populous *Oblasts*, such as South Kazakhstan, received significantly lower per capita net revenues than the less populous but oil-producing *Oblasts* of Atyrau and Mangistrau. This discrepancy in net revenues undoubtedly affected the capacity of the Republic to invest in education and health infrastructure (World Bank 2005b).

Kazakhstan's capitalism and economic performance

Throughout the 1990s Kazakhstan's economic performance was similar to that of other post-communist economies. The decline in GDP was similar to that of Russia and neighbouring countries and of many others from the former Soviet Union. In the mid 1990s macroeconomic policy in most former centrally planned economies, Kazakhstan included, became more restrictive, reducing inflation to single-digit figures, and slow growth was achieved. The IMF even commended Kazakhstan 'for continued prudent macroeconomic policies, which, supported by high oil prices and increasing foreign investment, have led to strong economic performance, broad based economic growth and the rapid accumulation of international reserves and assets in the National Fund' (Dzankobaeva and Piedra 2005). The pattern of slow growth continued in the late 1990s. In short, there was little difference in the economic performance of Kazakhstan compared with other former centrally planned economies.

At the end of the 1990s the economy showed signs of increased growth. Real GDP growth accelerated to reach 13.5 per cent in 2001 and by 2005 Kazakhstan was achieving the highest sustained rates of growth of all the former centrally planned economies. Oil was the driver. While the current account balance of most former centrally planned economies remained negative, the oil revenues, coming into play after 2000, led to a positive current account balance in Kazakhstan, something only China and Turkmenistan achieved in the period 2001–4. Budget receipts increased 59 per cent between 2002 and 2004, with corporate tax income increasing its contribution from 27.8 per cent to 32.3 per cent of total state budget receipts (ASRK 2005). Increases in public expenditure in the areas of education and health during this period, although significant, did not increase significantly either as a proportion of GDP or of state budget expenditure.

During the fifteen years of post-communist capitalism up to 2005, the structure of the economy changed dramatically, with a significant decline in the role of agriculture and basic industry, and an increase in the contribution of services. This was as dramatic as in any of the former centrally planned economies. However, Kazakhstan was firmly in the distinct group of countries for which fuel oils dominate, surpassing even Russia in their share in exports. This distinguishes its performance from that of most of its Central Asian neighbours. Among these resource-rich countries, Turkmenistan experienced a restoration of growth after a low point in 1997, but that country has been politically highly authoritarian and could not be regarded as an open economy.

The strong, stable political structure provided a strategic direction in the exploitation of Kazakhstan's natural-resources base by channelling resources to the National Fund and to social infrastructure such as health and education, and in ensuring relatively stable growth after 1997. Economic performance, particularly in the face of severe external shocks, such as the Russian crisis of 1998, was impressive. The government clearly played a significant role in the creation of laws and regulations and developing the policies for a business environment. President Nursultan Nazarbayev championed the Kazakhstan 2030 programme, proclaiming the aim of building an institutional framework that would position Kazakhstan as a competitive market economy, joining the list of the fifty 'most competitive' countries and gaining admission to the WTO. Thus the role of the state has been central as the driver of the reform process and as the prime coordinator of the parts of the economy that it dominates. It is this that sets Kazakhstan in a category of 'state-led' capitalism.

However, Kazakhstan remained a lower-middle-income country, according to World Bank criteria. Prior to the collapse of the Soviet Union, its citizens had enjoyed higher living standards than the average for lower-middle-income countries, thanks to the resources spent on the social infrastructure by the communist regime. They fell behind during the

Table 8.4 Development indicators during Kazakhstan's transformation

Country	Gini coefficient for per capita incomes		Life expectancy at birth		Infant mortality rate, per 1,000 live births		Basic education gross enrolment rate, per cent of 6-7-14/15 age groups	
	1987–90	1996–9	1990	2001	1990	2001	1989–90	1996–7
Kazakhstan	0.3	0.35	68	63	42	81	93.9	89.2
Russian Federation	0.26	0.47	69	66	17	18	93.0	90.8
Hungary	0.21	0.25	69	72	15	8	99.0	99.2
Czech Republic	0.19	0.25	72	75	11	4	97.6	99.1

Source: World Bank (2005a).

1990s and development indicators showed a rapid decline. This was partly due to the sharp economic downturn, the severity of which was exacerbated by the nature of industrialization introduced during central planning, reaching a higher level than would normally have been expected for countries of this level of income. Decline was very rapid with the collapse in markets after the fall of the Soviet Union and the opening of the economy. During the 1990s, development indicators in Kazakhstan experienced a rapid decline, to the level of that expected by lower-middle-income countries. Income inequality widened, levels of poverty increased and levels of overall health suffered. With the rapid increase in economic growth and recovery in government expenditure since 2000, these began to recover.

Table 8.4 shows the somewhat mixed picture. Health indicators showed a particularly severe decline after 1990 and it was worse than the decline in Russia. The same can be said of school enrolments. The Gini coefficient for individual incomes, measured by one method, rose from 29.1 to 53.0 between 1988 and 1995, the period of the most severe decline in GDP. Figures in Table A.8 in the statistical Appendix suggest a reversal in the following years to a level in 2003 comparable with some Central European countries and actually below the levels of Russia, the UK and the US.

Poverty remained widespread, reflecting the Republic's rural base and concentration of growth in the energy sector, but proportion of people with incomes below the subsistence level decreased significantly after 1998 albeit, according to figures in Table A.9 that provide an alternative measure, remaining substantially above the level found in Russia. The United Nations (2005) attributed this poverty in Kazakhstan primarily to unemployment and low incomes. Economic growth did not raise the

Table 8.5   Kazakhstan: selected indicators

	1995	2000	2004
Kazakhstan GDP per capita, constant $, 2000	1,007.0	1,214.7	1,822.4
GDP, bn KZT	1,014	2,600	5,870
Industrial output, KZT mn	646	1,762	3,734
Fixed capital investment, $ mn	149	519	1,531
Trade balance, $mn	114	2,168.4	6,785.6
Total exports, $ mn	5,250.2	9,288.1	20,603.1
Fuel exports (per cent of merchandise exports)	24.8	53.0	68.3
Gross international reserves, end year, $ mn	1,653	2,096	9,277
Assets of national (oil) fund, end year, $ mn	–	–	5,131
Gross foreign direct investment, $mn	984.3	2,781.2	8,293.0
Of which FDI for extraction of crude petroleum and natural gas	191.8	2,002.1	5,200.5
FDI for manufacturing	239.5	246.9	519.1
Public expenditure on education, per cent GDP	–	2.8	3.5
Public expenditure on health, per cent GDP	–	1.7	2.4

Sources: World Bank (2005a); National Bank of Kazakhstan (2005); ASKR (2005).

proportion of low-paid employees. This indicates that employment preservation was not high on the Kazakhstan agenda. The growth in SMEs and in self-employed people may in fact have represented the response to lack of employment opportunities elsewhere in the economy. Again, Kazakhstan was not heading in the CME direction with their high levels of social safety nets.

Table 8.5 summarizes the transformation to indicate the central role of fuel exports. Per capita GDP reached its lowest point in 1995 and, according to these figures, returned to its 1990 level only in 2003. Measured in KZT, industrial output grew more rapidly than GDP as a whole. The growth in fuel exports accounted for the great bulk of the increase in total exports. The resulting trade surplus contributed to growing reserves. Indeed, the assets of the National Fund in 2004 were equivalent to 38 per cent of the trade surplus over the time of its existence. There was an increase in FDI in manufacturing, alongside the obvious and massive growth relating to fuel extraction, but spending on health and education remained relatively low. Thus fuel exports had given the state immense power and resources, but it had yet to be decided how much of this would be used.

Conclusion: Kazakhstan's capitalism

Kazakhstan bore many of the hallmarks of the LME in the Hall and Soskice framework, but not all. Prices and markets drove decision making for the growing private sector, especially SMEs and foreign-owned firms. However, there was little indication of inter-firm relations, as the majority of large enterprises remained in state hands. There was little room for employee bargaining power in the state sector and no evidence of industrial relations in the growing private sector. There was little employment protection, apart from in the state sector, where low pay was still prevalent, a feature inherited from central planning.

Corporate governance and competition policy were still ineffective, at best in a process of development. All transition economies have found this the hardest part of the transition process. Although the banking sector and the stock exchange did not play the role one would expect in a developed LME, they were growing in importance. In particular, the increase in bank lending was significant, albeit still at very low absolute levels.

Policies to support social development, particularly education and health care, demonstrated an attempt to return to basic standards that had been lost with the collapse of the Soviet Union. However, the long-term trend remained unclear. Although the policy of the government was to promote equitable social support mechanisms, and health and education policies, there was little, if any, sign in 2005 of a trend towards a 'social-democratic' model of capitalism, with employment security, high social welfare, and coordinating wage bargaining, a 'Continental European' model, with well-developed financial markets, a 'Mediterranean' model with high employment protection, or an 'Asian' model of large corporations and collaboration with the state (Amable 2003). The role of general training, supported by the state, was high and there was little evidence of firm-led vocational training, as one might expect in a CME.

The continuing dominance of the state took Kazakhstan firmly outside the classic LME model. It retained ownership of many of the large enterprises and had not developed an arm's-length approach to governance and accountability. The state itself, led by the Presidential Administration, was undertaking a coordinating role, overseeing the introduction of laws and institutions intended to support a market economy.

Indeed, the President's office retained a central role. Many of the functions of government were actually replicated in both the Presidential Administration and in ministries. Decrees that were implemented by ministries were overseen by the Presidential Administration. Agencies, such as the Agency for Civil Service Affairs, mandated in 1998 to implement civil service reform, and the Agency for Fighting Corruption and Economic Crime set up in 2004, were established under the Presidential Administration specifically to oversee the reform process in ministries. The parliamentary chambers remained weak in comparison to the Presidential

Administration. Although the state had played a strong role in development of laws, effective enforcement remained an issue, and one that could shape the evolution of Kazakhstan's variety of capitalism. This was highlighted by Transparency International (2005) which placed Kazakhstan 107th out of 158 countries in the Corruption Perceptions Index. This represented a major impediment to the enforcement of laws. The authorities appeared committed to reducing the level of corruption. In 2004 the Agency for Fighting Corruption and Economic Crime, in its first year of establishment, challenged over 800 cases, ranging from violations of the tax code to breaches of competition and consumer law. The Committee for Financial Control and State Purchases was also established in 2004 to investigate misappropriation of budget funds and, according to the EBRD, uncovered misappropriation worth KZT 14 bn (over $100 mn) and filed 600 cases with law enforcement agencies. Disciplinary measures were taken against 700 officials. There is some evidence of the impact in results of BEEPS studies which show a significant improvement in the perception of corruption as an obstacle to business growth between the surveys of 2002 and 2005. As with most CIS countries, as shown in the survey, crime in 2005 was looked upon as becoming less of a problem over time. The key feature in Kazakhstan was the role of state agencies, created by the Presidential Administration, rather than a fully independent legal system. An arm's-length approach to governance, a key coordination mechanism of the LME, was a long way off for Kazakhstan.

A decade and a half after starting with capitalism, Kazakhstan was showing signs of two possible directions. The first would be movement towards the LME model. This would depend on privatization of state-owned joint-stock companies, further development of governance and regulation systems, a reduction in corruption, a lessening role for the state in economic activities and a bigger role for the stock exchange and banking system in coordination of firms' activities.

The second possibility is that Kazakhstan would continue to develop as a 'state-led liberalized market economy'. The market would provide the coordination mechanisms for the growing private sector, but the state sector would retain ownership and control in sectors of strategic interest. The dominance of state-owned joint-stock companies would replace the 'corporation *vis-à-vis* state' relationships that form the basis of CME models (Hall and Soskice 2001) and state-led models (Coates 1999; 2000). Huge growth in revenues would come from hydrocarbon exports, which would remain under state control, but growth in employment and income would be expected to develop from the private sector, supported by the state's policy on high levels of education and health care. The growth of this variant of the state-led LME would depend on the state's ability to create the environment for the *de novo* and foreign-owned firms to prosper. A strong state has a positive role to play in this respect. Accumulation of capital through the state budget can provide support for education and health systems. A legal infrastructure enforced by the Presidential Administration may substitute in part for the independent regulatory bodies found in LMEs, such as the UK. This is very different to the state-led capitalism as out forward by Coates (1999; 2000), where the role of the state is defined by the relationship with corporations. This is much more direct, but it may be one way in which resource-rich, former centrally planned economies can embrace the capitalist system. By 2005, the variety of capitalism in Kazakhstan was already different to that in Russia, where the role of big business *vis-à-vis* the government had become a defining characteristic. Kazakhstan's version, the state-led LME, provides a model that might be followed by other resource-rich former centrally planned economies, such as Azerbaijan and Turkmenistan.

References

Amable, B. (2003) *The Diversity of Modern Capitalism* (Oxford: Oxford University Press).

ASRK (Agency on Statistics of the Republic of Kazakhstan) (2005) *Statistical Yearbook of Kazakhstan 2005* (Almaty: ASRK).

Coates, D. (1999) 'Models of Capitalism in the New World Order: The UK Case', *Political Studies*, 47, 643–60.

Coates, D. (2000) *Models of Capitalism: Growth and Stagnation in the Modern Era* (Cambridge: Polity Press).

Dzhankobaev, T. and J. Piedra (2005) 'Kazakhstan's Capital Markets: Ahead of the Pack', *Journal of Structured Finance*, Spring, 66–72.

EBRD (European Bank for Reconstruction and Development) (1998, 2000, 2005) *Transition Report* (London: EBRD).

EIU (The Economist Intelligence Unit) (2004) *Kazakhstan Country Profile 2004* (London: Economist Publications).

ETC (Eurasian Training Centre) (2005) *Financial Management of Oil Reserves, Trainers Manual* (Astana: Eurasian Training Centre for Civil Servants).

Global Insight (2005) *Kazakhstan* (Boston: Sovereign Publications Limited).

Government of Kazakhstan (2004) *Medium-Term Plan of Social Economic Development of the Republic of Kazakhstan (2005–7)* <http://www.zakon.kz>.

Hall, P. and D. Soskice (eds) (2001) *Varieties of Capitalism: The Institutional Foundations of Comparative Advantage* (Oxford: Oxford University Press).

Hanson, P. and E. Teague, (2005) 'Big Business and the State in Russia', *Europe–Asia Studies*, 57, 657–80.

Kalyuzhnova, Y. (1998) *The Kazakstani Economy: Independence and Transition* (London: Macmillan).

Kazakhstan Stock Exchange (2004) *Annual Report of the Kazakhstan Stock Exchange* (Almaty) <www.kase.kz>.

National Bank of Kazakhstan (2005) *Statistical Bulletin*, No. 11.

Rysbekov, M. (1995) 'Privatization in Kazakhstan', *Comparative Economic Studies*, 37, 1–10.

Transparency International (2005) *Transparency International Annual Report* (Berlin: Transparency International).

United Nations (2005) *Millennium Development Goals in Kazakhstan* (Almaty: UN).

World Bank (2005a) *World Development Indicators 2005* (Washington, DC: World Bank).

World Bank (2005b) *Kazakhstan: Reforming Intergovernmental Fiscal Relations: Lessons from International Experience* (Washington, DC: World Bank).

9
Georgia: Capitalism as Organized Chaos

Barbara Christophe

To apply the Varieties of Capitalism (VoC) approach as formulated by Hall and Soskice (2001) to the far removed margins of the post-Soviet space without doubt involves a good deal of conceptual stretching. For a variety of reasons Georgia is a nut that is especially hard to crack. The expansion of a concept that has clearly been formulated with reference to the advanced economies of the OECD world is rendered difficult by more than just the sheer scale of the dramatic economic downturn Georgia has experienced after the dissolution of the Soviet Union, with a GDP of less than half the 1989 level in 2005.

There is even more at stake than the somewhat typical post-socialist discrepancy between a certain inclination towards neo-liberal policies and the still limited capacities of nascent and underdeveloped capital markets (see Chapter 1). In contrast to many other East European and even some post-Soviet countries, classification is not complicated by the legacy of the socialist welfare state, which translates into a share of social spending in GDP slightly above the average of even LMEs (see Table 6.2 below and Table A.10 in the Statistical Appendix). Quite the reverse: in the 1990s, Georgia was harshly criticized by international financial institutions for an almost total retreat of the state from the provision of public welfare. The Georgian mode of deviation from the ideal type of either LME or CME thus differs quite crucially from many other post-socialist cases.

Whereas most post-socialist economies offend against a core assumption of the VoC paradigm by failing to ensure institutional complementarity across *different* spheres of regulation, the Georgian type of infraction is somewhat more radical. What we do observe here rather is the institutionalization of mutually contradictory rules in a *single* domain of regulation. Most visibly this is in the sphere of corporate governance, which will be analysed in detail below. A close reading of legislative norms and regulations reveals significant inconsistencies which result from the constant blending of rules stemming from the competing regulatory traditions of LMEs and CMEs. The existence of a regulatory framework which directly prevents the emergence of any kind of predictability does not demonstrate the weakness of a state bureaucracy failing to set the rules of the game. It is neither the impact of competing pressure groups nor the influence of rival donor organizations which accounts for the inconsistency of norms. What we observe rather are the carefully planned effects of a strategy pursued by a political elite[1] which consciously creates legislative loopholes and contradictions as a means of generating insecurity. It is this kind of insecurity which forces economic actors to seek shelter with a state elite that has nothing to offer in terms of tangible benefits but much to take in terms of posing a serious threat to their very existence.

As this kind of logic is hardly comprehensible in the categories of the VoC approach, I shall test the explanatory power of the political capitalism thesis which, at least with regard to post-socialism, appears to be its main rival. I shall, however, reject its application to the Georgian situation for two reasons. First, in the original version coined by Max Weber, the term carries a certain notion of pre-modernism which prevents us from spotting the highly modern or even post-modern features of the Georgian economy, deeply entrenched in global networks of exchange. Though its transnationality index is rather low, due to the mostly informal and unrecorded nature of these exchanges, I shall demonstrate that Georgia depends heavily on the inflow of externally generated resources.

Secondly, in its application to post-socialist currents, as suggested among others by Jadwiga Staniszkis (1991), the concept emphasizes the successful conversion of political power possessed by former communist office holders into economic wealth based on ownership rights. To a certain degree this process is even described in terms of a primitive accumulation of capital. As I shall demonstrate, the story that has to be told about Georgia is not about struggling for property but about the preservation of control. The members of the Georgian power elite seem to have dismissed the chance of becoming proprietors as an option that obviously involved too much risk in an economic environment characterized by uncertainty and gloomy perspectives. In my concluding remarks I shall therefore suggest the alternative notion of capitalism as organized chaos.

The dynamics and contours of a shrinking economy

By early 1994 the Georgian economy was close to collapse, due to the combined effect of the break-up of the Soviet Union and internal turmoil.

The country had been hit hard by two secessionist conflicts with the break-away regions of Abkhazia and South Ossetia as well as by a civil war triggered by the violent deposing of President Gamsakhurdia in January 1992. GDP declined by 40 per cent and 30 per cent annually between 1992 and 1994. Due to a nearly total dissolution of even the most basic features of centralized statehood and the emergence of a wide range of entrepreneurs of violence filling in the gap, the budget-revenue-to-GDP ratio hit the ground with 2 per cent in 1994 (IMF 1996). Despite significant stabilization gains achieved under the former party secretary Eduard Shevardnadze, who returned to power in 1992, and notwithstanding the farreaching reform programme he launched with the assistance of the international donor community after the smashing of competing groups of warlords in 1995, economic recovery remained modest. By 2004 Georgia's GDP still stood at only 45 per cent of its 1989 level, compared with 98 per cent and 72 per cent in two other war-torn countries, Armenia and Azerbaidzhan, respectively. The only post-Soviet country to be worse off was Moldova with 44 per cent (EBRD 2005: 48). But when it comes to other macroeconomic indicators, Tbilisi beats even Kishineau in the race to the bottom. Whereas industrial production declined by 62 per cent between 1990 and 1998 in Moldova, it fell by 84 per cent in Georgia (Mancev 2000).

After 1998, which was a turning point of sorts, with economic restructuring bearing its first fruits, things did not improve in a clear and sustained way. On the contrary, the two-digit GDP growth rates that had been achieved during the honeymoon period of reforms in 1996 and 1997 were replaced by quite meagre results lingering between 2 per cent and 5 per cent until 2003, and then moving up to 6–8 per cent in 2004 (EBRD 2005: 137). An alarming growth of corruption, a sharp increase in smuggling and an accelerated reshuffling of government agencies became indicative of a deteriorating state performance (Christophe 2006). A report funded by USAID revealed that poor tax enforcement, and regular collusion between government agencies and well-entrenched networks of smugglers in the petroleum sector alone, imposed an annual loss of more than $200 mn, that is more than one third of revenues, on the budget (Stier 2002). Together with the disturbing effects of the Russian crisis, this resulted in a tremendous slowdown of economic recovery. A similar trend was to be observed in the realm of politics. The 1999 parliamentary and 2000 presidential elections were marked by widespread fraud, signalling a steady loss of the elite's ability to mobilize authentic support.

Georgia, along with Moldova, has without doubt experienced the deepest economic crisis among all Soviet successor states and is still far removed from any kind of sustainable recovery. The catastrophic events that have evolved in Georgia following the dissolution of the USSR left the country with an almost totally destroyed industrial infrastructure, an enormous burden of foreign debt, that amounted to 145 per cent of annual exports and 404 per cent of the annual state revenue in 2003, and a poverty rate of more than 60 per cent. Besides becoming a transit country for the export of Caspian energy resources, there hardly seems to be a viable economic strategy at hand. In the beginning of the twenty-first century, Georgia thus in many respects has come to resemble a 'classic' third world country. This refers first of all to the structure of the labour market, the provision of welfare and the structure of trade.

Although the official unemployment rate of 14 per cent of the active workforce appears to be quite moderate at first glance, the real picture is very much obscured by a 62 per cent share of self-employment. Moreover, totally in line with third world scenarios, self-employment is mainly concentrated in a highly unproductive agriculture with a share of 81.6 per cent. Though contributing only 20 per cent of GDP, agriculture accounts for roughly 50 per cent of employment. According to an official definition, 1 ha of agricultural land in the possession of a family automatically renders all its members self-employed (HRIDC 2002). Whether 1 ha is enough to provide for the subsistence minimum of an average family of four, however is, a quite controversial issue. Only 13–15 per cent of those employed in agriculture succeed in marketing their products. Whereas self-employment is still on the rise, the share of hired employment continues to shrink. This is mainly due to the contraction of the state sector which still accounted for 66 per cent of employment, as distinct from economic activity, in 2003 (GET 2003: no.4).

In spite of being a very much contested and scarce resource, which is mainly distributed via closely knit networks of friends and relatives, salaries from employment are far from assuring even the most modest standards of living. While only a small segment of 37 per cent of the active workforce is actually employed, only 3.5 per cent of them earn a salary that surpasses the officially established monthly subsistence minimum of $59 (IOM 2003). The average salary of $33 barely covers 60 per cent, the official minimum wage of $9 amounts to a miserable 16 per cent. It thus does not come as a surprise that external labour migration has become the most important factor in the country's socio-economic system. According to different calculations, average annual remittances from mostly illegal labour migrants heading as a rule to Russia, Turkey or Germany, range between $400 mn and $720 mn (IOM 2003) and amount to 10–18 per cent of GDP. In this respect, Georgia leaves far behind even traditional labour-exporting countries like Mexico and Turkey, each with a share of approximately 1.5 per cent of total remittances in GDP. Against the backdrop of these figures, the $49.4 mn salaries paid in 2003 to budget sector workers or the $131 mn of social security provision, appear to be negligible (GET 2004: no.1).

Without facing any serious opposition from a population that was primarily occupied with striving for survival, the Georgian government succeeded in adapting the scope of the socialist welfare state to the capacities of a shrinking economy. The most radical retreat of the state from the provision of public goods was to be observed in the sphere of education and health care. Having already fallen from $804 to $30 per pupil between 1990 and 1995 (GET 1996: no.1), the share of public expenditure on education in GDP continued to drop from 1.6 per cent to 0.8 per cent in 2000 (IMF 2001). In 1995, the Georgian government embarked on radical reforms in the health care system that were heralded as a big success but actually gave rise to a sharp decline in procurement of medical services (Gzirishvili and Mataradze 1999). The overall plan of reorienting a system of free health-care provision financed directly by the state to the standard social insurance model ended with the total fiasco that was to be expected. The idea to finance a State Medical Insurance Company (SMIC) by the contributions of employers and employees was based on clearly unrealistic assumptions about formal employment (Gotsadze 2002). Although the SMIC collects 3 per cent and 1 per cent in pay-roll taxes from workers and entrepreneurs respectively, it still receives 40 per cent of its budget from the state. But due to constant arrears in public sector contributions, which amount to $20 per person per annum and are thus far below the CIS average of $77, the actual impact of the SMIC is close to zero. While out-of-pocket expenditures by private individuals cover 87 per cent of health spending, public financing accounts for less than 8 per cent of total costs (Gamkrelidze *et al.* 2002).

A close look at the development of the Georgian trade balance strengthens the impression of rapid adjustment to the position of a marginalized economy. Although the ratio of imports to exports, which had soared to nearly 3:1 in 1998 but returned to a more modest proportion of 1.5:1 in 2003,[2] had improved significantly with the implementation of reforms, the reduction of the trade deficit looks considerably less impressive if one pays attention to the concomitant change in the overall structure of exported goods. These alarming figures reflect nothing less than a self-destructive move towards the crudest form of deindustrialization and disinvestment. Equipment and machinery from former state-owned enterprises, that had been squandered at dumping prices during zero price auctions from 1997, were sold in great quantities. Having acquired these assets far below their actual value, most of the new owners did not even spend a thought on reviving production. As a rule, they were solely interested in cannibalizing the production infrastructure and ended up exporting everything of value that survived the intensive pilfering by competing groups of warlords in the internal turmoil of 1992–5 (Christophe 2004). A telling example would be the case of JSC Medea, quite a famous wool-cloth factory located in the town of Kutaisi that had been equipped with Italian machines in the last days of *perestroika*. It was sold at a hugely discounted rate at the second zero auction in March 1998 (GET 1998: no.1). With an actual price of $0.06 a block of its shares that had been nominally valued at $1.41 attracted the lowest bid. The majority shareholding, which remained state-owned for another five years, was sold for $5,000 in 2002 (GET 2002: no.3).

The impact of competing donor organizations

Against the backdrop of this tale of deindustrialization, ruralization and disinvestment, Georgia hardly seems to be suitable for an analysis from the perspective of the VoC approach, initially designed to make sense of the typological divergencies observed in highly developed economies. The question of whether the country actually saw the emergence of any kind of modern capitalism after the beginning of the transformation process or rather ended up with a very specific and self-destructive form of pre-modern merchant capitalism, depicted by Burrawoy and Krotov (1992) in their study on the wood industry of northern Russia, might very justifiably be raised. But there is still one argument that can be brought up against this kind of sceptical reasoning.

Ever since the fragile stabilization brought to the war-torn country by Shevardnadze began to take root in 1995, the package of reforms that was launched immediately in the same year bears the heavy footprint of recommendations and policy prescriptions made by international financial organizations and Western donor organizations. Especially in the middle of the 1990s, the heavy dependence on external assistance left the country's elite with little choice but to accept externally set conditionality as a means of gaining access to desperately needed finances. Even in 1997, 57 per cent of state expenditure was financed by external credits and grants (UNDP 1998).[3] Having received $850 mn in assistance for a population of roughly 5 mn between 1992 and 2000 from the American development agency USAID alone, Georgia was soon to blossom as one of the largest recipients of US aid per capita. In 2000 the Clinton

Administration, which was mainly driven by the interest in assuring a minimum of stability as a precondition for turning the country into a transit space for the export of Caspian energy resources, spent $200 per person on Georgia. That was six times the amount spent on Ukraine and roughly 160 times the per capita aid received by Russia.

This extraordinarily high degree of dependence on development aid, conditional on the readiness to pursue an externally prescribed path of reforms, should obviously make us expect the political economy of Georgia to be shaped very much by the regulatory tradition of its respective donor countries. Bearing in mind the prominence of Georgia in the aid pro-grammes of other countries apart from the USA – the GTZ (the German company advising on international cooperation for sustainable develop-ment), for example, made Georgia one of its privileged partners at the end of the 1990s – we can reasonably assume that the contradictory impact of rival concepts made its regulatory regime less than homogeneous.

A convincing proof of a certain degree of tension in inter-donor relations would be the competition between American and German development specialists with regard to the institutionalization of landownership. Both sides converged in treating the granting of ownership titles on small plots distributed to farmers during privatization as an important factor in reviving an agriculture that had almost slipped back to a subsistence level. However, they very much disagreed on the strategy appropriate to achieve that goal. While the GTZ, in accordance with German traditions, invested heavily in building up a national land register, USAID, in what appears to be a diligent copy of American practices, started to distribute ownership titles right away, without bothering local authorities with the quest for an accurate measurement of plot boundaries. In search for an answer to the question of what went wrong in the Georgian transform-ation, it is therefore tempting to refer to the violation of the precept of institutional homogeneity inflicted on the country by donor competition, traces of which can be followed in more prominent domains as well.

The Georgian mode of corporate governance

To take an example more closely related to the issues focused in the VoC approach, the legal foundations of corporate governance reveal obvious contradictions. While the Law on Entrepreneurs, adopted in 1994, was very much influenced by the German model, the Law on the Securities Market that passed through parliament in 1998 was clearly shaped by Anglo-American standards (World Bank 2002). The areas of responsibil-ity covered by the two laws overlap. Thus the blending of American legal norms corresponding to the model of an LME with German legal standards close to the ideal type of a CME led to the emergence of a contradictory regulatory regime.

The Law on Entrepreneurs 1994 protects management from any kind of interference from outside. Though enterprises have to be registered at district courts, disclosing the amount of the founding capital as well as the identity of the management and the members of the supervisory board, they are not obliged to notify changes in ownership after establishment. Requirements on providing information to the public are already quite low so far as the letter of the law is concerned. They are softened still further by implementation that does not live up even to these modest standards. On the one hand, there is no centralized system of filing the information kept by district courts. On the other hand, the majority of judges tend to ignore their duty of making information available to the public. As a result, there is almost no form of efficient control over the performance of the management, a situation that led to quite frequent cases of unregistered asset transfer and thus resulted in a hidden legalization of asset stripping at the expense of shareholders.

In general, the law did almost nothing to help shareholders to exercise their ownership rights. While introducing a distinction between common shares with voting rights and preference shares without voting rights, it set no limits for issuing the latter. Enterprises could thus easily end up without any kind of oversight over management, not to mention over the active participation of owners in taking decisions. Only in 1999 was an amendment to the law prescribed, to the effect that managers have to get the written approval of shareholders if they want to impose restrictions on share transfers (World Bank 2002). This situation is all the more unsatisfactory as Georgia, in sharp contrast to other post-socialist countries, displays a highly dispersed structure of ownership, with institutional investors and investment funds playing an almost insignificant role (Djibouti 2003). As a result of the peculiarities of the Georgian process of privatization, there are about 500,000 individuals, that is more than 10 per cent of the population, performing at least nominally the role of shareholders. The German way of exercising corporate control via dense networks of cross-shareholding, which provides not only a constant flow of inside information but certain restrictions on opportunistic behaviour by rendering investment in reputational capital necessary, could thus not really fill the gap.

The Law on the Securities Market, enacted in 1998, seems to follow a totally different kind of logic (World Bank 2002). At least on a literal interpretation, it imposes quite heavy constraints on the concealment of information. A manager who owns more than 5 per cent of the assets in a joint-stock company (JSC) is obliged to disclose his holding to the National Securities Commission of Georgia (NSCG) and to the Georgian Stock Exchange (GSE). So-called reporting companies, meaning JSCs with more than 100 shareholders and other companies traded on the stock exchange, are committed to extended reporting standards. They have to hire independent share registrars and disclose annually audited financial statements which should include detailed information on financial categories such as the dividends paid and profits or losses made (Akhabadze 2004). Despite these legal provisions and certain improvements effected with the establishment of the stock exchange in terms of reducing the scope of informal transactions, the securities market is not in a position to deliver accurate information on the structure of ownership or the performance of tradable companies. While trading in securities outside official channels could have been reduced considerably from 94 per cent to 48 per cent between 2000 and 2002, the efforts of the GSE and NSCG at assuming an oversight function and imposing discipline on free-riding managers more interested in self-enrichment than in serving the interests of shareholders were doomed to almost total failure. There are mainly two, closely interrelated, reasons for this disaster.

First, we can observe a practice widely diverging from established legal norms. According to the results of an investigation by the NSCG, there are frequent cases of non-compliance with even the most basic requirements. This refers first of all to the holding of general shareholder meetings, as 80 per cent of JSCs held no meeting and even a third of the companies listed on the GSE failed to do so (World Bank 2002). Under these circumstances, shareholders can hardly exercise their right to elect members of the supervisory board, control the sale of assets, supervise the performance of management or appoint independent auditors. If one keeps in mind that in 2001 only 10 out of 1,773 JSCs paid dividends to shareholders (Djibouti 2003), one can easily comprehend that shareholders did not face any reasonable incentives to press for the observance of legal requirements. When it comes to meeting the legal obligation of submitting annual reports, the picture does not get much better. According to a World Bank review only 31 per cent of all reporting companies presented any kind of report and an even smaller share of roughly 27 per cent disclosed financial statements (World Bank 2002). As of January 2002, this figure showed some improvement, with the share of JSCs actually fulfilling the reporting duties increasing by 170 per cent. But even among those more or less law-abiding enterprises, there was little readiness to involve shareholders in oversight or decision making. Less than half of them bothered to convene shareholder meetings.

Secondly, despite the relatively high dose of consultancy involved in the completion of the respective legislation, the institutional framework of the Georgian securities market was of little significance. As we have already seen, the NSCG, which is actually a government agency, simply does not have the clout and administrative power to prevent the breeching of norms by imposing sanctions. Against the backdrop of the high density of severe violations of the law, the penalties of roughly $28,000 awarded to 275 enterprises in 2002 are a mere drop in the ocean (Djibouti 2003). Generally speaking, the significance of officially regulated trading of shares at the stock exchange is close to zero. Market capitalization was $114 mn in 2002, equivalent to less than 2.9 per cent of GDP, which is absolutely miserable even by poor post-Soviet standards. In 2002 only 284 JSCs out of a total of 1,773 were listed for trading at the GSE, with all the others obviously failing to meet the quite modest requirements for being admitted. In 2000, the year the stock exchange started to operate, two issuers accounted for 95 per cent of all dealings (Djibouti 2003). Even two years later the total volume of transactions per annum was hovering around the $4 mn mark, with 58 per cent accruing from dealings in three companies (Akhabadze 2004).

If we try to reflect these findings in the light of the predictions encouraged by the VoC approach, we cannot but conclude that they miss the crucial point. Basically there are two contentions that seem to bear some relevance for the explanation of post-socialist scenarios. To render things more complicated, they appear to be in conflict, at least when it comes to the implications that can be drawn from them.

On the one hand, culture is ascribed a prominent role in shaping the institutional framework of a political economy. Casting a closer look at the chain of arguments presented by the paradigm, we can go one step further and state more precisely that it is mainly the mode of strategic interaction characteristic of CMEs that is highly dependent on a specific form of cultural embedding. Culture, understood as 'shared understanding about what other actors are likely to do' (Hall and Soskice 2001), fulfils two functions: it contributes to the solution of collective action problems notorious for obstructing mutually advantageous cooperation and it prevents cooperation from developing into a form of collusion that totally excludes any kind of efficiency-enhancing competition. In an almost paradoxical manner, culture thus simultaneously *facilitates* and *restricts* cooperation. What the ideal-type CME really needs to achieve optimum efficiency are thus culturally fuelled mechanisms for the generation of trust that act in two directions. They have to produce trust *between* economic actors which are actually competing with one another and they have to generate trust *in* economic actors' commitment to resist the temptation of abandoning competition altogether. Emphasizing this punchline, the argument clearly lends plausibility to the conclusion that CMEs should be much more demanding in terms of cultural and institutional preconditions than LMEs. Bearing in mind the widespread thesis on the general lack of trust in post-socialist societies (Sztompka 1993; 1995), one would not hesitate to regard market-driven competition, which lies at the heart of LMEs, as an adequate solution to cooperation problems in a society like Georgia. The lack of trust is thereby treated as a common legacy of socialism as a defunct system marked by a common trend towards the routinization of corruption (Jowitt 1974) and the production of social anomie (Tatur 1995). In the case of Georgia, this conclusion seems to be all the more compelling as the country is said to suffer from paramount state weakness (Christophe 2003), which would act as an additional obstacle to institutionalizing an efficient CME.

This line of reasoning is, however, quite vulnerable to criticism from the perspective of another assumption supported by the VoC approach. Implicitly, the paradigm embraces a certain notion of path dependency when stressing the importance of past experiences in determining economic actors' expectations. Wherever people do share a memory of positive outcomes achieved by modes of non-market coordination, one could easily push further the implications of that argument to contend that they would be much more prone to engage in mutually beneficial cooperation. It would thus be a costly mistake to opt for the model of market competition tailored for the needs of societies that are not vested with this kind of historically evolved potential, and thereby deprive oneself of the opportunity to make use of a unique comparative institutional advantage. David Lane (2000) has translated this insight into an unambiguous statement in favour of a pattern of cooperative state-led capitalism as the mode that will fit the challenges of post-socialism best. Obviously, he abides by a completely different notion of socialism, stressing the record of a paternalistic state that at times was quite successful in coordinating economic activity, providing ample welfare and pushing through industrialization against the odds of global marginalization.

Faced with these quite contradictory and mutually exclusive assumptions about the most appropriate solution to coordination problems under the conditions of post-socialism, we cannot but face the truth that both of them seem to be quite misleading with regard to Georgia. As I have tried to elaborate in my brief review of the legislative foundations of corporate governance, the Georgian political economy constantly oscillates between the features of an LME and a CME. One short cut to an explanation of this rather irritating finding could be a reference to the impact of competing external actors and consultants. According to this view, Georgia would be perceived as something like a playground for the implementation of rival blueprints for institutional reforms. Looked at from this angle, the country and its elite appear to be a kind of passive victim of donor competition, doomed to the adoption of contradictory and therefore rather damaging regulatory norms. Recalling the evidence I have given above and paying attention to the quite ample space for arbitrary action obviously left to the Georgian elite, this perspective, however, seems to be less convincing. Despite considerable pressure from the international donor community, the government did not really seem to face tight constraints and more than once-tolerated crucial deviations from externally imposed legal norms on behalf of economic actors. Local actors obviously succeeded in manipulating the reform agenda of external actors, which did not really make a convincing effort at enforcing conditionality, to their own advantage.

Another way of approaching a Georgian regulatory regime notable for its rather unexpected blending of contrasting models would be to start by noting the rather wide hole gaping between what appears to be appropriate and what turns out to be probably the case. Obviously, the peaceful coexistence of legal norms which are normally regarded as belonging to mutually exclusive modes of regulation was rendered possible by a quite selective attitude towards less than binding rules. Official ones were not completely irrelevant, but they did not steer social interaction in a clear-cut way. This insight leads us to a rather critical review of another assumption favoured by the VoC approach.

Hall and Soskice expended quite a lot of thought on revisiting standard models for explaining the relationship between institutional logics and the conduct of economic actors. In what is their novel contribution to the debate, they stress that economic actors are most likely to be conditioned by institutional incentive structures in their choice of a specific mode of strategic interaction. In line with a general trend in new institutional economics, their approach, though mainly actor-centred, explicitly recognizes the capability of institutions to influence the cost–benefit analysis of rational individuals. In emphasizing a 'relational view' (Hall and Soskice 2001) of firms, and underlining the necessity to engage in different kinds of coordinative games with external actors, the advantage of their paradigm clearly consists of defining more precisely the specific link between institutions and economic actors. Inspiring as this perspective may be, it seems to be less relevant to the Georgian situation. According to the analysis presented so far, a simple adaptation of these findings is complicated by two aspects.

First, the shrinking of the economy, and especially the clear dominance of trade over production, significantly reduces the scope and density of cooperative relations in which economic actors are actually embedded. The logic of that argument is quite simple. In order to cannibalize an enterprise acquired at a zero auction by organizing the sale of machines and equipment to Turkey, all the new owner needs are more or less sporadic relations with tax and custom officers to facilitate export. These contacts can be established on the basis of personal relationships, but do not require an elaborated framework of institutionalized guarantees. On the contrary, the informal nature of these networks allows for a secure exclusion of potential competitors who do not have access to the advantages offered by acquaintance or kinship. The typical Georgian entrepreneur is thus more interested in staying close to the political elite than in forging horizontal ties with fellow entrepreneurs. As a consequence, the more successful among them are as a rule striving to become members of parliament, whereas business associations as a means of furthering interests clearly play a minor role (Jones 2000).

A similar tendency is to be traced in the sphere of industrial relations. An entrepreneur who heavily relies on self-employed sub-contractors for getting things done is simply saved the necessity to coordinate relations with a hired workforce. In contrast to dependent employees, self-employed sub-contractors are effectively disciplined by sharing the risks of economic transactions. At first glance, all this may appear to resemble the features of market-driven coordination typical of LMEs. However, if we take a closer look at the incentives to get involved in networks or at why self-employed persons seek shelter with more influential entrepreneurs, this analogy loses much of its plausibility. The case of self-employed mini-bus drivers offers quite telling evidence in this respect. Most of them work under the protection of so-called transport bases which are, as a rule, run by members of the local councils (Christophe 2005). Asking for the reasons that made them subordinate to these bases and pass a quite crucial share of their profit to them, one comes across a wide range of bureaucratic obstacles rendering the transport business quite difficult. To mention just the most absurd detail, the ordinary bus driver has to pass a daily medical examination proving that he or she is not drunk and does not suffer from high blood pressure. There are always drunken drivers on Georgian streets having worked much more than their due quota of eight hours, but you will hardly ever spot a single one who is not able to produce a written document that proves the opposite. As it is hardly possible for the individual transport entrepreneur to handle the ever-increasing number of bureaucratic obstacles lying between him and entrepreneurial activity on his own, he is almost compelled to look for protection.

Secondly, the conceptualization of relations between institutions and economic actors suggested by Hall and Soskice implicitly takes for granted that processes of institutionalization will always lead to the emergence of incentive structures that will shape the conduct of actors in a way consistent with the abstract societal interest in the promotion of economic growth. This is an optimistic expectation, heavily driven by normative assumptions, the validity of which is circumscribed by the presence of a form of democratic governance assuring a more or less equitable articulation of social interests. Only under these circumstances will economic actors face severe constraints on pushing forward their interests at the expense of society as a whole. Georgia seems to be far removed from meeting these demanding conditions.

Political capitalism as an alternative model?

We can now state that the structure of the political economy in Georgia is characterized by a quite peculiar intermingling of rude forms of market-driven competition, which extend even to the sale of political decisions, with selective state intervention to the advantage of privileged clients of the political elite. The chapter thus arrives at an insight that serves as a point of departure for the political capitalism approach (King and Szelenyi 2005). In making a distinction between the autonomous type of *political* capitalism and the different modes of *modern* capitalism that the concept of Hall and Soskice is concerned with, it follows a Weberian mode of reasoning. While it clearly abstains from the notion that modern capitalism is inevitable, the model rather stresses the uniqueness and the persistence of a deviant type. Although our analysis of the Georgian economic order seems to have produced results that are very much in line with these predictions, two objections make me hesitate to reformulate them in the categories of the political capitalism approach.

First, in accordance with the Weberian project of spotting the peculiarities of modernity, the paradigm explicitly characterizes the political and economic structures corresponding to the type of political capitalism as pre-modern. This is, in my view, hardly plausible with regard to Georgia. As I have shown with respect to migration, the Georgian political economy is not only dependent on integration in global networks, it also reaps stability from a kind of hybridity that rests upon a combination of modern and pre-modern forms. This is most obvious with regard to the system of domination, which mixes up a patrimonial mode of exercising rule with bureaucratic elements and thus avoids what has been termed the Achilles heel of patrimonialism, namely uncontrolled decentralization and the creeping feudalization of power (Christophe 2005). To a certain extent, the same holds true in the realm of economics as well. On the one hand, we observe a constant ignorance of even such fundamental principles of modernity as the definition and recognition of clear-cut property rights. But on the other hand, as I have shown in the sphere of corporate governance, the Georgian regime was notable for the adoption of highly modern forms of regulation. Although these imported elements quite frequently remained a kind of façade which did not have very much relevance for everyday interaction, they nevertheless are not completely irrelevant. As they primarily aim at creating confusion and unpredictability, they without doubt acquired a totally new content, but they are not without function.

Secondly, at least in the version that has been widely applied to postsocialism, the political capitalism approach was very much concerned with the problem of state capture by powerful oligarchs.[4] As I have argued, in Georgia this more or less typical phenomenon was mainly replaced by a kind of regulatory capture. Members of the apparatus of rule have succeeded in using their regulatory power to create a market for selling dispensations from partly absurd regulations. The ease with which the new government of Saakashvili has succeeded in depriving the clients of the Shevardnadze regime not only of political power but also partly of wealth points to the same phenomenon.

Conclusion

Having rejected the taxonomy suggested by the Varieties of Capitalism approach as well as the typology offered by the model of political capitalism as an adequate key to describing and understanding the Georgian economic system, it may appear tempting to analyse the resulting order as a variant of what David Lane (2000) has described as *chaotic capitalism*. However, if we take a closer look at the concept he has developed on the basis of empirical findings from Russia, we will detect crucial differences.

According to Lane, chaos and disorder in Russia are something that simply emerges as the result of an uncoordinated interplay between competing social forces. Whereas he clearly emphasizes disorganization, lack of cohesion, elite disunity and the absence of a dominant class system as the hallmark of Russian capitalism, chaos in Georgia is staged and exploited by a tiny, and therefore highly integrated, elite. Looked on from the angle of their narrow interests, the blending of contradictory modes of regulation appears to be rather rational. The result is a kind of non-systemic system with a lot of structural holes built into it, which assure for a reliable generation of insecurity as a means of exercising power and control. This somehow perverse and parasitic order is obviously quite successfully adapted to the opportunity structure of a shrinking economy, in whose potential for sustainable development actually nobody seems to believe. Having been deprived of the rent-seeking opportunities provided by the Soviet economy of shortage, and without any kind of natural wealth to be sold on the world market, the Georgian power elite has thus encouraged the emergence of an organized chaos, designed to channel the distribution of wealth generated in transnational spaces. This appears to be a much more attractive option than struggling for the acquisition of property. Power thus does not aim at the creation of predictability. It rather concentrates on the organization of small-scale explosions designed to steer the directions these resources take on their transfer into the local context.

Notes

1. Speaking of political elites I do not intend to suggest that we observe anything like a clear separation of political and economic power in Georgia. Quite the reverse, as in many other post-soviet countries the political and economic elites are rather merged. However, what I do want to emphasize by insisting on the political character of the elite is the fact that political power still has priority over economic power as a source of influence *and* wealth. Whereas it is still control over political decision-making power which opens up access to economic resources, the possibilities of translating economic power into political clout are rather limited.
2. Own calculations based on figures from GET.
3. This figure already indicates a certain improvement. In 1993 grants alone amounted to 76 per cent of total revenue (GET 1995).
4. To a certain extent political capitalism was implicitly identified with the phenomenon of state capture. However, as indicated in Chapter 7, the appropriateness of this equation can reasonably be questioned even with regard to Russia.

References

Akhabadze, T. (2004) 'Compliance of Security Industry Operations in Georgia with International Norms', *Georgian Economic Trends*, 1, 109–14.

Burrawoy, M. and Krotov, P. (1992) 'The Soviet Transition from Socialism to Capitalism: Worker Control and Economic Bargaining in the Wood Industry', *American Sociological Review*, 57, 16–38.

Christophe, B. (2003) 'Bringing Culture back into a Concept of Rationality. State-Society Relations and Conflict in Postsocialist Transcaucasia', in J. Köhler and C. Zürcher (eds), *The Potential of Post-Soviet (Dis)Order* (Manchester: Manchester University Press), 193–207.

Christophe, B. (2004) 'Parastaatlichkeit und Schattenglobalisierung: Das Beispiel Georgien', in P. Lock and S. Kurtenbach (eds), *Kriege als (Über)Lebenswelten: Schattenglobalisierung, Kriegsökonomien und Inseln der Zivilität* (Bonn: EINE Welt).

Christophe, B. (2005) *Metamorphosen des Leviathan in einer postsozialistischen Gesellschaft. Georgiens Provinz zwischen Fassaden der Anarchie und regulativer Allmacht* (Bielefeld: Transcript Verlag).

Christophe, B. (2006) *Country Report Georgia*, Bertelsmann Transformation Index <www.bertelsmann-transformation-index.de/150.0.html>.

Djibouti, M. (2003) 'Securities Market of Georgia in 2002', *Georgian Economic Trends*, 2-3, 79–91.

EBRD (2005) *Transition Report 2005* (London: EBRD).

Gamkrelidze, A. *et al.* (2002) *Health Care System in Transition: Georgia* (Copenhagen: European Observatory on Health Care Systems).

GET, *Georgian Economic Trends*, various issues (Tbilisi: Georgian–European Policy and Legal Advice Center)

Gotsadze, G. (2002) 'Health Care Financing in Georgia', in H. L. Fuenzalida-Puelma (ed.), *Health Care Reform in Central and Eastern Europe and the Former Soviet Union* (Budapest: Open Society Institute), 50–3.

Gzirishvili, D. and G. Mataradze (1999) *Health Care Reform in Georgia* (Tbilisi: UNDP).

Hall, P. A. and D. Soskice (eds) (2001) *The Institutional Foundations of Comparative Advantage* (Oxford: Oxford University Press).

HRIDC (Human Rights Information and Documentation Center) (2002) *An Alternative Report on Economic, Social and Cultural Rights in Georgia* <www.humanrights.ge/eng/files/ecososgeo_d.PDF>.

IMF (1996) *Georgia: From Hyperinflation to Growth* (Washington, DC: IMF).

IMF (2001) *Georgia: Recent Economic Developments and Selected Issues* (Washington, DC: IMF).

IOM (International Organisation for Migration) (2003) *Labour Migration from Georgia* <http://tcc.cm.int/icm/images/uploads/Georgia- per cent20Labour per cent20Migration_1074510721.pdf>.

Jones, S. F. (2000) 'Democracy from Below? Interest Groups in Georgian Society', *Slavic Review*, 59, 42–73.

Jowitt, K. (1974) 'An Organisational Approach to the Study of Political Culture in Marxist-Leninist Systems', *American Political Science Review*, 78, 1171–91.

King, L. and I. Szelenyi (2005) *Varieties of Post-Communism: Patrimonial and Liberal Regime*, Paper to be presented at the Conference VoC, Riga, 28 April–1 May.

Lane, D. (2000) 'What Kind of Capitalism for Russia? A Comparative Analysis', *Communist and Post-Communist Studies*, 33, 485–504.

Mancev, D. (2000) 'Strany Central'noi Azii I Kavkaza v SNG: Ekonomicheskij Aspekt', *Central'naja Azija I Kavkaz*, 1, 55–67.

Staniszkis, J. (1991) *The Dynamics of Breakthrough* (Berkeley: California University Press).

Stier, Ken (2002) 'Report Details Failure in Georgian Petroleum Tax Collection', *Eurasia News*, 12 December.

Sztompka, P. (1993) 'Civilizational Incompetence: The Trap of Post–Communist Societies', *Zeitschrift für Soziologie*, 22, 85–95.

Sztompka, P. (1995) 'Vertrauen: Die fehlende Ressource in der postkommunistischen Gesellschaft', in B. Nedelmann (ed.), *Politische Institutionen im Wandel* (Opladen: Westdeutscher Verlag), 254–78.

Tatur, M. (1995) 'Interessen und Norm: Politischer Kapitalismus und die Transformation des Staates in Polen und Russland', *Leviathan Sonderheft*, 15, 93–116.

UNDP (1998) *Human Development Report: Georgia* (Tbilisi: UNDP).

USAID (2000) *Development Plan for Georgia 2000–2003* (Washington, DC: USAID).

World Bank (2002) *Report on the Observance of Standards and Codes. Corporate Governance Country Assessment Georgia* (Washington, DC: World Bank).

10
The Western Balkans*
Will Bartlett

The political background

The break-up of Yugoslavia in 1991 following proclamations of independence by the republics of Slovenia, Croatia, Macedonia, and in 1992 of Bosnia and Herzegovina established several new states in the region. It was followed by a decade of conflict. Wars broke out in Croatia in 1991, in Bosnia and Herzegovina from 1992 to 1995, in Serbia and Kosovo 1999, and serious insurgency occurred in Macedonia in 2001. Albania, already well established as an independent state, did not escape a violent civil conflict following the collapse of a number of pyramid savings banks in 1997. The turbulence in the region calmed down following the intervention of international institutions, including armed intervention by NATO in the Kosovo conflict, and active diplomatic intervention by the EU in resolving the Macedonian conflict in 2001.

Croatia, Macedonia and Albania are unitary states, and have achieved a degree of stability. However, two less stable federal states have been established. The Federal Republic of Yugoslavia, established in April 1992, changed its name to Serbia and Montenegro in 2003. Within it, the province of Kosovo was placed under United Nations administration following the end of the Kosovo war. In 2002 a provisional government of Kosovo was elected to which some less strategic state powers were delegated. In practice, Montenegro has many features of an independent state, with autonomy to design its own institutions of economic management and social welfare and, like Kosovo, has adopted the euro as legal tender. Montenegro is due to hold an independence referendum in 2006, and discussions on the final status of Kosovo have begun. Whatever the outcome, the uncertainty over the political constitution of the state union of Serbia and Montenegro has provided weak incentives for the development of a coherent set of complementary institutions.

The other federal state, Bosnia and Herzegovina (BiH), is composed of two 'entities', the Republika Srpska (RS) and the Federation of Bosnia and Herzegovina (FBiH), and the autonomous District of Brčko. Following the Dayton Agreement in 1995, the United Nations appointed a High Representative to oversee the implementation of the peace agreement. The Office of the High Representative has wide powers to intervene in the political and economic affairs (Chandler 1999). Since most economic policy-making powers are in any case decentralized to the level of the two entities, and within FBiH further decentralized to ten canton governments, the powers of the central government to formulate economic policy and to design the institutions of a new market economy are extremely limited.

In the 1990s those south-east European states that were least affected by the wars and conflicts in the Balkans, namely Slovenia, Romania and Bulgaria, became early candidates for EU membership. Slovenia achieved EU membership in 2004, while Romania and Bulgaria have signed Treaties of Accession and are due to become EU members in 2007. The European Commission has designated the remaining Balkan states the 'Western Balkans', with a perspective for eventual EU membership. Thus far, Croatia and Macedonia are the leaders in this process, having signed Stabilization and Association Agreements (SAAs) in 2001.[1] Croatia became an official candidate for EU membership in 2004 and Macedonia in 2005. Albania has been negotiating for an SAA for several years while Serbia and Montenegro and BiH are at the start of their SAA negotiations. Kosovo is waiting for a resolution of its status before joining in that process while taking early steps through the implementation of a European Partnership.

One important condition for EU entry is the creation of a functioning market economy. But as recent research has shown, there is a wide variety of different forms of capitalist market economies. Key dimensions of the discussion of the 'diversity of modern capitalism' have been identified by Amable (2003) who identifies five key dimensions which distinguish capitalist systems: institutional configurations of product markets; labour markets; systems of finance and corporate governance; the welfare system; and the education system.

This process of institutional evolution has not been available to the transition countries which have had to adopt institutions on a more or less experimental basis borrowing ideas and examples from other more advanced capitalist countries. The Western Balkan countries have additionally relied heavily on international assistance and aid donations in the aftermath of the devastation of the various armed conflicts that beset the region in the 1990s. This assistance has very often come on highly conditional terms and has involved the transplantation of policies and institutional solutions from elsewhere. The institutional mix which has emerged has typically been based on policy transfer from a variety of sources and on uncoordinated policy advice. This has resulted in a rather exotic mixture of economic and social reforms, and the institutional configurations that have emerged have often been neither complementary nor compatible. The emergent forms of capitalism therefore do not fall neatly into the boxes identified in the varieties of capitalism literature. Moreover, the important role of informal as opposed to the formal institutions which are the focus of the theory presents a further difficulty for classification.

In the rest of this chapter I attempt to identify some of the main directions of institutional change in the region since the collapse of Yugoslavia and the overthrow of the communist system in Albania. I follow the five-dimensional typology of formal institutions established by Amable, and in the final section present some necessarily imperfect and preliminary conclusions about the types of capitalism that seem to be emerging from this period of rapid change.

Finance and corporate governance

Privatization legislation was introduced early after independence in Croatia in 1991, and in Macedonia in 1993.[2] While implementation was rapid in Croatia, the process did not take off in Macedonia until 1995. In BiH, as a consequence of the armed conflict, privatization legalization was not passed until 1999. Initial attempts at privatization in Serbia had been reversed in the mid 1990s and new privatization legislation was not introduced in Serbia until 2001 after the overthrow of the Milošević regime. Privatization has been most delayed in Kosovo where privatization administered by the UN through the Kosovo Trust Agency only began in 2003. The principal difference between these successive waves of privatization was the important role of insider privatization to employees and managers in the Croatian and Macedonian and Albanian cases, the use of voucher privatization in Bosnia and Herzegovina and the adoption of direct sales through auctions and tenders in the Serbian case. Paralleling these developments, financial deepening took place relatively early in Croatia, where bank credit to the private sector increased as a share of GDP from about 1994 (Cottarelli *et al.* 2003). Financial deepening did not begin in BiH until 2001 and in Serbia and Montenegro until 2002, and was not noticeable in either Albania or Macedonia at the time of the Cottarelli *et al.* study.

The Croatian privatization law envisaged the compulsory privatization of all enterprises and the elimination of social ownership.[3] Privatization transferred ownership to a new class of politically well-connected individuals many of whom were returned expatriates or local businessmen with close links to the governing party, or even members of it. Other beneficiaries included enterprise managers who were able to acquire shares with loans offered by state-owned banks to individuals favoured by the ruling party (Petričić 2000: 207–8). Such loans would typically be repaid from company profits, or through mortgaging company assets. Shares acquired by managers through such management buy-outs were often sold on the basis of undervalued assets. Employees also benefited from the discounted sale of shares, but many sold them to managers at the first opportunity or simply ceded them to the managers in return for preserving their jobs. With a few exceptions, the new 'tycoons' stripped the assets of many Croatian industries rather than reinvesting for long-run growth. By 1998 these excesses led to a full-blown banking crisis and the collapse of some important regional banks. The economy entered into a recession in 1999, unemployment reached unprecedented levels (Bartlett 2003). Within a few years the Croatian banking sector had been largely taken over by foreign banks, mainly from Italy and Austria. Nevertheless some of the privatized enterprises survived and became large and successful companies which have subsequently driven the growth of the Croatian economy.

In Macedonia, the privatization programme was carried out quickly and was largely completed by the end of 1997, by which time over 1,000 enterprises had been fully privatized and only 234 remained in the privatization process. The main methods of privatization adopted were management and employee buy-outs, with management buy-outs being the most prevalent in terms of both employment and the value of equity involved. Managers were required to put up only 10 per cent of the purchase price with the remainder to be paid in instalments over ten years. Typically, the most profitable, or potentially profitable, enterprises were sold to managers at substantial discounts, often on the basis of severely undervalued asset valuations. Weaker and smaller enterprises were sold to employees often at more inflated valuations of assets. In a number of cases managements acquired further shares from employees by dubious methods, or appropriated the voting rights of the employee shareholdings, consolidating majority holdings to the management group. By the end of 2003, some 1,678 companies had been privatized. Of these, 393 companies, with assets of just €77 million, had been privatized through employee buy-out, and 234 companies with assets worth €705 million had been privatized by management buy-out. The disparity in value of the two sets of companies indicates that, one way or another, the managers had acquired by far the most valuable part of the privatized company base. The rest of the companies were privatized through other methods. Just 155 companies with capital assets of €25 million were sold to foreign owners. Thus insider privatization has been the predominant form of ownership transformation in Macedonia.

In Bosnia and Herzegovina about two thousand socially owned and state-owned enterprises, worth an officially estimated $10 billion, were included in the privatization process. The approach adopted in FBiH was based on mass voucher privatization, avoiding the direct sales to insider workers and managers that had characterized privatization in Croatia and Macedonia. Vouchers were awarded to all citizens who were over 18 years old in December 1997, and who had been citizens of the Socialist Republic of Bosnia-Herzegovina in March 1991. Only 65 per cent of any purchase of assets or shares could be made with vouchers, the remaining amount had to be paid for with cash. This was intended to raise revenue for the government, but it effectively excluded many people with limited means. The first phase of privatization involved the sale of small enterprises and flats, mostly owned by the municipalities. The sale of larger enterprises took place after a number of Privatization Investment Funds had been established which were the main buyers. Individuals could participate in the purchase of large enterprises by investing their vouchers in the investment funds. However, in the absence of effective financial institutions many individuals sold their vouchers on the open market to raise much-needed cash (Donias 2002). In the fractured Bosnian state privatization inevitably took on an ethnic dimension, with vouchers being accumulated in the hands of wealthy individuals based in the different ethnic communities. While many smaller enterprises have been privatized, larger enterprises have remained in state ownership especially in RS.

In Serbia the initial privatization process ground to a halt after the imposition of United Nations sanctions in 1992. Some public utilities were nationalized and many other enterprises were converted into so-called 'mixed ownership' in which the state had effective control. Previously privatized enterprises were brought back into state ownership through a revaluation of capital assets (Lazic and Sekelj 1997). The state-owned banks often had a dominant shareholding, and controlled many firms which were formally privatized. The other major shareholders were often managers who had bought large shareholdings at heavily discounted prices. A new privatization programme initiated in 2001 was designed, with the assistance of the World Bank, to make a radical break with the past, basing the process on cash sales through public tenders and auctions

(Dabla-Norris and Wade 2002: 35). Privatization proceeded rapidly in the first two years with most small and medium-sized enterprises sold off mostly through auction, but since 2003 the process has slowed down following the assassination of Prime Minister Djindjić in 2003, an event which revealed the strong hold of organized crime in the country (Vasić 2005). The new government elected in December 2003 adopted a more populist approach, returning to the policy of protecting large state-owned industries (Begović 2005).

In Albania small-scale privatization had been largely completed by the end of 1994. An Enterprise Restructuring Agency, established in 1993 with assistance from the World Bank to restructure the largest enterprises before their privatization, was responsible for the thirty-two largest enterprises in Albania. By 1996, when the agency was closed, the restructuring pro-gramme had reduced the workforce from 50,000 to less than 7,000 and ten of the thirty-two enterprises had been privatized (Vaughan Whitehead 1999: 157). In 1995 a voucher scheme was introduced to complete the privatization of the large state-owned enterprises. However, this was unsuc-cessful and the large enterprise sector was privatized through direct sales gradually over the following years. Although privatization was pushed through rapidly, there was no parallel development of a properly regu-lated financial system. In its place a set of 'pyramid' schemes emerged in Albania in the early 1990s. These attracted savings because the popula-tion did not trust the state-owned banks. Many individuals and families had placed their life savings in the schemes, which offered unrealistically high rates of return. The pyramid schemes also provided opportunities for recycling profits earned from smuggling petrol and other goods into the Federal Republic of Yugoslavia during the period of UN Sanctions. Several pyramid schemes collapsed in January 1997, and the naïve depositors lost hundreds of millions of dollars. Violent protests against the closures soon turned into serious riots in several towns. In the south of the country protestors set fire to government buildings. In March the prime minister resigned and a state of emergency was declared. But rather than quelling the riots, the use of armed police and military units sparked a widespread uprising against the government. Factories and shops were looted and weapons were seized from military arsenals. Armed gangs took over several towns in the south of the country, and rebel committees were established. In the face of the revolt the army and police authority disintegrated and the country slid into anarchy. The government was overwhelmed and forced to resign. An interim government appealed for international assist-ance and eventually Italy took the leading role in an international force which entered Albania to restore order.

Table 10.1   Privatization and ownership in the Western Balkans

	Large-scale privatization	Small-scale privatization	Governance and enterprise restructuring	Private sector as per cent of GDP	Bank credit as per cent of GDP, 2002
Albania	3	4	2	75	4.9
Bosnia and Herzegovina	3−	3	2	50	21.9
Croatia	3+	4+	3	60	45.6
Macedonia	3+	4	2+	65	17.1
Serbia and Montenegro	3−	3+	2+	50	14.7

Note: The EBRD uses a five-point scale running from 1, low, to 5, high.
Sources: EBRD (2005); Cottarelli et al. (2003).

Table 10.1 provides a summary picture of the outcome of the privatization process in the Western Balkans. The privatization process has been most advanced in Croatia and Macedonia, although there are still significant sectors in state ownership, such as the large shipyards in Croatia. The share of private ownership is highest in Albania, indicating the collapse of state involvement in the economy, although corporate governance arrangements are relatively weak. The effects of the delayed privatization process in Bosnia and Herzegovina and in Serbia are reflected in the relatively low indicators for large-scale privatization and the low share of the private sector in the economy.

Product markets and barriers to entry

As noted above, the privatization process in the Western Balkans has been relatively slow in Serbia and Montenegro and in BiH. In these two cases the state has maintained a close involvement in the economy, albeit at entity level in the case of BiH. Political parties have been able to control the economy to their advantage by retaining control over the enterprise sector and controlling appointments to top managerial positions. In the former cases the retention of political power was focused on the connection between political parties and state-owned enterprises, combined with a disinclination to foster the growth of the private sector. In Croatia and Macedonia, insider privatization involved transfers of ownership to politically favoured individuals. Governments gained political advantage through fast privatization to insiders. These different approaches impacted on the policies towards the entry of new private firms, being less accommodating in the case of Serbia and Montenegro and BiH than in the case of Croatia and Macedonia. In Albania, following the pyramid bank collapse of 1997, economic policy became more liberal, guided by the strong influence of the IMF and the World Bank which supported the economic recovery. These trends are reflected in the data on the entry of SMEs presented in Table 10.2, which shows the greater difficulty of registering a company and the lower density of SMEs in Serbia and Montenegro and in BiH, compared to the other three countries.[4]

The reduction of barriers to entry and growth of SMEs has been a main focus of policy towards the improvement of competitiveness of the Western Balkan states and to the creation of a more favourable 'investment climate'. In Bosnia and Herzegovina, the High Representative formed a so-called 'Bulldozer Commission' in 2003 to sweep away restrictive legislation. This was to some degree effective and led to a reduction in the number of days needed to register a company from 74 in 2002 to 54 in 2005. In Serbia recent reforms have led to a significant fall in the number of days needed to register a company and propelled the country to the top of the league of the World Bank's best performers in 2005. Nevertheless, the effect of restrictive regulations over the years has been to push much economic activity into the informal economy. Levels of informal economy activity have been high in Serbia and Montenegro and in Bosnia and Herzegovina, also due to the effects of UN sanctions which generated a strong black market and criminal economy in Serbia (Andreas 2005). The war in BiH had similar effects (Andreas 2004). The informal economy appears to be especially evident also in Albania where a recent report

Table 10.2   Entry of SMEs in the Western Balkan countries

	Number of days to register a company (2002)	Number of days to register a company (2005)	Number of procedures to register a company (2002)	Number of procedures to register a company (2005)	SMEs per thousand inhabitants (2002)
Albania	62	41	11	11	18.2
Bosnia and Herzegovina	74	54	12	12	7.9
Croatia	50	49	13	12	14.3
Macedonia	48	48	7	13	16.4
Montenegro	4	15	4	10	8.5
Serbia	71		16		

Sources: OECD (2003); data for 2005 are taken from the World Bank *Doing Business* Database.

estimates the non-agricultural informal economic activity at around one quarter of GDP (OECD 2003).

Labour markets

In former Yugoslavia the system of worker self-management provided a high degree of job security to employed workers, while the decentralized relations between enterprises and absence of central planning led to open unemployment (Bartlett 1991). Although employee participation within enterprises has been abolished in all the successor states, institutions of social dialogue between employers, trade unions and governments have been established in all the Western Balkan countries at national level. These institutions are, however, generally weak and ineffective (Djurić 2003). The exception is Croatia where an Economic and Social Council (ESC) was established in 1993 and operates through eighteen regional branches. It is a tripartite body on which each of the social partners has six seats and consults government on labour legislation. Elsewhere the institutions of social dialogue are only weakly developed. In BiH there is no ESC at state level because the trade unions are divided on ethnic lines. Two ESCs operate at entity level. The RS ESC was established in 1997 but meetings are infrequent and the RS government has little interest in the process of social dialogue, while the FBiH ESC was established only in 2002. ESCs were established in Macedonia (1996), Serbia (2001), Montenegro (2001) and Kosovo (2001) but the social partners are relatively weak in those countries. In Albania the National Council of Labour was established in 1997 as the main tripartite body. It consults the Ministry of Labour and Social Affairs on issues of social policy and labour policy but in practice meets infrequently.

Unemployment has continued to be a major problem in the Western Balkans (see Table 10.3). In 2003, registered unemployment rates ranged from lows of between 15 per cent and 16 per cent in Albania and 19 per cent in Croatia to highs of 44 per cent in Bosnia-Herzegovina, 45 per cent in Macedonia, and as high as 53 per cent in Kosovo. Labour force survey measures of unemployment, where available, are lower than registered unemployment but still high.

The countries in the region inherited a set of employment laws which offer relatively high levels of protection to incumbent workers (Arandarenko 2004). High dismissal costs have created labour markets with low rates of labour force turnover, simultaneously boosting the informal economy. Young people have found it difficult to obtain employment in the formal sector, increasing rates of youth unemployment. Workers who

Table 10.3   Unemployment data for the Western Balkans, 2003

	Registered unemployment rate, %	% of total who are long-term unemployed	% of unemployed below 25 years	Labour Force Survey unemployment rate
Albania	15.0	92.6	7.7	15.2
Bosnia and Herzegovina	44.0	n/a	n/a	n/a
Croatia	18.7	59.6	35.8	14.3
Macedonia	45.3	87.0*	58.4^	36.7
Serbia and Montenegro	28.0	75.6^	46.5^	15.2

Notes: * 2001; ^ 2002.
Source: CEB (2005).

lost their jobs through restructuring have found it hard to return to employment, and consequently the rate of long-term unemployment is high in most countries. Part of the explanation can be found in the degree of rigidity in labour market institutions and the extent of employment protection. Arandarenko (2004) identified Croatia as the country with the most restrictive employment legislation and the most inflexible labour markets in the region. A World Bank report noted a reduction of employment protection in Macedonia during the 1990s, which, however, remained relatively high in relation to other transition countries (World Bank 2003: 40). Another explanation in the Yugoslav successor states, which have adopted Bismarkian health insurance systems, is the incentive to register as unemployed merely to ensure payment of health insurance contributions by the Employment Bureau.

Employment policy reforms moved several countries away from passive measures to active labour market policies. In both Croatia and Serbia new employment laws were introduced in 2003 designed to improve the flexibility of the labour market, and in Kosovo a new employment law was enacted in 2004. The Croatian reforms led to a reduction in the level of employment protection, which brought the country into line with the average restrictiveness of old EU member states such as France (Šošić 2005). Less is known about the effects of legislation in Serbia but anecdotal evidence points towards weak effects, and continuing rigidities in the labour market. National Employment Action Plans, inspired by the European Employment Strategy, provide a framework for active labour market policy measures and have been developed in Croatia, Macedonia and Serbia.

Systems of social protection

At the beginning of the 1990s new legislation was introduced to reform the social welfare systems. In Albania a Law on Social Assistance and Welfare was passed in 1993 which established a market-oriented and means-tested system of social assistance, administered by a new institution known as the State Social Services. In September 2004 a new draft Law on Social Assistance and Welfare, prepared with support from the World Bank, was discussed in the Albanian parliament. It aims to develop community-based social services involving NGOs and other civil society organizations in the provision of social services.

Social services and welfare benefits were well developed in former Yugoslavia and administered through local Centres for Social Welfare, responsible to government ministries. These continue to exist in all the Yugoslav successor states, with the responsibility to assess needs, distribute social assistance payments and provide social welfare services. Average social assistance payments are extremely low, highlighting the importance of active labour market measures that would provide income-earning opportunities for the poorest groups. In some countries badly affected by the conflicts of the last decade the issue of the social welfare of war veterans and war victims and their families has been contentious. In FBiH, in RS and in Croatia war veterans and their families are entitled to more favourable levels of social assistance benefits than other citizens. Attempts to reduce the privileges of this social group led to protests in RS, while in Croatia their political support played some role in the election outcome in Croatia in 2003. In RS a specialized department of the Ministry of Veterans' Affairs provides them with privileged access to social services.

Due to the large number of pensioners, pensions form a central element of the social protection systems in the Western Balkans. However, pension systems are under severe strain due to low employment rates and a poor record in contribution collections and the dependency ratio, the ratio between pensioners and employees, is unfavourable since early retirement had been widely used to facilitate enterprise restructuring. Relatively high contribution rates have lead to widespread avoidance by businesses and stimulated the growth of the grey economy. The countries of former Yugoslavia inherited an income-related pay-as-you-go system with relatively high replacement rates and pension expenditures absorb high proportions of GDP in Montenegro (17 per cent), Croatia (13.5 per cent), Serbia (12 per cent) and Macedonia (9 per cent). Pensions are lower in Albania where pension expenditures amount to just 5 per cent of GDP.

Nevertheless, pensions are low in relation to subsistence needs in all the Balkan countries, with average pensions of just €100 per month in FBiH, €90 in Serbia and Montenegro, €50 in Albania, and €40 in Kosovo. In RS, even the limited pension entitlements are often not fully paid.

The World Bank has been influential in driving forward pension reforms in the region, and several countries have embarked upon pension reform programmes. Pension and disability insurance laws were introduced in Croatia in 1998, in Macedonia in 2000, in Serbia and Montenegro in 2003, while in BiH the reform effort has focused on harmonization of the provisions of the pay-as-you-go system between the two entities. In Kosovo an entirely new pension system was introduced following the 1999 war.

The Croatian pension reform laws introduced a three-pillar pension model. The first pillar maintains a reformed compulsory pay-as-you-go system with an extended retirement age. The second pillar, introduced in 2002, is based upon individual compulsory contributions to private pension funds. The third pillar envisages voluntary top-up contributions but has not yet been implemented. The Macedonian pension reform, which began in September 2004, introduced a three-pillar pension system similar to the Croatian model. The privately managed and fully funded second pillar will be compulsory for new entrants to the labour market, and is to be implemented in 2006. In Kosovo a three-pillar pension system has also been introduced under the guidance of World Bank and USAID assistance. The publicly managed first pillar provides a flat-rate pension of €40 to all citizens aged over 65. This was introduced because contribution records of many Kosovar workers had been lost during the 1999 conflict. The second pillar consists of a privately managed and fully funded pension system based upon a 5 per cent contribution by employees on gross wages. It is administered by the Kosovo Pensions Savings Trust which, extraordinarily, has placed the scheme members' individual savings accounts entirely outside the country in a mutual investment fund managed by ABN AMRO in Belgium. The third pillar consists of a small number of occupational schemes, of which there are just six in operation.

In contrast to these multi-pillar pension reforms, the Serbian government has resisted introducing multi-pillar pension reforms and is focusing instead on the reform of the compulsory pay-as-you-go system by raising the retirement age, changing the pension formula, changing the pension indexation, and reviewing the level of the minimum pension. In Montenegro a new pension law envisages the eventual introduction of a three-pillar pension system, pending the strengthening of the pension system administration (half of potential contributors evade payment). In BiH the reform of even the first-pillar pension system is hampered by inefficiencies in the public pension funds at entity level, which are unable to pursue unpaid contributions effectively. A recent agreement between the two entities to harmonize the pension systems and to recognize acquired rights across entities appears not to have been implemented. In Albania a social insurance-based pay-as-you-go pension system was introduced in 1993. It consists of a compulsory part, a voluntary part and a supplementary part, all administered by the State Insurance Institute. Pensions are income-related, with a minimum pension to support the incomes of the poorest pensioners, which is 75 per cent of the minimum wage. There are no plans to introduce multi-pillar reforms.

In all the emergent states of former Yugoslavia health-care services are financed through compulsory health insurance contributions paid in proportion to wages and salaries, and collected by National Health Insurance Funds, which are the successors of the old Republican Health Insurance Funds. Although compulsory national health insurance systems are supposed to cover the whole population, in practice the system has broken down in BiH, where 37 per cent of the population of FBiH and 15 per cent of the population of RS are uncovered. This situation has come about due to the extensive spread of the informal, grey economy and the failure of employers even in the formal economy to pay health contributions. In Albania, although a compulsory health insurance system exists, the services covered are limited to polyclinics and some drugs. A new Health Care Insurance Law presented to parliament in 2004 envisages extending coverage to hospital health-care services. Most health services are provided through a tax-funded public health-care service covering the whole population.

Health expenditures are highest in Croatia where health-care costs amount to almost 9 per cent of GDP, close to the EU average. Health expenditures in FBiH are low and facilities are often duplicated at canton level, while administrative expenses are high due to the existence of ten separate cantonal health insurance funds. Unequal access to health-care services resulting from the lack of cross-financing between cantons has led to significant spatial inequality in health-care provision. Health expenditure from public sources is lowest in Albania, where it amounts to just 2.9 per cent of GDP, although supplemented by almost equivalent private expenditures and patients are often required to make significant informal private contributions to access public health-care facilities in the form of side-payments to doctors and other health workers.

Education

In the former Yugoslav states, the share of education in GDP has remained around 4 per cent, low by international standards (the EU average is 5 per cent), while in Albania the share of public education expenditure in GDP was just 2.9 per cent in 2003 (see Table 10.4). This is supplemented by private resources as parents make additional informal contributions or send their children for additional lessons in the private sector. Schools in the main cities are overcrowded. In FBiH, although education expenditure is relatively high, the multiplication of administration in the various levels of government and facilities are duplicated within cantons. There are different curricula for the three ethnic groups, and children from the ethnic groups are often taught in different classrooms in the same school. In Serbia and Montenegro the school system has suffered from a chronic lack of investment. In Kosovo the education system has had to be rebuilt both physically and academically in the aftermath of a decade of exclusion of the Albanian minority from the school system and following the destructive impact of war. In addition, a high rate of illiteracy among girls reflects the widespread phenomenon of early school drop-out especially in traditional rural villages, which represents a challenge to policy makers concerned with issues of gender equality and social inclusion. In Croatia, due to the higher level of GDP the education system is better funded than in other countries, although problems remain in relation to damaged school buildings in the war-affected areas. The most pressing problem in Croatia is the low pay of teachers, which, in relation to other sectors in the economy, has led to demoralization among teaching staff.

Table 10.4   Health and education expenditures as per cent of GDP

	Total expenditure on health, 2000	Total expenditure on education, 2000	Public expenditure on health, 2003	Public expenditure on education, 2003
Albania	3.4	2.7	2.1	2.9
Bosnia and Herzegovina	4.5	6.3	n/a	5.8
Croatia	8.6	5.1	7.2	4.2
Macedonia	6.0	4.1	n/a	n/a
Serbia	5.6	4.4	5.6	3.5
Montenegro			7.3	5.9
EU average	8.7	n/a	n/a	n/a

Sources: UNECE (2005); ILO (2005).

For Vocational Education and Training (VET) systems most countries of the region have been given assistance by the EU Cards programme for cooperation with the Western Balkans, which has been involved in VET reform projects in Albania, Croatia, Macedonia, Serbia, Montenegro, and Kosovo. These VET reform projects have been directed essentially at the secondary-school system. This assistance has reflected a Continental European approach to VET education. They have rarely addressed the pressing problem of retraining the unemployed and redundant workers who have been left stranded in mid-life by the widespread deindustrialization and loss of career expectations that have affected thousands of adult workers.

Conclusion

Four of the five countries of the Western Balkans began their transition towards a capitalist economy from similar if not identical initial conditions as members of the same federal state. The institutions of self-managed market socialism in former Yugoslavia were the most liberal market-oriented institutions of the socialist world. The fifth, Albania, started its transition from a diametrically opposed position as one of the most centralized command economies. As indicated in the introduction, the circumstances of transition and post-conflict reconstruction have necessitated a chaotic mix of institutional borrowings from experiences in other countries. The institutional configurations that have emerged have seldom been based on strong institutional complementarities. However, in the light of the analysis provided by Amable and other analysts of the Varieties of Capitalism approach, it is possible broadly to discern three types of capitalist economies seem to be emerging in the Western Balkans.

The first group of countries are the early reformers which comprise Croatia and Macedonia. These countries were both privatized relatively early during the 1990s through predominantly insider privatization. Government policy has been pro-market and efforts have been made to reduce the barriers to SME entry and growth, especially in Croatia. Consequently the density of SMEs in the population is relatively high. Both countries have relatively high employment protection, although this is reducing following labour market reforms, and social dialogue is active although weak. On the social side, both have adopted market-based three-pillar pension schemes, Bismarkian health insurance, and spend relatively high proportions of GDP on health, but less on education. Overall, while the picture is mixed, it seems reasonable to conclude that these two countries are evolving towards a classic Continental European model of capitalism. This is likely to become more emphasized as these candidate states move increasingly closer towards the goal of EU entry. The position of Macedonia in this group, however, is tenuous. The mix of institutions is unstable and ambiguous and, given the significant presence of organized crime (Mappes-Niediek 2004), the country could potentially gravitate towards the third group described below.

The second group comprises Albania and Kosovo. Albania made rapid early progress with small-scale privatization and, although privatization stalled temporarily in the late 1990s, it now has the highest share of private activity in GDP of all Western Balkan states. Kosovo began transition with a state sector that was highly inefficient and under Serbian domination. The underground economy established by the Albanian population in the 1990s was essentially in the private sector. Both economies are highly reliant on the private sector, and Albania has the highest density of SMEs in the population of all Western Balkan countries. The informal economy is prevalent, and there is a medium level of barriers to SME entry. Unemployment rates are relatively low in Albania partly due to mass emigration, while unemployment in Kosovo is extremely high due to the greater difficulty of exit. Social protection is based on a residual model with means testing and the pension system is pay-as-you-go, but income-related. In Kosovo pensions are flat-rate with a compulsory second private pillar. The share of public expenditure on health and education is low and individuals are expected to make private contributions to pay for both services either formally or informally. Overall, despite a number of anomalous institutional features, this pair of countries corresponds broadly to the image of a liberal market economy, or at least they appear to be moving in that direction. However, the low level of financial intermediation, and the correspondingly high degree of informalization based upon cash-economy principles, combined with ineffective public administration and high scope for the operation of organized crime, suggest that this liberalism is quite unlike that in the more developed market economies. The strong reliance on informal rather than formal institutions to ensure contract compliance (Xheneti 2006) suggests that, if not a uniquely 'Balkan' form of liberal capitalism at least it corresponds to the more unregulated forms of transitional economic systems discussed elsewhere in this book.

The third group are the late reformers, comprising Serbia and Montenegro (although Montenegro has more recently adopted some more liberal market features) together with Bosnia and Herzegovina, especially RS. This pair of countries had the slowest start to privatization, and consequently has the lowest share of private activity in the economy. At the same time the informal economy is a significant factor, including black economy and criminal activities. The density of SMEs in the population is relatively low, and there are many obstacles to new firm entry, although this has improved in Serbia and Montenegro in recent years. Employment protection in the formal sector is strong, yet social dialogue is poorly developed. Both have resisted World Bank-sponsored pension reforms, although pension and social transfers are low and inefficient. Health and education services are poorly funded, and in BiH also inefficiently provided. This pair of countries has many similarities to the Mediterranean model identified by Amable, but, due to the additional prevalence of black market activities and stalled reforms, could perhaps qualify as a *sui generis* Balkan model of capitalism.

Notes

* Earlier versions of this chapter were presented at the 13th Research Seminar of the MET Network, held at the Jean Monnet Centre for Excellence, University of Cambridge, Friday 12 March 2004, and at a seminar of the Baltics to Balkans Research Workshop, Institute for Advanced Studies, University of Bristol, 1 February 2006. I am grateful to the participants at these events and to Peter Sanfey, for helpful comments and suggestions.

1. The Macedonian SAA came into force in 2004, the Croatian SAA in 2005.
2. For an overview of privatization in the Yugoslav successor states in the first half of the 1990s see Uvalić (1997).
3. Social ownership was the unique form of Yugoslav property, equivalent to state ownership in other socialist countries. Socially owned enterprises were formally under the supervisory control of workers' councils under the Yugoslav system of workers' self-management.
4. Bartlett and Bukvič(2002) present evidence of higher barriers to SME growth in BiH compared to Macedonia, while Broadman et al. (2004) discuss entry barriers for SMEs in all south-east European countries.

References

Amable, B. (2003) *The Diversity of Modern Capitalism* (Oxford: Oxford University Press).
Andreas, P. (2004) 'The Clandestine Political Economy of War and Peace in Bosnia', *International Studies Quarterly*, 48, 29–51.
Andreas, P. (2005) 'Criminalizing Consequences of Sanctions: Embargo Busting and Its Legacy', *International Studies Quarterly*, 49, 335–60.
Arandarenko, M. (2004) 'International Advice and Labor Market Institutions in South-East Europe', *Global Social Policy*, 27–53.
Bartlett, W. (1991) 'Economic Reform, Unemployment and Labour Market Policy in Yugoslavia', *MOST-MOCT Economic Policy in Transition Economies*, 3, 93–110.

218   *The Western Balkans*

Bartlett, W. (2003) *Croatia: Between Europe and the Balkans* (London: Routledge).
Bartlett, W. and Bukvić, V. (2002) 'What are the Main Barriers to SME Growth and Development in South-East Europe?', in W. Bartlett, M. Bateman and M. Vehovec (eds), *Small Enterprise Development in South-East Europe: Policies for Sustainable Growth* (Boston: Kluwer), 17–38.
Begović, B. (2005) 'Post-conflict Reconstruction in Serbia: A Political Economy View', *Economic Reform Feature Service May 25* (Beograd: Centre for International Private Enterprise).
Broadman, H.G. *et al.* (2004) *Building Market Institutions in South Eastern Europe: Comparative Prospects for Investment and Private Sector Development* (Washington, DC: World Bank).
Council of Europe (CEB) (2005) *Social Challenges in South East Europe* (Paris: Council of Europe Development Bank).
Chandler, D. (1999) *Bosnia: Faking Democracy after Dayton* (London: Pluto Press).
Cottarelli, C., G. Dell'Ariccia and I. Vladkova-Hollar (2003) *Early Birds, Late Risers and Sleeping Beauties: Bank Credit Growth to the Private Sector in Central and Eastern Europe and the Balkans* (Washington, DC: IMF Working Paper No. 03/213.)
Dabla-Norris, E. and P. Wade (2002) *The Challenge of Fiscal Decentralization in Transition Countries*, (Washington, DC: IMF Working Paper No. 02/104.)
Djurić, D. (2003) *Social Dialogue, Tripartism and Social Partnership Development in the South East European Countries, Including Recommendations for Serbia and Montenegro* (Budapest: Centre for Policy Studies Central European University).
Donias, T. (2002) 'The Politics of Privatization in Post-Dayton Bosnia', *Southeast European Politics*, 3, 3–19.
EBRD (2005) *Transition Report* (London: European Bank for Reconstruction and Development).
ILO (2005) *Social Security Spending in South Eastern Europe: A Comparative Review* (Budapest: International Labour Office).
Lazić, M. and L. Sekelj (1997) 'Privatization in Yugoslavia (Serbia and Montenegro)', *Europe–Asia Studies*, 49, 1057–70.
Mappes-Niediek, N. (2004) *Balkanska mafija* (Zagreb: Durieux).
OECD (2003) *South East Europe Region Enterprise Policy Performance: A Regional Perspective* (Paris: Organisation for Economic Cooperation and Development).
Petričić, D. (2000) *Kriminal u hrvatskoj pretvorbi* (Zagreb: Abakus).
Šošić, V. (2005) 'Poverty and Labour Market Policies in Croatia', *Financial Theory and Practice*, 29, 55–73.
UNECE (United Nations Economic Commission for Europe) (2005) *The Statistical Yearbook of the Economic Commission for Europe* (Geneva: United Nations).
Uvalić, M. (1997) 'Privatization in the Yugoslav Successor States: Converting Self-Management into Property Rights', in M. Uvalić and D. Vaughan-Whitehead (eds), *Privatization Surprises in Transition Economies: Employee-Ownership in Central and Eastern Europe* (Cheltenham: Edward Elgar), 266–300.
Vasić, M. (2005) *Atentat na Zorana* (Beograd: Narodna Knjiga).
Vaughan-Whitehead, D. (1999) *Albania in Crisis: The Predictable Fall of the Shining Star* (Cheltenham: Edward Elgar).
World Bank (2003) *FYR Macedonia Country Economic Memorandum Tackling Unemployment*, Report No. 26681-MK (Washington, DC: World Bank).
Xheneti, M. (2006) 'Barriers to SME Growth in Transition Economies: The Case of Albania', Draft Ph.D dissertation, School for Policy Studies, University of Bristol.

Part IV
Statist Market Economies

11
Belarus: Heading towards State Capitalism?

Julia Korosteleva

This chapter focuses on the evolution of various institutional forms in the Belarusian economic model, aiming to identify the type of capitalism, if any, that has developed. The analysis starts by sketching the origins of the Belarusian economic strategy. Political and institutional changes in 1996 provide the backdrop to the major economic developments of the late 1990s, resulting in the formation of a state capitalist economy. The question 'how capitalist is Belarus?' is addressed further through examining institutional developments in the core areas pinpointed by Amable (2003), namely the product market, labour market, financial-intermediation sector and social security system. The Belarusian pattern of extensive state intervention in all economic areas suggests that the typologies of capitalist economies established in both Hall and Soskice's and Amable's works are not applicable in this case. The Belarusian economy can be characterized neither as a liberal market economy nor as a coordinated market economy. It rather appears to possess features typical of state capitalism. Finally, the question of the efficiency of the Belarusian economic model, in terms of the extent to which it can claim to be successful as an alternative pathway, is addressed.

The economic consequences of authoritarian politics

The fall of the Berlin Wall in late 1989 marked the beginning of transition to capitalism for socialist countries. The near simultaneity of regime changes often contributed to the perception that the former Soviet republics and the Central and Eastern European countries (CEECs) by and large fit a common model of post-socialist transition, in which differences mainly lie in the degree or sequence of market-oriented reforms. The reality of transition has proven more complex, with country-specific factors, such as cultural and historical preconditions and institutional developments, playing substantial roles. In some, most notably Poland, Hungary and Czechoslovakia, which were considered the most advanced in their progress towards building democracy and market economies, there was from the start widespread support among leaders and the population for a 'return to Europe' and for a 'complete break with the communist past', leading to the rapid formation of competitive markets free from government intervention (Lavigne 1999: 99–100, 119).

Belarus made a different choice after the dismantling of the USSR. Independence in 1991 was not the result of a Belarusian societal protest against Soviet domination, or of an aspiration for national self-identification. National identity did not exist in pre-transition Belarus. It had been eroded by a policy of Belarus's russification starting from 1795, by extermination of the Belarusian elite in the Stalin epoch, by the Nazi occupation and, finally, by a second wave of Sovietization after the Second World War. Moreover, Belarusians, like most of the nations of the former Soviet Union, had little understanding of market economy values as, unlike in CEECs, Soviet domination had lasted for nearly seven decades. The first major political and economic reforms did not start until Gorbachev's *perestroika* in 1986.

Thus the Belarusians were not prepared for a radical political and economic transformation. Their first experiences of transition were rocketing prices, the erosion of savings and real incomes, and layoffs. This happened against the background of enrichment of the dominant political elites, the so-called *nomenklatura*. These factors turned the majority of Belarusians into opponents of market reforms, pushing them to elect a populist leader, Alexander Lukashenko, who came as an outsider from the corrupt political corps and whose election platform was to fight sleaze and to support Belarus–Russia unification. It has been argued that 'reforms are more likely to occur when political outsiders challenge the authority of incumbents' (Denizer *et al.* 1998: 9) and the beginning of Lukashenko's presidency in 1994–1995 was marked by some fragmented market reforms, including domestic financial market liberalization. However, these were primarily the result of the liberal economic policy pursued by the government headed by Prime Minister Chygir and the policy of Bogdankevich, a chief of the National Bank of Belarus in 1994–95. As is argued below, the nature of Lukashenko's politics pushed economic policy in a different direction.

Political oppression started in 1995 when Lukashenko's attempts to extend his presidential powers brought him into conflict with parliament and the Constitutional Court. A referendum in November 1996 allowed

Table 11.1 The index of economic freedom in selected transition economies

Country	1996		2000		2003	
	OS	Rank out of 140	OS	Rank out of 161	OS	Rank out of 156
Poland	3.3	75	2.8	52	2.8	61
Estonia	2.4	23	2.2	21	1.7	3
Belarus	3.5	84	4.2	141	4.2	146
Russia	3.7	104	3.8	121	3.5	116
Turkmenistan			4.4	148	4.2	147
Ukraine	4	122	3.7	119	3.6	124
Uzbekistan			4.5	153	4.3	149

Note: OS denotes an overall score that is an average of ten factors measuring economic freedom. The Heritage Foundation defines economic freedom as 'the absence of government coercion or constraint on the production, distribution, or consumption of goods and services beyond the extent necessary for citizens to protect and maintain liberty itself'. The measure of economic freedom includes: trade policy, fiscal burden of government, government intervention in the economy, monetary policy, capital flows and foreign investment, banking and finance, wages and prices, property rights, regulation, and informal market activity. Indicators range from 1 to 5, where 1–1.99 means 'free', 2–2.99 – 'mostly free', 3–3.99 – 'mostly unfree' and 4–5 – 'repressed'. Scores are rounded to one decimal place.
Source: <http://www.heritage.org>.

the amendment of the constitution to extend the presidential term and to replace the parliament with a 'smaller and wholly subordinate National Assembly', paving the way 'for the establishment of an increasingly authoritarian regime' (White and Korosteleva-Polglase 2006: 155). In turn, economic policy became a means to protect the position of the dominant political elite by avoiding some of the more direct negative social costs of transition (Korosteleva 2004). Thus the political changes from 1996 had a complementary impact on economic activity.

After more than a decade of transition Belarus developed a reputation as one of the least-transformed economies of the post-socialist region with a private sector share accounting of only 25 per cent of GDP compared to 65 per cent in Ukraine and 70 per cent in Russia (EBRD 2004). As demonstrated in Table 11.1, the Heritage Foundation gives Belarus the worst ranking, outdoing Turkmenistan and Uzbekistan, amongst transition economies in 1996–2003. Belarus falls under the 'repressed' category, while most of its neighbours, including Ukraine and Russia, have made some progress in transformation and have moved to a category of 'mostly unfree'.

The Belarusian economy was heavily controlled and regulated by the state with intervention present in nearly all spheres of economic activity. This is revealed in the high degree of state ownership, a golden share rule, caps on trade mark-ups and producer profit margins, government-mandated redistribution of financial resources to 'priority' sectors of the economy and centrally set wage targets. Interpreting low aggregate demand as one of the factors causing output decline, the Belarusian government stimulated demand with an unprecedented credit expansion, backed by negative real interest rates (Korosteleva 2004). Capital control and foreign exchange restrictions and tariff and non-tariff barriers to trade were put in place to accompany the demand-management strategy. In fact, mechanisms that laid the foundation of the Belarusian economic development strategy bore a strong resemblance to those typical of a planned economy, including state ownership, production plans, administrative allocation of resources, price subsidies, and repressed inflation (for further discussion, see Nuti 1999, Lawson 2003; Bakanova *et al.* 2003; and Korosteleva 2004). However, elements of a market economy, although very limited, continued developing alongside the dominating practices of a planned economy.

The authorities portrayed this Belarusian model as a socially oriented market economy with some degree of state control that should ultimately bring Belarus closer to something between the social-democratic model and the Continental European one, if expressed in terms of the Amable approach. This is not convincing. Nor can it be equated with the models developed in China and Vietnam where the emphasis was on 'social welfare and stability' through state control over some economic activities and gradual liberalization (World Bank 2002). China did not rush to privatize its state enterprises or to liberalize prices, preferring instead a two-tier system with free market prices for goods produced in excess of quotas (Stiglitz 2002). However, as the World Bank (2002) argues, the resemblance 'ends there' as China and Vietnam were gradually reforming their economies. The Chinese strategy triggered an average annual economic growth rate of over 10 per cent in the 1990s and a reduction in poverty rates. The key to China's success was the growth of the private sector while maintaining employment in the state sector. Belarus can hardly be placed in the same policy box. Nor does the Belarusian economic model fit with any ideal capitalist models advocated by Hall and Soskice (2001) or Amable (2003). Government intervention in economic regulation in Belarus created a type of state capitalism (for discussion of the term, see Radygin 2004), combining elements attributed to the capitalist system with state ownership and substantial state control over the economy.

This is elaborated in discussion of individual points in the sections that follows.

Product market competition

State control, barriers to entrepreneurship and barriers to trade and investment are the key institutional areas explored here. State control can easily be maintained by preserving and increasing state ownership. This became possible with the reversal of a privatization programme which had been based primarily on management–employee buy-outs and, to a lesser extent, on vouchers (EBRD 2000). After 1995 privatization became rather artificial. It presupposed turning state enterprises into joint-stock companies, with a state share dominant or at least exceeding 25 per cent, resulting in preservation of state control over managerial decisions (Korosteleva 2004).

This was strengthened further by a 'golden share' rule introduced by the government in 1997 for joint-stock enterprises with a continuing state share. This gave the state an unlimited right to veto any shareholders' decisions on restructuring and liquidation of the enterprise, profit distribution and managerial appointments. It even gave the state the ultimate authority over operational matters. An updated version in March 2004 gave even more discretionary powers to the authorities and required the introduction of the 'golden share' in any privatized enterprise. The retroactive character of the document completely 'undermines the institution of private property' in Belarus (Romanchuk 2004).

Furthermore, measures allowing administrative price controls on a number of socially important goods were reintroduced in 1996. A variety of administrative measures were used to suppress price increases, including monthly price-increase ceilings, caps on trade profit margins and the regulation of prices by the cost of inputs. These were mostly eliminated by 2002, but a presidential decree of 19 May 1999 on the regulation of prices and tariffs remained in force in 2005 and the practice of administrative price controls was still in use (see, for example, IMF 2005).

As far as barriers to entrepreneurship are concerned it is worth noting that administrative control mechanisms continued, including business licensing, registration and certification, production plans, limitation of access of private enterprises to credits, discretionary regulatory exemptions and an increasing tax burden. The registration procedure was complicated and exclusively based on the 'permissive principle'. Between 1996 and 2005 there were two mandatory re-registrations of Belarusian legal entities, significantly reducing the number of functioning enterprises.

As a result of the first re-registration in 1996–97 the number of enterprises decreased by 35 per cent. The procedure required an enterprise manager and chief accountant to submit a document signed by the tax and state control bodies to a special commission. The manager and chief accountant were then asked to attend a commission meeting, at which the commission members would decide whether to allow the enterprise to continue in operation. One of the common reasons for many private enterprises not passing reregistrations was their inability to comply with high statutory minimum requirements set by the government (Daneiko *et al.* 2003).

Licensing of certain economic activities was used to crowd out potential competitors from the market. After the adoption of a presidential decree in July 2003 on licensing certain types of economic activities, the total number that required licensing was reduced from 165 to 49, while the number of state bodies issuing licences was reduced from 45 to 39 (Daneiko *et al.* 2003). This might appear as a step towards liberalization of market entry for businesses, but the opposite is suggested by the revocation of licences from two private medical centres in 2005, 'Ekomedservice' and 'Nordin', which were potential rivals to state clinics, on the grounds that they supposedly lacked qualified staff. Thus, licensing continued to be a state tool for suppressing competition (for discussion see *Belorusski Rynok*, 11–18 July 2005; 25 July–1 August 2005; 1–8 August 2005). Moreover, along with rationing access to cheap natural resources and price distortions, licensing also became a source of rent seeking. For example, such highly profitable and lucrative businesses as the import of oil and gas, fish and seafood products were fully nationalized, while others such as the import of cars, chemical fertilizers, alcohol and tobacco goods remained under heavy state control (Daneiko *et al.* 2003).

Other administrative measures impeding enterprises' economic activity included unstable, contradictory and often retroactive legislation, setting of production targets for industry, discretionary regulatory exemptions for strategic state-owned enterprises, an increased tax burden, complicated book-keeping and finally endless state inspections of enterprises' activities. Regarding the latter, Rakova (2003) notes that 'Belarus is the only civilized country where receipts from fines appear to be an official item in the budget.'

Despite the *de jure* official declaration of equality in treatment of enterprises, *de facto* discrimination against private enterprises continued through the limitation of their access to credits, state support of some 'strategic' state-owned enterprises, relief for the latter from paying some taxes and customs duties at the expense of increasing the tax burden on the private sector and rationing of access to cheap natural resources (Korosteleva 2004). Business regulations also created barriers to trade and investment. The inflow of foreign direct investment became very limited with the reversal of the privatization programme in 1996–97 and the introduction and further expansion of the golden share rule in 1997 and 2004. In the aftermath of the Belarusian currency crisis in early 1998, and later in the August 1998 financial crisis in Russia, wide-ranging controls on exchange rates and cross-border payments were reintroduced. It should be noted that even with some fragmentary attempts to ease restrictions over the period of transition, general macroeconomic instability and an unfavourable business climate appeared as *de facto* impediments for attracting private capital. World Bank figures (2005: 10) show that the cumulative direct investment inflow per capita for the period of 1989–2003 amounted to only $200, one tenth the average level for CEECs. Moreover, contradictory and often retroactive legislation further aggravated the functioning of domestic economic agents and frightened off foreign companies expressing any initial interest in dealing with their Belarusian counterparts.

In 1999, after some years of a multiple exchange rate regime, the authorities switched to a single exchange rate and convertibility for current account operations. By September 2000 the official exchange rate had devalued to the market level and then remained relatively stable. Moreover, there was some liberalization of import and export controls in 2000–2002. As of 2004 the EBRD evaluated progress in the trade and foreign-exchange systems as '2+', denoting some progress in the elimination of import and export restrictions and in achieving almost full current account convertibility.

At the same time, as Table 11.2 suggests, Belarus continued to be a laggard in promoting corporate governance and enterprise restructuring. It demonstrated the least progress in this area with the EBRD index of enterprise reform, shifting from 1.7 in 1995, indicating moderately tight credit and subsidy policy, to 1 in 1997–2003, meaning a return to soft budget constraints. This is the lowest among the twenty-seven transition economies with only Turkmenistan performing as badly. With privatization stalled, little progress was made in improving the state of competition in Belarus.

Indeed, Belarus in 2005 appeared to have undergone only a partial transformation away from the practices of central planning. The strength of the state sector is clear, with figures from the Ministry of the Economy showing a majority state share in 49 per cent of joint-stock companies in 2000 and 48 per cent in 2005. Only 20 per cent of such companies

Table 11.2   Selected indicators denoting product-market competition

Indicators	1995	1996	1997–2002	2003
Private sector share in GDP, %	15	15	20	25
EBRD index of small-scale privatization	2	2	2	2.3
Large-scale privatization	1.7	1	1	1
Enterprise reform	1.7	1.7	1	1
Competition policy	2	2	2	2

Note: The EBRD index of small-scale privatization is scored from 1, meaning little progress to 4+, meaning the standards and performance typical of advanced industrial economies, or no state ownership of small enterprises. The index of large-scale privatization takes the value 1 for little private ownership and 4+ for more than 75 per cent of enterprise assets in private ownership with effective corporate governance. The index of enterprise reform is scored from 1, denoting reliance on soft budget constraints and little progress in promoting corporate governance to 4+ meaning effective corporate control exercised through domestic financial institutions and markets. The index of competition policy is scored 1 for no competition legislation and institutions, 2 for competition policy legislation and institutions set up and some reduction of entry restrictions occurred and 4+ for effective enforcement of competition policy.
Source: EBRD (2000; 2004).

had no state share in 2000, rising to 29 per cent in 2005. The continuing authority over the day-to-day operations of private enterprises can also be documented from a survey by the Institute of Privatization and Management in which 20 per cent of managers indicated that the government imposed production targets on them (Daneiko *et al.* 2003: 54): the percentage increased with enterprise size such that over 70 per cent of managers of private enterprises with over 200 employees confirmed that the authorities were setting plans for their businesses. This was not full central planning, but nor was it, in view of the level of state intervention and direction, a free-market system.

The wage–labour nexus

The analysis of wage and labour relations centres on employment policy and industrial relations. In 1996, worried by the social and political costs, the government abandoned the IMF-backed approach of setting macro-economic stabilization as the priority. Instead, it favoured keeping the economy as close as possible to full employment through an expansionary macroeconomic policy, based mainly on lax credits, subsidies to state enterprises and negative real interest rates. Speaking at the inaugural session of the 13th Supreme Council, Lukashenko warned that 'in this difficult time, the people should be supported, the workers and peasants should be protected, and not thrown outside the factory gates' (Silistki 2002: 13). The rate of registered unemployment became one of the lowest across the region, averaging 2.4 per cent in 1997–2002, compared to 10.2 per cent in Russia or 11.7 per cent in Poland (Haiduk *et al.* 2004). Employment protection in 1996–1999 closely resembled a planned economy with employees protected from layoffs. However, a presidential decree of July 1999 on 'extra measures on improving labour relations and strengthening labour discipline' gave unlimited power to employers, meaning the state, over hiring and firing. The document envisaged a new employment policy based on contracts, primarily of a short-term character, usually for one year. However, making the labour market more flexible and reducing employment protection did not bring Belarus closer to a market-based model, as the state remained the main employer. The new employment system was significant rather in a political context and in its implications for trade unions, and hence collective bargaining.

Two trade union confederations have operated in Belarus, the Federation of Trade Unions (FTUB), with about 4 mn members, and the Belarusian Congress of Democratic Trade Unions (BCDTU), with about 20,000 members. Both confederations, but especially the FTUB, came under strong attack from the government after the 2001 presidential election in which Vladimir Goncharik, at that time the FTUB head, was Lukashenko's principal rival. The government found various means to exert pressure that led to Goncharik's resignation in December 2001 and to changes within the FTUB which ensured its loyalty to the state. This had an effect at enterprise level where managements could use their powers to threaten dismissal for individual activists, thereby limiting any scope for independent union activity. Thus authoritarian politics reduced unions to effective irrelevance both in politics and in the system of wage determination.

Wage setting remained centralized with no collective bargaining over levels or pay structures. Instead, it was built from the old Soviet system. Wages were primarily formed on the basis of an official pay-scale with twenty-seven categories. The authorities set the first-step wage which was used for calculating other wages by multiplying the latter by a special coefficient differentiated in terms of qualifications and seniority. The pay-scale system applied to all enterprises, albeit with some exceptions. Thus individual enterprises set their own first-step wage in line with their performance by stating this in a collective agreement (Haiduk *et al.* 2004).

The finance sector

After 1996 the Belarusian government re-established state control over the financial system and effectively reintroduced the practice of soft budget constraints. Assigning the central role in maintaining the Belarusian economic model to the banking system, the government halted reforms in that sector, which had been partly liberalized. Renationalization followed a presidential decree of 24 May 1996 after which state ownership rose from 55 per cent (IMF 1995:33) to reach 80 per cent in September 2004. The authorities also legitimized the subordination of the central bank with a presidential edict in March 1998 which formalized and enhanced the powers of the head of state over the National Bank of Belarus. Subordination was further strengthened in the Banking Code, enacted in 2000, within which the President acquired the right to appoint and remove not only the bank's chairperson, but also the members of the Board of Directors (Korosteleva 2004), the body responsible for setting the main directions of the central bank's activities.

A resolution of the Council of Ministers on 2 October 1996 officially defined six large banks as state agents for socio-economic projects and government debt. These were subsequently termed 'System-Forming Banks' (hereafter SF banks). They were of exceptional importance to the economy, dominating the market for banking services. As of September 2004 only one of these six banks, Priorbank, was under foreign ownership, controlled by the Austrian Raiffeisen group, but the expansion of the golden share rule in 2004 gave the government the continuing right to take decisions concerning the bank's activities.

They effectively monopolized banking, controlling over 90 per cent of total assets, 90 per cent of enterprise lending, almost 100 per cent of lending to households and their capital accounted for 77 per cent of total banking capital. The term 'state monopolization' is used here to show that the banking sector is mainly represented by the six system-forming banks. However, to be more precise, each of the six banks operated in a specific market segment and, in these specific segments, there was no competition between the banks, which meant that each had a monopoly over the market segment in which it operated (Korosteleva 2004). The SF banks, as agents of state policies, were expected to channel directed credits, primarily designed to support the agricultural sector and house construction, and serve other governmental programmes of 'high priority' on 'favourable terms', meaning that the lending rate was only half the refinancing rate, at the expense of banks' own resources. In turn, SF banks were supported by the authorities setting them relatively soft individual indicators of banking performance, allowing less provision for losses on loans than required by banking regulation rules and providing for regular recapitalization by the state. Together then, these changes in banking re-established the basis for soft budget constraints in favoured parts of the economy.

Domestic credit provided by the banking sector to the economy accounted for only 21 per cent of GDP in 2003, far below many CEECs. A loose monetary and credit policy, aimed at keeping enterprises afloat, drained the banks' financial resources. Many loans were never repaid and inflation eroded the real value of bank deposits and capital, thus leading to serious liquidity problems and undercapitalization of the banking sector. Priority financing of loss-making state-owned enterprises triggered problems of adverse selection and moral hazard. Thus, access to credit by 'good borrowers', who could have paid competitive interest rates, was restrained by liquidity constraints and low capitalization of the banking sector. At the same time, state-owned enterprises, convinced that they were too big for the state to let them sink, took bank loans for granted, often failing to repay them and expecting new bank loans to bail them out.

The capital market was very shallow and barely played any role in enterprise financing. The securities market was represented by government securities such as treasury bills which, along with credit emission, were the main method for financing the government deficit and the most liquid financial instrument. However, it should be noted that, in comparison to its neighbours Ukraine and Russia, the volume of such bills issued in Belarus remained low. Corporate securities, mostly shares in privatized enterprises, were weakly developed, reflecting the low level of privatization.

Social protection

Unlike many transition economies, Belarus developed a relatively extensive social security system. It moved away from reliance on price controls for basic food, housing and communal services, all features of a planned economy. However, the move was gradual as the state continued to direct banks to provide wage credits to enterprises to assure timely wage payments to employees. There were periodic increases in nominal wages to adjust for inflation. The share of social transfers in total money income of private households grew from 16.4 per cent in 1990 to 18.2 per cent in 2002. The pension system underwent no reform and there were no private pension funds.

The World Bank, as indicated in Table A.9 in the Statistical Appendix, estimated that, at the international yardstick of $ 4.3 per day, only about 21 per cent of the Belarusian population should be considered poor in 2002, compared with 41 per cent in Russia or 27 per cent in Poland. However, this figure was substantially higher than in 1999 when it had been under 10 per cent (World Bank 2002:4). Belarus had the lowest rate of inequality in income distribution in the countries of the former Soviet Union, measured by the Gini coefficient, as shown in Table A.8.

Institutional complementarities and economic performance

The financial system, being almost entirely bank-based, gave Belarus some apparent similarities to a coordinated market economy. However, the institutional interactions and complementarities within the system show up substantial differences. The strategy of output growth, based on the government setting production targets for industry, was complemented by state demand-management policies primarily in the form of the loose monetary and credit policy, interest rates ceilings and periodic wage increases. The balance between the wage bill and consumer spending was a key condition for equilibrium. Thus centralized wage setting and administratively fixed prices were necessary, complementary, measures to prevent any unwanted macroeconomic imbalances.

A loose monetary and credit policy appeared to complement a fiscal policy aimed at offsetting the losses from direct taxes through an implicit form of taxation, namely inflation tax. Since most government debt took the form of non-indexed nominal assets, the value of that debt was eroded when prices rise. Since an inflation tax cannot easily be extracted from private securities markets, the authorities' actions inhibited the development of the latter.

The domination of state ownership over enterprises matched a resumption of the practice of soft budget constraints to avoid large-scale bankruptcies. Had the authorities allowed gradual privatization, they could have limited the dependence of enterprises on state support while using a selective industrial policy to target investment to specific sectors with high technological potential. Thus, although the institutional practices that developed in Belarus had an internal coherence that together assured the viability of the chosen economic strategy, they differed from those of established kinds of capitalism and this had important implications for economic performance.

The beginning of the transition to a market economy was marked by a sharp decline in GDP and industrial production and a huge price jump fuelled by price liberalization. During 1991–5 GDP declined by 12 per cent per annum and yearly inflation rates were far in excess of 1,000 per cent. Five years after transition began, against the background of continuing transition recession and a range of currency and banking crises shaking the transition economies in the region, the revival of the Belarusian economy, with economic growth averaging at 7 per cent per annum in 1996–4 (see Table A.1 for year-by-year figures), created an impression that its alternative strategy had succeeded. The policy of money-led stimulation of aggregate demand triggered a surge in households' consumption and investment, as indicated in Table 11.3. It should be noted that the share of inventories declined between 1997 and 1999, demolishing arguments that economic growth could be explained solely by an increase in the stock of unsold goods. An increase in inventories was registered first in 2000, after several years of growth.

The surge in investment activity was mainly due to the strong growth of housing construction financed primarily by directed credits at highly preferential rates. The main branches of the economy contributing to growth in the late 1990s were industry and housing construction. It is worth noting that by 2000 the share of investment in housing construction exceeded that of industry, reaching 29.6 per cent in total investment in fixed assets. This strategy of extensive financing of housing construction, agriculture and poorly performing, large, state-owned enterprises has been identified as a primary source of economic inefficiency, in the sense that resources are clearly misallocated (Bakanova *et al.* 2003; Daneiko *et al.* 2003).

There are some doubts over the accuracy of published GDP figures. The persistent current account deficit has led to an overestimate due to the use in the national statistics of the official exchange rate, which was

Table 11.3 GDP by expenditure, real percentage changes over previous year, 1996–2002

	GDP	Households	Government	Gross capital formation	Net exports
1996	2.8	5.7	−1.3	−3.1	−4.1
1997	11.4	11.4	7.1	20	−5.9
1998	8.4	14.1	6	24.5	−4.9
1999	3.4	9.5	5.6	−11.1	−2.4
2000	5.8	8	6.6	−0.9	−3.2
2001	4.7	17.9	1.8	−6.5	−3.6
2002	5	9.3	1.8	3.2	

Source: Haiduk *et al.* (2004: 37).

60 per cent lower than the market rate (Daneiko *et al.* 2003:117). However, GDP was underestimated due to the failure to measure the contribution of the shadow economy. These two effects may balance each other out (*ibid.*:117). World Bank and IMF experts have also expressed some concerns over GDP data, but concluded that 'statistical problems are not sufficient to radically change the reported trend of real GDP'(World Bank 2002:1).

The role of Russia appears to have been significant in sustaining economic growth in Belarus. Economic integration contributed to the revitalization of the Belarusian economy by providing it with a valuable alternative in the aftermath of the international isolation which the country suffered after the November 1996 referendum. Russian assistance commenced with a write-off of the Belarus $1 bn debt in March 1996. Then Belarus received unlimited access to the Russian market and the opportunity to purchase oil and gas at 50 per cent of the world price level for oil and 16 per cent for gas. A customs union between the two states established in 1995 put Belarus in control of almost all Russian exports and imports to the West, as they crossed the Belarusian border.

The significant losses in customs payments to the Russian side finally led to the collapse of the customs union which had clearly not been properly thought through at the start. However, a more important help was a Russian agreement to conduct 92 per cent of trade by barter. The terms meant, in effect, that Belarus exchanged its overpriced industrial goods for underpriced oil and gas from Russia. Russia–Belarus trade grew rapidly as barter schemes proliferated and was actively lobbied for by Lukashenko when he visited Russian regions (Korosteleva 2004). Altogether, the annual amount of hidden Russian subsidy to the Belarusian economy has been estimated at $1.5–2 bn in 1997 and 1998 (Silitski 2002: 252), which is equivalent to 11 per cent and 14 per cent of the Belarusian GDP in those two years respectively. It can be concluded that, without such subsidization, Lukashenko would not have been able to sustain the Belarusian 'transformation' model.

The weakness of the model is revealed in other features, particularly in relation to the financial system and how it was tied in with the process of growth. This was primarily consumption-led and stimulated through wage increases, often in excess of labour productivity. Enterprises were frequently unable to pay wages on time and had to resort to bank credits, which were in turn directed by the government. Short-term growth was also driven by a surge in investment in 1997 and 1998. Housing construction was financed primarily by directed credits at highly preferential rates of under 5 per cent per annum, well below the rate of inflation, to be repaid over forty years. Credits on favourable terms also went into agriculture and industry to support loss-making enterprises. The impact of this credit expansion can be seen in the inflation rate which rose from 52.7 per cent in 1996 to 293.7 per cent in 1999, creating the so-called inflation tax on households, enterprises and banks, a consequence of which was a drastic reduction in real cash balances. The government switched to tight monetary policy from 2000, cutting down on directed credits, but the SF banks were still directed to continue granting preferential loans. The rate of inflation fell over the following years, but was still 19.3 per cent in 2004.

Despite the distorting role of the state, this was substantially different from a system of fully directed credits in which enterprises would have no financial independence at all. State-owned enterprises, including joint-stock companies with a state share, had access to bank loans when running a deficit. Other enterprises were also formally eligible for bank loans, but Belarusian banks were not able to finance major projects, not least in view of their commitments to loss-making enterprises. This explains a surge in enterprise arrears and a widespread use of monetary surrogates. While a problem of liquidity constraint was also typical of many CEECs at the early stage of transition, it was mainly attributed to a short-term tightening of monetary policy. In Belarus a policy of credit expansion, aiming to keep enterprises afloat, drained the banks' resources, leading to widespread liquidity problems. The private sector was primarily financed by small and medium-sized commercial banks that, in the highly inflationary environment prior to 2000, often preferred to concentrate on foreign-currency speculation, government securities and short-term loans to SF banks on the inter-bank market.

In contrast to the Soviet system, where the deposits of enterprises were not freely usable and were controlled through branch ministries, at least until the 1987–89 reforms, managers of enterprises in the Belarus of the Lukashenko period could dispose of the retained profits as they wished. Moreover, unlike fully state-owned enterprises, joint-stock companies had an incentive to make a profit. In a Soviet system, meeting a production target was almost the only incentive for an enterprise and financial deficits were common.

However, the partial nature of finance-sector reform had further systemic consequences, including a demonetization and unofficial dollarization of the economy. On average, between 1996 and 2002, only 70 per cent of the economy was monetized. The policy of low interest rates discouraged savings, one of the main sources of financing enterprises in Belarus. Retained profits could not play a significant role in maintaining enterprises' economic activity in Belarus in the 1990s as the number of loss-making enterprises increased, reaching 35 per cent of all enterprises in 2002, as against 7.3 per cent in 1994. Overall, profits tended to decrease, amounting to only 11.8 per cent of GDP in 2002 against 52.9 per cent in 1994. Moreover, credit expansion and state subsidies to loss-making enterprises, combined with high taxation of profitable firms, exhausted the financial resources of the healthier enterprises. Furthermore, borrowing from foreign markets was restricted and a market for corporate securities did not exist due to the delayed privatization. Financing therefore remained mainly inflationary, relying on current and lagged emissions from the central bank.

A likely consequence of this form of operation of the finance system is a decline in the average productivity of capital, due to the replacement of high-yielding investment that can be generated in the private sector or in the branches of the economy with high technological potential by low-return investment, directed mainly to loss-making or low-return agricultural and industrial sectors, and to stimulate household consumption through wage increases. This pattern of financing could not sustain long-term growth. The slowdown in 1999–2001, with mounting inventories, an increase in the number of loss-making enterprises and a significant deterioration in Belarus's competitive position, all provide evidence of the inefficiency of the Belarusian economic strategy.

This strategy can be viewed as survival-oriented rather than growth-oriented (Bakanova *et al.* 2003) aiming, above all, at serving the government's own needs in ensuring political survival. After 2000, government policies gradually adjusted towards reducing economic distortions and GDP growth surged again from 4.5 per cent in 2002 to 11 per cent in 2004. Nevertheless, the sustainability of this growth pattern, and therefore social stability, remains questionable. This is due to the delay in economic restructuring and the vulnerability of the Belarusian economy to any change in its external environment. After 2001 this was favourable to Belarusian economic development. Rising oil prices, expanding exports of oil products and rising demand in Russia contributed to the high rates of economic growth (World Bank 2005). However, continued evasion of fundamental reforms put the country at risk of a severe transition crisis that could inflict even greater economic and social costs than those after the Soviet Union's collapse.

Conclusion

This examination of the political economy of Belarus within the Varieties of Capitalism approach has focused on the system that emerged after political changes in 1996. Excessive state control and regulation appeared to complement the establishment of an authoritarian regime. This high degree of state involvement in all fundamental institutional domains turned Belarus into a state capitalist economy. It incorporated some elements of a planned economy, including state ownership, price controls, lax credits, plan targets and centralized wage setting, alongside some elements of a market economy, including private property, although very constrained, and partly liberalized domestic markets. The elements from the planned economy appeared to dominate. The Belarusian economic model is therefore clearly distinct from any of the ideal types of capitalism established by Hall and Soskice (2001) or Amable (2003). Instead, Belarus developed a type of state capitalism in which rent-seeking mechanisms existed and, despite the official declaration of all enterprises to be treated equally, discrimination against private enterprises continued. However, even without undertaking structural reforms as such, the Belarusian economy grew after 1997 and this puzzled many economists. The evidence here suggests that this growth was ultimately unsustainable as it depended on a specific international situation and an economic model that was fundamentally inefficient.

References

Amable, B. (2003) *The Diversity of Modern Capitalism* (London: Oxford University Press).
Bakanova, M., L.V. de Souza, I. Kolesnikov and I. Abramov (2003) *Explaining Growth in Belarus* <www.gdnet.org/pdf/draft_country_studies/Belarus_final.pdf>.
Daneiko, P. *et al.* (2003) *Beloruski Business: State, Trends, and Perspectives* (Minsk: Institute of Management and Privatization).
Denizer, C., R. Desai and N. Gueorguiev (1998) *The Political Economy of Financial Repression in Transition Economies*, Policy Research Working Paper Series, 2030 (Washington, DC: World Bank).
EBRD (2000) *The Transition Report 2000: Employment, Skills and Transition* (Oxford: Oxford University Press).
EBRD (2004) *The Transition Report 2004: Infrastructure* (Oxford: Oxford University Press).
Haiduk, K., H. Herr, T. Lintovskaya, S. Parchevskaya, J. Priewe and R. Tsiku (2004) *The Belarusian Economy at a Crossroads* (Moscow: International Labour Organization).
Hall, P. and D. Soskice (eds) (2001) *Varieties of Capitalism: The Institutional Foundations of Comparative Advantage* (Oxford: Oxford University Press).
IMF (1995) *Belarus – Recent Economic Developments*, Staff Country Report, 95/99 (Washington, DC: IMF).
IMF (2005) *Republic of Belarus: 2005 Article IV Consultation*, Country Report, 05/214 (Washington, DC: IMF).
Korosteleva, J. (2004) 'Continuity over Change: Belarus, Financial Repression and Reintegration with Russia', in N. Robinson (ed.), *Reforging the Weakest Link* (Burlington: Ashgate), 61–80.

Lavigne, M. (1999) *The Economics of Transition: From Socialist Economy to Market Economy*, 2nd edn (Basingstoke: Palgrave).

Lawson, C. W. (2003) 'Path-dependence and the Economy of Belarus: The Consequences of Late Reforms', in E.A. Korosteleva, C.W. Lawson and R.J. March, (eds), *Contemporary Belarus: Between Democracy and Dictatorship* (London, New York: RoutledgeCurzon), 125–36.

Nuti, D. M. (1999) 'Belarus: A Command Economy without Central Planning', presented at the Fifth Dubrovnik Conference on transition economies, Ten Years of Transition: What Have We Learned and What Lies Ahead, 23–25 June.

Radygin, A. (2004) 'Rossiya v 2000–2004 Godakh: Na Puti k Gosudarstvennomu Kapitalismu?', *Voprosy Ekonomiki*, 4, 42–65.

Rakova, E. (2003) *U Belorusskogo Businessa Dve Problemy: Plokhie Zakony i Mnogo Raznykh Vysokikh Nalogov* <www.belapan.com/ru/analit/420-8.html>.

Romanchuk, J. (2004) *State of Corruption in the Republic of Belarus* <http://liberty-belarus.org/english/2004076195140.shtml>.

Silitski, V. (2002) 'Political Economy of Belarus-Russia Integration', in V. Bulhakau (ed.), *Belarus-Russia Integration* (Minsk: Encyclopedix), 222–69.

Stiglitz, J. E. (2002) *Globalization and Its Discontents* (London: Penguin).

White, S. L. and E. A. Korosteleva-Polglase (2006) 'The Parliamentary Election and Referendum in Belarus, October 2004', *Electoral Studies*, 25 (March), 155–60.

World Bank (2002) 'Memorandum of the President of the International Bank for Reconstruction and Development and of the International Finance Corporation to the Executive Directors on a Country Assistance Strategy for Belarus', 23401-BY (Washington, DC: World Bank).

World Bank (2005) *Belarus: Window of Opportunity to Enhance Competitiveness and Sustain Economic Growth*, Country Economic Memorandum for the Republic of Belarus, 23246-BY (Washington, DC: World Bank).

12
China's Transformation towards Capitalism

Jeanne Wilson

Since embarking on a programme of economic reform in late 1978, China has moved, albeit in an incremental fashion with periodic stops and starts, towards market capitalism. In 1993 the Chinese Communist Party (CCP) deleted the description of China as a planned economy under public ownership from the state constitution, proclaiming it a 'socialist market economy'. Further amendments legitimated the ownership rights of private entrepreneurs (1999) and the sanctity of private property (2004). In a related development, entrepreneurs were granted the right to join the CCP in 2002. While China undoubtedly constitutes an example of economic transformation from the Soviet-style planning system, its experience must be distinguished from that of its former socialist brethren. First, most obviously, China was one of the few remaining examples, at least ostensibly, of a Marxist-Leninist state, governed by a Communist Party. Secondly, China was still, despite a record of remarkable growth, a developing economy, setting it apart from the states of Eastern Europe and the more industrialized states of the former Soviet Union.

China also differed significantly from the variety of capitalism models set forth by Hall and Soskice and Amable. Both models are concerned with the forms of capitalism encountered in advanced industrialized states. In particular, Hall and Soskice's reliance on the firm as the unit of inquiry holds little relevance for China. Both approaches also tend to assume the existence of a democratic polity, in which policy decisions are the result of negotiations and bargaining among a multitude of diverse actors pursuing specific vested interests. This view corresponds to political processes in the states of Western Europe and North America but does not capture the complexities of the Chinese political system. The Chinese movement to capitalism reflects the conscious actions of the Chinese state under the leadership of the CCP, a situation that is not considered in the Varieties of Capitalism analyses. Despite the lack of absolute congruence, these models are nonetheless useful as a starting point for analysis of the process of economic transformation in China. Here, I am concerned with two interrelated issues: the extent to which China can be considered a capitalist economy and the format of China's evolving economic system, viewed in the context of the models set forth in the Varieties of Capitalism analyses.

I argue that China's economic transformation to 2006 was characterized by a distinctive, and arguably dysfunctional, dualism. On the one hand, the dominant thrust of reforms was towards the adoption of neoliberal economic policies, most consistent with the liberal market economy (LME) of Hall and Soskice or the Anglo-Saxon market economy of Amable. On the other hand, the Chinese leadership simultaneously embraced a strategy of promoting key pillar industries. This quest to establish large-scale conglomerates, in effect a policy of developing national champions, looked more towards Amable's Asian model of capitalism and to the practising of close collaboration between the state and large corporations, as seen in the *Chaebol* of Korea and the *Keiretsu* of Japan. This system, as it evolved, indicates less the development of some hybrid form of capitalism Chinese-style than the uneasy coexistence of two separate economic policies pursued by the government. China's status as a late developer, however, located it in a markedly different international environment from that encountered by its East Asian neighbours. To a greater extent, moreover, than most of its post-socialist counterparts, China's movement towards the market was closely linked to integration into the global economy.

The initial thrust of the Chinese economic reforms was somewhat reminiscent of earlier reform efforts undertaken within the socialist bloc, notably in Yugoslavia and Hungary (Kornai 1992). Chinese reformers followed a previously trodden path in their efforts to decentralize the locus of decision making to the enterprise as a means of stimulating competition and increasing allocative efficiency. However, the Chinese reform agenda far superseded the circumscribed efforts of an earlier generation of socialist reformers. This discussion considers the extent to which China has adopted capitalist features making use of the criteria set forth by David Lane in Chapter 1 and how far changes have set China on the road to a recognizable variety of capitalism, with Hall and Soskice's LME appearing, in some respects, a strong candidate.

The next sections set different aspects of development against this framework. Privatization and market liberalization appear consistent with a trend away from state control and the section on internationalization indicates the strong pressure from China's integration into the world economy. However, evidence on developments in financial intermediation is more mixed. In this case a strong state role appears as a constraint on moves in the LME direction. Growing inequality is consistent with the nature of economic growth, but changes in labour relations demonstrate specific features that reflect the authoritarian political structure and the continuation of some of the more traditional practices from the communist period. The section on complementarities demonstrates that this does not include those practices that gave unions one of their significant roles in the past. Indeed, the appearance here is of a conscious effort to create the necessary institutional structure for a market system.

Privatization and price liberalization

By the late 1990s, the private sector had emerged as the most dynamic component of the Chinese economy, and a critical source of jobs. Between 2000 and 2003 the number of workers employed in private enterprises in China's urban areas more than doubled to over 25 million (ZGTJNJ 2004: 119). Nonetheless, the actual extent of privatization within the Chinese economy is difficult to gauge. It is no simple matter to distinguish between private and public forms of ownership. In certain instances, property rights were detached from ownership *per se*. For example, even after agriculture had been decollectivized for over two decades, the state retained ownership of the land, although peasants had the legal right to lease land for up to fifty years, buy and sell land contracts, and hire labour. Conversely, privately owned enterprises, especially town and village enterprises in the countryside, often preferred to register as collective operations, so-called red hat firms, as a matter of convenience in doing business.

During the 1990s, the state embarked upon its ambitious quest of changing the ownership structure of state-owned enterprises (SOEs), a process that gave rise to an often bewildering assortment of operational arrangements. Many firms, especially smaller ones owned by local authorities, were privatized. A 2000 study carried out by the International Finance Corporation, an affiliate of the World Bank, reported that around 80 per cent of the SOEs owned by governments at the county level or lower had been transformed into private enterprises (Gregory *et al.* 2000: 14). Other SOEs were restructured to include some sort of private component through such procedures as leasing and contractual arrangements, employee buyouts and share ownership, the opening up of SOEs to foreign and domestic private investment and the establishment of joint ventures

(Mako and Zhang 2003). The total number of SOEs declined from 238,000 to 150,000 from 1998 to the end of 2003 (Naughton 2005: 65).

Chinese statistical analyses do not provide detailed information about the composition of private firms, much less the share of GDP originating in the private sector. This task was first attempted by the International Finance Corporation which concluded that the private sector constituted 33 per cent of GDP in 1998, compared with a state sector share of 37 per cent. Adding the contributions of individual peasants and collectives raised the non-state sector share of GDP to 62 per cent (Gregory *et al.* 2000: 16–17). Subsequent Chinese official assessments corroborated this estimate. A 2004 report commissioned by the Ministry of Commerce indicated that the non-state sector contributed 63.37 per cent of GDP in 2001 (*China Daily*, 21 April 2004). Moreover, the private sector share of GDP was markedly higher in the southern coastal regions. In Zhejiang province, for example, the private sector was reported in 2003 to generate 90 per cent of provincial GDP, a figure that reached 99.9 per cent in the city of Cixi (*China Daily*, 24 December 2004).

Over time, China shifted from a centrally administered system of mandatory production quotas to an indicative system, giving the localities some decision-making authority, and then to a reliance on the market as a regulator of productive outputs, save for large-scale infrastructure projects. In 1998, the State Planning Commission was abolished, symbolizing the end of an era. Price liberalization accompanied this process, with a parallel evolution from set prices through a dual-track pricing system to the abolition of price controls for most items. Price liberalization was a necessary prerequisite for China's entrance into the World Trade Organization (WTO) and in 2004 over 90 per cent of retail prices, over 80 per cent of farm products and almost 90 per cent of producer goods prices were estimated to be set by the market (*South China Morning Post*, 8 January 2004).

Integration into the global economy

From their onset, China's economic reforms were predicated on an opening to the outside world, indicating a rejection of the Maoist policy of self-reliance. The regime courted foreign investment, originally seen as a means of technology transfer, and pursued a trade policy oriented towards the export of labour-intensive consumer goods. By the late 1990s China had emerged as a major player in global trade, increasingly enmeshed in a relationship of interdependence with its primary trading partners, notably the United States and Japan. Despite considerable opposition among the ideologically wary, the Chinese leadership successfully pushed for admittance into the WTO, viewing further integration into the global economy as a necessary prerequisite of its goal of economic modernization. China ranked second to the United States as the destination point for foreign direct investment (FDI) for most of the 1990s. In 2003 it replaced the United States at the top. In 2003 FDI amounted to 3.8 per cent of GDP and 12.4 per cent of gross fixed capital formation. Accumulated stocks were equivalent to 36.6 per cent of GDP and the foreign funded sector of the economy employed 3.2 per cent of the urban labour force. This was the source of 57 per cent of Chinese exports (http://englishpeoplesdaily. com.cn). WTO requirements that China ease restrictions on foreign investment in services can be expected to bring about a shift in FDI flows towards that sector. China also became increasingly active as a foreign investor in its own right with outward FDI stocks estimated to have reached $37 bn by the end of 2003 (UNCTAD 2004: 25; Wu 2005). In the same year, China ranked as the third largest trading nation, behind the United States and Germany. Manufactured goods made up 92 per cent of China's exports with an increasing share for high-technology exports. Rodrik (2006:4), moreover, notes that China is an outlying case in this respect: its export mix was that of a state with three times its level of per capita income.

This internationalization had a pronounced impact on some geographical areas and economic sectors, while bypassing others. The coastal regions in Southern China, notably Zhejiang, Fujian and Guangdong provinces, were far more penetrated than inland and northern areas. In general, the growth of export production took place outside the state sector of industry, within foreign-funded, rural and township, and privately owned enterprises. Zweig (2002) has persuasively argued that many rural areas of China are far more internationalized than the urban SOEs, which produce goods that are uncompetitive on world markets.

Financial intermediation

China's performance on measures related to capital markets and financial structures presents something of a paradox. Comparative performance on indicators published by the global financial institutions is impressive, often implying that China ranks within a select cohort of established capitalist states. Stock market capitalization was 48.1 per cent of GDP in 2003, above that of Germany at 44.9 per cent and considerably higher than the average for post-socialist states, as indicated in Table A.5 in the Statistical Appendix. As Table A.6 further indicates, domestic credit provided by the banking sector was 177.9 per cent of GDP in 2003, compared with 150.4 per cent in Germany and 27.6 per cent in the Russian Federation. However, a closer examination of Chinese financial institutions indicates that they were still at a preliminary stage of development. The explosive growth of the economy had outstripped the establishment of corresponding regulatory frameworks. Moreover, the entire system still bore the legacy of socialist planning, placing constraints upon its operation and impeding the optimum allocation of financial resources.

The incomplete nature of China's transformation was readily apparent in the operation of China's equity markets (Kim *et al.* 2003). China had two equity markets, not counting the Hong Kong Stock Exchange, the Shanghai Securities Exchange established in 1990 and the Shenzhen Securities Exchange which began operations in 1991. At the end of 2003, they had a total market capitalization of RMB 4,240 bn, with 1,287 companies listed (ZGTJNJ 2004: 769). China's equity markets were originally established to provide an infusion of capital into the SOEs, a function which continued as of 2006. Private firms were not legally excluded from the exchanges, but technical rules impeded their participation. Of 976 companies listed in 1999, only eleven were non-state firms (Gregory *et al.* 2000: 46). Foreign investment was also highly constricted, primarily limited to Class B stocks which trade on both exchanges in foreign currency (110 of the total in 2003). Moreover, regulations specified that only one third of the shares of SOEs issued on the equity markets were actually tradable, a factor that served to reduce supply and contributed to the overvaluation of shares. Stock market operations lacked transparency, with the consequence that stock prices conveyed little information about the performance of listed firms (Durnev *et al.* 2004). A government effort in 2001 to sell off shares in SOEs to finance pension system reform increased market volatility, leading to its abrupt cessation. By 2006 the government had embarked on a new pilot programme to convert state-owned shares to tradable shares in listed companies (IMF 2005: 25).

The tensions between plan and market were similarly in evidence in efforts to reform China's banking sector. During the pre-reform period, Chinese banks functioned not as banks conceived of in capitalist practice, but as administrative conduits for the transfer of funds, notably to SOEs, from the state budget. In 1993 the government started to reform the system, bringing it into line with commercial criteria, a process that was accelerated in the late 1990s in the midst of negotiations over WTO entry. The terms allowed foreign banks, albeit with considerable constraints, access to China's domestic market in 2006. Although four state-owned banks continued to dominate the banking system, China also began to encourage locally owned regional banks as well as a private banking sector. Nonetheless, despite considerable efforts at restructuring, the banking system still appeared as a weak link in the transformation to market practices. Although a 1999 initiative established four asset-management companies to assume non-productive loans from the four major state banks, those banks continued to give loans to struggling SOEs without sufficient regard to performance indicators.

The result was the insolvency of the banking system. Between 25 per cent and 50 per cent of bank loans were estimated as non-performing and the entire system was somewhere between $300 bn and $500 bn in debt (Mulcahy 2003; Steinfeld 2004: 643). At the same time, private entrepreneurs faced considerable obstacles in acquiring bank loans, thus restricting credit to the most productive area of the economy. This also led, along with low official interest rates, to the proliferation of a parallel credit structure, an informal and unregulated, if not necessarily illegal, shadow banking system that challenged the state-owned banks, encouraging Chinese citizens to withdraw their money and seek greater gains in various pooled investment projects (Tsai 2002; Bradshaw 2004).

While the government was formally committed to the development of institutional investors, these remained in a nascent form, their construction further impeded by the restrictions on investment in China's capital markets. As with the banking sector, the terms of WTO accession dictated the opening up of China to foreign insurance companies, although not to full private ownership. It also meant broadening foreign access to fledgling collective investment institutions, but on a considerably reduced scale. According to a World Bank study, China's formal institutional assets were 10.6 per cent of GDP at the end of 2002, a figure much lower than the 207.3 per cent of GDP for the United States but similar to the 10.7 per cent for Hungary (Kim *et al.* 2003: 12, 25–6).

Income redistribution and inequality

Unlike the situation in a number of post-socialist states, China's transition to the market was a remarkable success, at least in terms of growth rates which for many years reached double-digit figures, as indicated in Table A.1. By the mid-2000s, China's Gross National Income had quadrupled since the onset of the reform movement. This lifted millions out of abject poverty. The number of people living in poverty, using the World Bank's measure of less than $1 per day per capita, declined from about 490 million in 1981 to 88 million in 2002 (World Bank 2003: 9; see also Table A.9). However, the rate of poverty reduction was most rapid in the early 1980s as rural incomes rose following agricultural decollec-tivization. Subsequent government policy measures tended to favour urban residents at the expense of rural peasants, contributing to an increase in income inequality.

By the early 2000s, 99 per cent of those living in poverty resided in rural areas, with high levels in Western China and remote mountainous regions. China had the dubious distinction of a faster rise in the Gini coefficient than any other state, starting from a level of 20 at the beginning of the 1980s to reach 44.9 in 1993 (World Bank 2003: 12–13; see also Table A.8). The Chinese government itself released reports in 2005 indicating that the Gini coefficient had risen to 48 (*Xinhua Financial Network News*, 20 June 2005). Such levels are comparable to those in many other devel-oping states, but considerably above the average of either the post-socialist states or the advanced industrial economies shown in Table A.8. By all accounts, including those of a concerned Chinese government, income inequality in China was considered likely to widen before declining, straining the social fabric of a society which touted egalitarian-ism as a key value during the Maoist era.

Labour conditions

Despite the Maoist ethos of egalitarianism, the industrial labour force in the pre-reform era was highly stratified in terms of the provision of wel-fare benefits and subsidies (Walder 1986). Nonetheless, the Chinese ver-sion of the social contract, widespread throughout the Communist bloc, specified the responsibility of the state to provide employment for its urban residents. The inability of the government by the late 1970s to ful-fil this obligation was undoubtedly a factor in the decision to open up the economy to private ventures as a means of absorbing surplus labour.

Economic reforms initiated a major shift in the relationship of the state to its working class, notably those workers in the state-owned sector. The state disavowed responsibility to provide employment for urban residents. With the hardening of budget constraints, many SOEs became finan-cially insolvent and began extensive layoffs. It is difficult to determine the extent of industrial unemployment in China. As elsewhere in the post-socialist bloc, workers were often maintained on employment rosters, even if they had not set foot in the factory for years. According to a report by the IMF (2004: 20), more than 28 million workers had been laid off from SOEs since 1998. Workers in the newly emergent private sector and foreign-funded enterprises typically received few, if any, welfare benefits and subsidies and the work was generally arduous. Sweat-shop labour conditions were prevalent in the joint-ventures in Southern China, especially those owned by Korean, Taiwanese and, to a lesser extent, Hong Kong entrepreneurs. Migrant rural workers, many of them young women, were compelled to work long hours in dangerous circumstances, under a brutally harsh labour regime (Chan 2000; Chan 2001).

The decline in life circumstances among the Chinese proletariat led to a dramatic upsurge in labour protests, especially in the cities that formed the core of China's industrial heartland during the Maoist era. The scale of worker protests is difficult to quantify but these incidents clearly numbered in the thousands on an annual basis. In 1998, for example, 85,000 labour disputes were recorded (Weston 2002: 722). Worker protests tended to be directed towards issues of wage arrears, layoffs, and other conditions of livelihood. Pensioners who failed to receive their retirement benefits also played a prominent role (Hurst and O'Brien 2002). These incidents tended to be tolerated by the authorities, who often offered some sort of short-term palliative to redress worker grievances, as long as they did not directly challenge the authority of the regime and remained unorganized, spontaneous expressions of discontent. The evidence indicated that Chinese worker protests were essentially economist in nature, rather than raising political questions about the legitimacy of the reform undertaking (Blecher 2002).

Worker protests elicited anxiety among the leadership which was highly sensitive to the potential for labour unrest to evolve into a political attack on the regime, in the manner of the Solidarity movement in Poland. Attempts to establish autonomous trade unions in China, most evident at the time of the Tiananmen democracy movement, were immediately quashed, with harsh punishment for the instigators. What is striking in this scenario, however, is the virtual absence of the official Chinese trade unions, the All-China Federation of Trade Unions, from disputes between labour and management.

China's trade unions have historically led a beleaguered existence, simultaneously representing the interests of both management and the working class. Periodic efforts to play a more assertive role, representing the genuine interests of the workers, invariably ended in failure, with the purge of offending cadres. Despite efforts post-1978 to provide a greater voice to the workers through the reinstitution of Workers' and Staff Representative Congresses and the promulgation of labour legislation, the overall impact of the economic reforms was further to weaken trade unions within the enterprise. In many cases the union leadership overlapped with the enterprise management, as was also the situation in the Maoist era. Union chairs commonly assumed the position as a part-time job, in conjunction with other managerial roles in the enterprise (Baek 2000). The transition to the market economy also meant the transfer of responsibility for administering welfare benefits from the enterprise to local government, depriving the unions of a traditional role within the enterprise.

Rates of unionization were very low in the newly established private enterprises and foreign-funded joint-ventures. The local authorities had little interest in enforcing labour standards as they were typically the joint-venture partners in these operations (Chan 2000). The ineffectiveness of the unions was reflected in membership figures, falling to 133.3 mn in 2003 from 144.6 mn in 2002: the number of grass roots units plunged from 171,300 in 2002 to 90,600 in 2003 and the number of full-time union personnel fell to 46,500 in 2003, compared with a high of 60,500 in 1996 (ZGTJNJ 2004: 875).

Complementarities

Although the vocabulary used differs from that of Hall and Soskice and Amable, the importance of complementary institutions has been reaffirmed in virtually every World Bank and IMF assessment of China, and by the Chinese leadership itself. However, these complementary institutions and processes were at best a work in progress. Moreover, the Varieties of Capitalism literature implicitly assumes the evolution of corresponding structures and processes over time, based on the particular configuration of a nation's cultural and historical attributes. This does not directly address the issues faced by leaders of post-socialist economies engaged, to a greater or lesser extent, in a deliberate attempt at economic engineering. The Chinese leadership set out on a course that necessitated a radical restructuring of the economy towards the market, as well as the development of corresponding processes and institutions.

Early on in the reforms, the Chinese government began to stress the imperative need to 'break the iron rice bowl', referring to the extensive structure of benefits and entitlements, including lifetime guaranteed employment, available to the elite stratum of workers in China's SOEs. The policy as it developed was to move the administration of welfare benefits from the enterprise to government bodies, with primary responsibility assumed by the localities. This included the establishment of state-wide pension, health insurance, disability, unemployment and maternity benefits. Typically these plans provided for employer and employee contributions with pooled benefits. In the long run, coverage was intended to extend throughout the urban employed population, including private enterprises and self-employed workers. The level of benefits was lower than under the previous system. For example, the replacement rate for pensions was set to decline from 80 per cent to 58 per cent for the average worker, while health insurance no longer extended to dependants (Kim *et al.* 2003: 7–8; Duckett 2004). As with China's financial reforms, all of these schemes were in an embryonic phase, subject to numerous difficulties with compliance, financing and administration. In effect, this social welfare policy was an attempt by the state to construct a social safety net as a complementary component of its market-oriented economic policies.

China also embarked on its economic reform programme minus the benefits of a legal system capable of supporting interactions in a market economy. After 1978, the Chinese leadership devoted considerable attention to establishing a series of economic and labour laws, in addition to the promulgation of criminal and civil codes. This commitment to legal structures was not rooted in the abstract belief, promoted in the Anglo-Saxon tradition, of the value of the rule of law as an end in itself. The regime seemed convinced that the development of a functioning legal system in China was a prerequisite to China's successful modernization. However, a number of factors impeded its institutionalization, including a cultural propensity to value personal relationships (*guanxi*) over the impartial application of rules, political intervention by the CCP, and structural constraints that made it difficult to implement a host of economic laws, such as bankruptcy proceedings. Thus, in practice, many laws were not enforced.

The Asian variant: building national champions

While the Chinese reform agenda focused largely on the liberalization of the economy, a parallel effort was directed to the development of large industrial conglomerates. In this respect, Chinese reform policy followed more closely Amable's Asian model of capitalism with the regulatory state retaining supervision over elite, strategic industries (cf. Pearson 2005). This tendency was visible by the second half of the 1980s (Nolan 2004: 36–7) and received further impetus in 1995 with the government's decision to restructure the state sector of industry, severing or loosening its administrative levers over the majority of SOEs, while retaining control over the largest state enterprises. This policy, known as 'grasping the large and releasing the small', bolstered the government's commitment to promoting a select group of large enterprises as national champions.

In the late 1990s, a number of critics, in particular Chinese economists, questioned the viability of the policy, pointing to Korea's experience in the Asian financial crisis and the widespread collapse of the *Chaebols*. However, in 1999 the CCP plenum dealing with SOE reform called for 'fostering strong and competitive large enterprises and groups' that could become 'the pillars of the national economy, and major forces of China in participating in international competition' (Mako and Zhang 2003: 1). The government designated six companies in the late 1990s as recipients of financial support with the goal of aiding them to achieve membership on the Fortune Global 500 by 2010. The establishment of the State Asset Supervision Administration Commission (SASAC) in 2003 ensured continued state supervision over the largest SOEs. In 2005 the director of SASAC, Li Rongrong, noted that the commission would reduce the 179 companies under its direct supervision to about 80, and create from 30 to 50 giant enterprises and group companies, on a par with international standards, within five years. This perspective was reaffirmed by Premier Wen Jiabao in his March 2005 speech to the National People's Congress in which he noted that China would 'energetically develop large companies and large enterprise groups that own intellectual property rights, have brand name products and are internationally competitive' (www.china.org.cn/english).

The Chinese policy of building national champions is an integral component of its 'go global' strategy to increase China's international economic presence. This endeavour, however, is motivated to a large extent, although not completely, by political goals which threaten to take precedence over calculations of market efficiency. It reflects the ascendance of bureaucratic over market forms of coordination and it is not clear how this can turn SOEs, often saddled with high levels of debt and low operational efficiency, into global competitors (Ting 2005). This strategy, moreover, implicitly assumes the maintenance of bank loans and subsidies to designated target enterprises, irrespective of economic performance, despite a commitment to the WTO to establish independent regulatory structures.

The Chinese government's goal faces significant challenges, both domestic and external. China is considerably more decentralized than Japan or Korea, with highly variant patterns of state–firm relations. Throughout most of the reform period, it lacked a coherent industrial strategy, which left local authorities to pursue their own ambitious schemes for regional development, discouraging outside domestic competition. Chinese firms are smaller, more geographically concentrated, and lacking in the networks of interdependence with financial institutions and other corporate structures characteristic of the Korean and Japanese economies. Thun (2004) argues that the Chinese leadership at the national level found it very difficult to support the development of large firms, due to a lack of bureaucratic capacity. Provincial resistance to mergers and acquisitions hindered state efforts at consolidation. Repeated efforts, for example, to use administrative measures to consolidate China's highly diversified auto industry resulted in failure, due to opposition by governmental authorities at the local level (Thun 2004; Noble *et al.* 2004: 21).

China, moreover, was seeking to construct national champions in an international environment markedly different from that encountered by its Asian neighbours. In an earlier period, Korea and Japan were able to create large enterprise groups through the use of protectionist measures that shielded nascent industries from foreign competition. This option was not available to China, especially since its admittance into the WTO. It did not have, nor was it likely soon to establish, a purely domestic automobile industry of international stature. Rather, the Chinese auto industry was dominated by joint-ventures with major international companies. Despite the barrage of criticism, primarily from American sources, for unfair trading practices, the terms of Chinese entrance into the WTO were stringent (Lardy 2002), requiring a series of liberalization measures that were, in the words of Charlene Barshefsky, the US Trade Representative, 'broader actually than any World Trade Organization member has made' (Branstetter and Lardy 2005: 12). Strictly speaking, China's WTO commitments did not preclude developing national champions, but the opening to global multinationals implies that China's industrial structure will evolve differently from Korea and Japan.

Japan and Korea, moreover, had the luxury of industrializing in an era that imposed fewer demands for technological innovation. Thun (2004) argues that China's utilization of FDI in high-technology sectors was driven not by the need for capital but by the need for technology and access to the most effective managerial practices. As a late developer, China faced an intensely competitive international environment in its quest to establish a global economic presence. A key motivation for Chinese firms seeking international acquisitions was to secure advanced technology and managerial expertise (Wu 2005). The main destination point of Chinese FDI at the end of 2003 was Hong Kong, followed by the United States. In this respect, China's outward FDI profile conforms to Hall and Soskice's (2001: 57) prediction that companies locate to LMEs in order to secure institutional support for innovation.

The role of the state

The Chinese movement to capitalism indicates the importance of the state as a transformative agent, in contrast to Hall and Soskice's focus on the firm.

Those authors take a democratic polity as a given. Economic policy is the outcome of bargaining among actors and institutions are the product of compromise between socio-political groups. Amable's model of Asian capitalism goes further in identifying the state as a decisive actor but his emphasis remains on the relationship of the government to business interests and its role in coordinating economic policy. These models, which assume the existence of mature capitalist states as the outcome of an evolutionary process of development, fail to match with Chinese experience.

The initiation of the Chinese reform movement reflected the conscious decision of the Chinese leadership, under the recently consolidated authority of then paramount leader Deng Xiaoping. The CCP, by its own admission, did not have a master plan for reform. This proceeded in an incremental and halting fashion, referred to as 'feeling for stones while crossing the river'. Structural economic factors, such as the regime's inability to provide jobs for urban dwellers, played a role in its onset, and continued to shape economic policy. The reforms themselves contributed to the growth of pluralist interests, with a group of emergent domestic actors, including joint ventures, regional authorities and town and village enterprises, able to lobby the government, often successfully, in pursuit of their economic agendas. This development is evocative of Hall and Soskice's assumptions regarding the input of multiple actors into economic policy making and has led to some optimistic assessments that China is on the path to a democratic future (Gilley 2004). These perspectives, however, do not capture the complexities of economic decision making in China.

As previously noted, the Chinese reform movement was such that the extent of market coordination varied according to the sector of the economy. Much of the economy, including agriculture, and forms of private, collective, and joint-venture ownership, functioned largely according to market criteria. In contrast, enterprises designated as of strategic importance, including pillar industries earmarked as potential national champions, remained sheltered from market competition, subject to bureaucratic forms of coordination.

This was roughly paralleled by a similar differentiation within the Chinese government. Local and provincial leaderships, at least those in geographic regions that benefited from the reforms, tended to support the transition to a market economy, entering into collaborative arrangements with local business interests. This did not mean unquestioned obeisance to laissez-faire precepts. Rather, local governments typically sought to resist national directives aimed at eliminating regional barriers to competition. Nor has the national government spoken with one voice. The central leadership promoted the development of strategic pillar industries, but it also sought the further liberalization of the Chinese economy, mobilizing the resources at its command to induce compliance at the regional levels. It is a clear oversimplification to contemplate the Chinese state as a unitary actor, single-mindedly directing China's economic transformation, immune to domestic and international influences. But it is also misleading to interpret the state as a sort of facilitator, mediating between a diversity of group interests. The Chinese central leadership rather played a decisive role in the articulation and implementation of China's reform agenda.

The spectre of the CCP leading China on a path of capitalist transformation points to a seemingly fundamental contradiction: how can a Marxist-Leninist regime, ostensibly legitimated by the realization of a socialist future, embrace a series of policies that appear to threaten its very survival? The political science literature has dedicated considerable attention to the question of the political consequences of economic reform, leading to the widely held expectation that the development of a market economy provides the preconditions for societal democratization (Lipset 1959; Inglehart 1997; Huntington 1991). It may well be that the CCP set into motion a series of processes that will result in its ultimate demise. In the short run, however, the Chinese leadership showed remarkable abilities at adaptation, enduring in the midst of the collapse of communist regimes throughout most of the rest of the formerly socialist bloc. The internationalization of the Chinese economy appears often to have operated to strengthen rather than dissipate CCP control. Zweig (2002) argues that the opening up of China's rural areas has served to increase CCP controls at the local levels, while Gallagher (2005) contends that the infusion of FDI into China retarded the forces of political liberalization. Preliminary evidence also indicates that the newly admitted entrepreneurs into the CCP were more willing accomplices than agents of political change (Dickson 2003). In this sense, it is possible, as Kornai (2000:33) suggests, that the CCP was increasingly interpenetrated by private business, leading to its transformation from an anti-capitalist into a pro-capitalist political force.

Conclusion

China's path to capitalism reflects both the legacy of its heritage as a socialist-style economy and its status as a late developer, still engaged in the process of economic modernization. The leadership's decision to initiate economic reforms was rooted in a pragmatic recognition that capitalist methods produced superior results to those achieved under socialist planning. As Deng Xiaoping famously remarked, it did not matter if the cat was black or white as long as it could catch mice. Nonetheless, the Chinese leadership was not able to bring itself explicitly to embrace capitalism as an operational construct, taking refuge in the vague designation of China as a 'socialist market economy'. Whereas the Chinese leadership sought to dismantle many of the structures standard to the Soviet-style planning system, it held fast to the preservation of the largest SOEs, identified as potential national champions in the mode of the Korean and Japanese conglomerates.

Nonetheless, the dominant strain of Chinese capitalism was towards the steady, if incremental, liberalization and opening of the economy. In this respect, the variety of capitalism developing corresponds more closely to Hall and Soskice's description of the LME. It is ironic that China, one of the remnant Communist Party regimes, should be widely hailed in the global economic community as a model of economic reform policy. China's particular path to the market defied the standard prescriptions outlined by the international financial community, notably the IMF. Nonetheless, as Rodrik (2004: 10) has noted, in the Chinese case 'unorthodox institutions worked precisely because they produced orthodox results, namely market-oriented incentives, property rights, macroeconomic stability, and so on'. In this sense, China's reform outcomes bear a resemblance to a number of points set forth by Williamson in his 1990 articulation of the Washington Consensus, with its emphasis on such precepts as privatization, liberalization of trade and FDI and fiscal reform (Williamson 1990; Williamson 2003).

The emphasis of the Varieties of Capitalism assessments on postindustrial economies leads them to disregard the role of the state as an agent of economic transformation, an important consideration for both postsocialist and developing economies. The Chinese state has not functioned as a monolithic unitary actor, unconstrained by structural factors and immune to domestic and external pressures. Nonetheless, it has played a dominant role in articulating China's economic transformation, setting forth strategic objectives in its reform agenda. In this sense, the CCP, acting through the state apparatus, served to coordinate the economy in its transition from socialism. At the same time, the state gradually ceded a large proportion of the operation of the economy to market imperatives. This did not include the designation of capital markets as the chief mechanism for capital allocation, a defining feature of the LME. It is difficult to imagine the Chinese leadership surrendering its control over capital to the impersonal mechanism of the marketplace, especially given its simultaneous commitment to fostering pillar industries. However, as

Steinfeld (2004: 650) has noted, the Chinese leadership consistently moved along the path of decontrol, such that 'most observers of the Chinese scene ... have yet to discern a figurative Rubicon across which Chinese reformers are unwilling to tread'. The evolution of China's economic transformation will be affected by any number of unknown domestic and external factors, such that prediction is a perilous exercise. The transition under way throughout the post-socialist bloc indicates that the act of establishing capitalist structures does not guarantee their operation according to market precepts. Despite its endorsement of market operations at the lower tiers, the CCP has been concerned to maintain political control at the upper echelons. This situation challenges fundamental precepts of the market as an autonomous regulator but it is hardly unique to communist regimes. The Chinese economy encompasses forms of both market and bureaucratic coordination, differentiated according to the sector of the economy. It is no easy task to define when a state has transformed itself from a socialist to a capitalist system, a historically unprecedented phenomenon. Kornai (2000: 30) notes that the changes made in the system must be irreversible. China's transition is obviously unfinished and its final outcome unknown, but judged by this criterion, China has definitively moved into the capitalist fold.

References

Amable, B. (2003) *The Diversity of Capitalism* (Oxford: Oxford University Press).
Baek, S. W. (2000) 'The Changing Trade Unions in China', *Journal of Contemporary Asia*, 1, 46–66.
Blecher, M. J. (2002) 'Hegemony and Workers' Politics in China', *China Quarterly*, 170, 283–303.
Bradshaw, K. (2004) 'Bankless Lending in China Sends out a Global Tremor', *New York Times*, 20 November.
Branstetter, L. and N. Lardy (2005) 'China's Embrace of Globalization', in L. Brandt, T. Rawski, and G. Lin (eds), *China's Economy: Retrospect and Prospects*, Asia Program Special Report, 129, 6–12, 365 (Washington, DC: Woodrow Wilson International Center).
Chan, A. (2000) 'Globalization, China's Free (Read Bonded) Labour Market, and the Chinese Trade Unions', in C. Rowley and J. Benson (eds), *Globalization and Labour in the Asia Pacific Region* (London: Frank Cass), 260–81.
Chan, A. (2001) *China's Workers under Assault: The Exploitation of Labor in a Globalizing Economy* (Armonk, NY: M.E. Sharpe).
Dickson, B. (2003). *Red Capitalists in China* (New York, NY: Cambridge University Press).
Duckett, J. (2004) 'State Collectivism and Worker Privilege: A Study of the Urban Health Insurance Reform', *China Quarterly*, 177, 155–73.

Durnev, A., K. Li, R. Mørck, and B. Yeung (2004) 'Capital Markets and Capital Allocation: Implications for Economies in Transition', *Economics of Transition*, 12, 593–634.

Fewsmith, J. (2001) *China since Tiananmen: The Politics of Transition* (Cambridge: Cambridge University Press).

Gallagher, M. (2005) *Contagious Capitalism: Globalization and the Politics of Labor in China* (Princeton, NJ: Princeton University Press).

Gilley, B. (2004) *China's Democratic Future: How it Will Happen and Where it Will Lead* (New York, NY: Columbia University Press).

Gregory, N., S. Tenev, and D. Wagle (2000) *China's Emerging Private Enterprises: Prospects for the New Century* (Washington, DC: International Finance Corporation).

Hall, P. and D. Soskice (eds) (2001) *Varieties of Capitalism* (Oxford: Oxford University Press).

Huntington, S. (1991) *The Third Wave: Democratization in the Late Twentieth Century* (Norman, OK: University of Oklahoma Press).

Hurst, W. and K. J. O'Brien (2002) 'China's Contentious Pensioners', *China Quarterly*, 170, 345–60.

IMF (2004) *People's Republic of China: 2004 Article IV Consultation*, (Washington DC: IMF Country Report, No. 04/351).

IMF (2005) *People's Republic of China: 2005 Article IV Consultation*, (Washington DC: IMF Country Report, No. 05/411).

Inglehart, R. (1997) *Modernization and Postmodernization: Cultural, Economic, and Political Change in 43 Societies* (Princeton, NJ: Princeton University Press).

Kim, Y., I. Ho, and M. St. Giles (2003) *Developing Institutional Investors in the People's Republic of China*, (Washington DC: World Bank).

Kornai, J. (2000) 'What the Change of System from Socialism to Capitalism Does and Does Not Mean', *Journal of Economic Perspectives*, 14, 27–42.

Kornai, J. (1992) *The Socialist System: The Political Economy of Communism* (Princeton, NJ: Princeton University Press).

Lardy, N. (2002) *Integrating China into the Global Economy* (Washington DC: Brookings Institution Press).

Lipset, S.M. (1959) 'Some Social Requisites of Democracy: Economic Development and Political Legitimacy', *American Political Science Review*, 1, 69–105.

Mako, W. P. and C. Zhang (2003) *Management of China's State-Owned Enterprises Portfolio: Lessons from International Experience* (Beijing: World Bank Office).

Mulcahy, J, W. (2003) 'Banking Means Never Having to Repay a Loan', *Asia Times*, 20 August.

Naughton, B. (2005) 'China's Political System and China's Future Growth', in L. Brandt, T. G. Rawski, and G. Lin (eds), *China's Economy: Retrospect and Prospects*, Asia Program Special Report, 129, 62–7, 351 (Washington, DC: Woodrow Wilson International Center).

Noble, G., J. Ravenhill, and R. Doner (2004) 'China's Auto Industry: National Strengthening and Globalization?' (unpublished manuscript).

Nolan, P. (2004) *Transforming China: Globalization, Transition and Development* (London: Anthem Press).

Pearson, M. (2005) 'The Business of Governing Business in China: Institutions and Norms of the Emerging Regulatory State', *World Politics*, 57, 296–322.

Rodrik, Dani (2006) *What's So Special about China's Exports?* (Cambridge, MA: John F. Kennedy School of Government, Harvard University) Working Paper No. RWP06-001.

Rodrik, Dani (2004) *Growth Strategies*, (Cambridge, MA: John F. Kennedy School of Government, Harvard University) <www.ksg.harvard.edu/rodrik/>.

Steinfeld, E. (2004) 'Market Visions: The Interplay of Ideas and Institutions in Chinese Financial Restructuring', *Political Studies*, 52, 643–63.

Thun, E. (2004) 'Industrial Policy, Chinese-Style: FDI, Regulation, and Dreams of National Champions in the Auto Sector', *Journal of East Asian Studies*, 4, 453–89.

Ting, S. (2005) 'State-Owned Firms to Face Faster Cuts', *South China Morning Post*, 14 March, 7.

Tsai, K. S. (2002) *Back Alley Banking: Private Entrepreneurs in China* (Ithaca, NY: Cornell University Press).

UNCTAD (United Nations Conference on Trade and Development) (2004) *World Investment Report 2004: The Shift toward Services*. (Geneva: UNCTAD).

Walder, A. G. (1986) *Communist Neo-traditionalism: Work and Authority in Chinese Industry* (Berkeley, CA: University of California Press).

Wang, X. (2004) 'China's Pension Reform and Capital Market Development', *China and World Economy*, 4, 3–16.

Weston, T. (2002) ' "Learn from Daqing": More Dark Clouds for Workers in State-Owned Enterprises', *Journal of Contemporary China*, 33, 721–34.

Williamson, J. (2003) 'A Short History of the Washington Consensus and Suggestions for What to Do Next', *Finance and Development*, 10–13 September.

Williamson, J. (1990) 'What Washington Means by Policy Reform', in J. Williamson (ed.), *Latin American Adjustment: How Much Has Happened?* (Washington, DC: Institute for International Economics), 7–20.

World Bank (2003) *China: Country Economic Memorandum: Promoting Growth with Equity*, (Washington DC: World Bank) Report No. 24169-C-A.

Wu, F. (2005) 'The Globalization of Corporate China', (Seattle, WA: National Bureau of Asian Research Analysis).

ZGTJNJ (*Zhongguo Tongji Nianjian*) (2004) (China Statistical Yearbook) (Beijing: China Statistics Press).

Zweig, D. (2002) *Internationalizing China: Domestic Interests and Global Linkages* (Ithaca, NY: Cornell University Press).

Statistical Appendix

Prepared by Vlad Mykhnenko

Table A.1 Annual percent change in real GDP: post-communist and selected advanced capitalist economies, 1990–2006

Country	1992	1993	1994	1995	1996	1997	1998	1999	2000	2001	2002	2003	2004
Post-communist economies:													
Albania	-7.2	9.6	9.4	8.9	9.1	-10.2	12.7	10.1	7.3	7.2	3.4	6	5.9
Armenia	-52.6	-14.1	5.4	6.9	5.9	3.3	7.3	3.3	6	9.6	13.2	13.9	10.1
Azerbaijan	-22.7	-23.1	-19.7	-11.8	1.3	5.8	10	7.4	9.2	6.5	8.1	11.5	10.2
Belarus	-9.6	-7.6	-11.7	-11.3	2.8	11.4	8.4	3.4	5.8	4.7	5	7	11
Bosnia and Herzegovina	-6.4	-2.2	11.1	16	62.6	29.9	15.9	9.6	5.5	4.3	5.3	4	5.7
Bulgaria	-8.4	-11.6	-3.7	-1.6	-8	-5.6	4	2.3	5.4	4.1	4.9	4.3	5.6
China	14.2	13.5	12.6	10.5	9.6	8.8	7.8	7.1	8	7.5	8.3	9.5	9.5
Croatia	-11.7	-8	5.9	6.6	5.9	6.8	2.5	-0.9	2.9	4.4	5.2	4.3	3.8
Czech Republic	-0.5	0.1	2.2	5.9	4.3	-0.8	-1	0.5	3.3	2.6	1.5	3.2	4.4
Estonia	-21.6	-8.2	1	4.5	4.4	11.1	4.4	0.3	7.9	6.5	7.2	6.7	7.8
Georgia	-44.9	-29.3	-10.4	2.6	10.5	10.6	2.9	3	1.9	4.7	5.5	11.1	6.2
Hungary	-3.1	-0.6	2.9	1.6	1.3	4.6	4.9	4.2	5.2	3.8	3.5	2.9	4.2
Kazakhstan	-5.3	-9.2	-12.6	-8.3	0.5	1.6	-1.9	2.7	9.8	13.5	9.8	9.3	9.4
Kyrgyz Republic	-13.9	-13	-19.8	-5.8	7.1	9.9	2.1	3.7	5.4	5.3	0	7	7.1
Latvia	-32.1	-11.4	2.2	-0.9	3.8	8.3	4.7	3.3	6.9	8	6.4	7.5	8.5
Lithuania	-21.3	-16.2	-9.8	3.3	4.7	7	7.3	-1.7	3.9	6.4	6.8	9.7	6.7
Macedonia, FYR	-6.6	-7.5	-1.8	-1.1	1.2	1.4	3.4	4.4	4.5	-4.5	0.9	3.5	2.4
Moldova	-34.6	-1.2	-30.9	-15.3	-5.9	1.6	-6.5	-3.4	2.1	6.1	7.8	6.6	7.3
Mongolia	-9.5	-2.9	2.3	6.3	2.4	4	3.5	3.2	1.1	1	4	5.6	10.6

Poland	2	4.3	5.2	6.8	6	6.8	4.8	4.1	4	1	1.4	3.8	5.4
Romania	-8.8	1.5	3.9	7.1	3.9	-6.1	-4.8	-1.2	2.1	5.7	5.1	5.2	8.3
Russia	-14.5	-8.7	-12.7	-4.1	-3.6	1.4	-5.3	6.3	10	5.1	4.7	7.3	7.2
Serbia and Montenegro	-2.2	6.7	7	6.3	7.3	0	2.5	-18	5	5.5	3.8	2.7	7.2
Slovak Republic	-6.7	-3.7	6.2	5.8	6.1	4.6	4.2	1.5	2	3.8	4.6	4.5	5.5
Slovenia	-5.5	2.8	5.3	4.1	3.6	4.8	3.6	5.6	3.9	2.7	3.3	2.5	4.6
Tajikistan	-28.9	-11.1	-21.4	-12.5	-4.4	1.8	5.2	3.8	8.3	10.2	9.1	10.2	10.6
Turkmenistan	-5.3	-10	-17.3	-7.2	-6.7	-11.3	6.7	16.4	18.6	20.4	15.8	17.1	17.2
Ukraine	-9.7	-14.2	-22.9	-12.2	-10	-3	-1.9	-0.2	5.9	9.2	5.2	9.6	12.1
Uzbekistan	-11.1	-2.3	-4.2	-0.9	1.6	2.5	2.1	3.4	3.2	4.1	3.1	1.5	7.1
Vietnam	8.7	8.1	8.8	9.5	9.3	8.2	5.8	4.8	6.8	6.9	7.1	7.3	7.7
Advanced capitalist economies:													
Germany	2.3	-0.8	2.6	1.8	1	1.7	2	1.9	3.1	1.2	0.1	-0.2	1.6
Japan	1	0.2	1	2	3.4	1.8	-1	-0.1	2.4	0.2	-0.3	1.4	2.7
Spain	0.8	-0.8	2.1	2.8	2.4	4	4.3	4.2	5.8	3.5	2.7	2.9	3.1
Sweden	-1.2	-2	4.2	4.1	1.3	2.4	3.6	4.6	4.3	1	2	1.5	3.6
United Kingdom	0.3	2.4	4.4	2.9	2.7	3.2	3.2	3	4	2.2	2	2.5	3.2
United States	3.3	2.7	4	2.5	3.7	4.5	4.2	4.4	3.7	0.8	1.6	2.7	4.2

Definitions: Gross domestic product (GDP) at purchaser prices is the sum of gross value added by all resident producers in the economy plus any product taxes (less subsidies) not included in the valuation of output. It is calculated without deducting for depreciation of fabricated assets or for depletion and degradation of natural resources.

Source: International Monetary Fund (2005) *Economic Outlook Database: September 2005* (Washington, DC: The Fund, available at <http://www.imf.org/external/pubs/ft/weo/2005/02/data/index.htm>).

Table A.2 GDP per capita, post-communist and selected advanced capitalist economies, US$ at PPP

	1990	1995	2000	2004
Post-communist economies:				
Albania	2,785	2,749	3,719	4,937
Armenia	3,609	1,433	1,986	3,806
Azerbaijan	3,958	1,808	2,561	3,968
Belarus	4,385	3,197	4,809	6,646
Bosnia and Herzegovina	990	1,213	4,394	5,504
Bulgaria	7,145	5,731	6,229	8,500
China	1,330	2,496	3,853	5,642
Croatia	8,099	7,061	9,080	11,568
Czech Republic	12,182	13,084	15,163	18,370
Estonia	8,708	6,800	10,284	15,217
Georgia	3,995	1,272	1,995	2,774
Hungary	8,949	9,088	12,264	15,546
Kazakhstan	4,793	3,609	4,675	7,418
Kyrgyz Republic	2,080	1,171	1,561	1,934
Latvia	8,528	5,517	8,187	11,980
Lithuania	9,652	6,286	8,895	12,980
Macedonia, FYR	6,244	5,394	6,543	7,237
Moldova	3,796	1,599	1,515	2,119
Mongolia	1,500	1,362	1,602	1,918
Poland	5,827	7,233	10,061	12,452
Romania	5,353	5,541	5,707	7,641
Russia	8,622	6,032	7,219	10,179
Serbia and Montenegro			3,795	4,858
Slovak Republic	9,715	9,121	11,777	15,066
Slovenia	11,339	12,401	16,615	20,306
Tajikistan	1,635	679	810	1,246
Turkmenistan	5,138	3,368	3,936	7,266
Ukraine	7,559	4,025	4,115	6,554
Uzbekistan	1,560	1,370	1,536	1,766
Vietnam	957	1,468	1,989	2,570
Advanced capitalist economies:				
Germany	18,317	22,107	26,074	28,988
Japan	18,789	22,524	25,894	29,906
Spain	13,036	15,710	20,194	23,627
Sweden	16,943	19,305	24,467	28,205
United Kingdom	16,319	19,738	24,695	28,938
United States	22,921	27,420	34,344	39,496

Definitions: PPP (purchasing power parity) means that an international dollar has the same purchasing power as a US dollar has in the United States.
Source: International Monetary Fund (2005) *Economic Outlook Database: September 2005* (Washington, DC: The Fund, available at <http://www.imf.org/external/pubs/ft/weo/2005/02/data/index.htm>).

Table A.3 Size and structure of output in selected economies: total GDP in US$ and value added by sectors as percentage of GDP, 1990–2003

Country	Gross domestic product US$ millions		Agriculture % of GDP		Industry % of GDP		Manufacturing % of GDP		Services % of GDP	
	1990	2003	1990	2003	1990	2003	1990	2003	1990	2003
Post-communist economies:										
Belarus	17,370	17,493	24	10	47	30	39	23	29	60
China	354,644	1,417,000	27	15	42	52	33	39	31	33
Czech Republic	34,880	89,715	6	3	49	39	–	27	45	57
Estonia	5,010	9,082	17	4	50	28	42	18	34	67
Georgia	7,738	3,988	32	20	33	25	24	19	35	54
Kazakhstan	26,933	29,749	27	8	45	38	9	16	29	54
Poland	58,976	209,563	8	3	50	31	–	18	42	66
Russia	516,814	432,855	17	5	48	34	–	–	35	61
Slovenia	17,382	27,749	6	3	46	36	35	27	49	61
Ukraine[a]	81,456	49,537	26	14	45	40	44	25	30	46

(*Continued*)

Table A.3 (Continued)

Country	Gross domestic product US$ millions		Agriculture % of GDP		Industry % of GDP		Manufacturing % of GDP		Services % of GDP	
	1990	2003	1990	2003	1990	2003	1990	2003	1990	2003
Advanced capitalist economies:										
Germany	1,671,335	2,403,160	2	1	39	29	28	23	59	69
Japan	3,039,693	4,300,858	2	1	39	30	27	21	58	68
Spain[a]	509,997	838,652	6	3	35	30	–	17	59	67
Sweden	240,153	301,606	3	2	32	28	–	21	64	70
United Kingdom	989,524	1,794,878	2	1	35	27	23	17	63	72
United States	5,757,200	10,948,547	2	2	28	23	19	15	70	75

Note: [a] Components are at basic prices.

Definitions: (1) gross domestic product is converted to US dollars at current market exchange rates. (2) GDP value added is the net output of an industry after adding up all outputs and subtracting intermediate inputs. The industrial origin of value added is determined by the International Standard Industrial Classification (ISIC) revision 3. Agriculture corresponds to ISIC divisions 1–5 and includes forestry and fishing. Industry covers mining, manufacturing (also reported separately), construction, electricity, water, and gas (ISIC divisions 10–45). Manufacturing corresponds to industries belonging to ISIC divisions 15–37. Services correspond to ISIC divisions 50–99. This sector is derived as a residual (from GDP less agriculture and industry) and may not properly reflect the sum of services output, including banking and financial services. For some countries it includes product taxes (minus subsidies) and may also include statistical discrepancies.

Source: World Bank (2005) *World Development Indicators 2005* (Washington, DC: The World Bank, available at <http://devdata.worldbank.org/wdi2005/index2.htm>).

Table A.4 Foreign trade as percentage of GDP and shares of selected product groups in exports, 1990–2003

Country	% of GDP				% of exports, 2003			
	Exports of goods and services		Imports of goods and services		Food and agriculture	Fuels	Ores and metals	Machinery and transport equipment
	1990	2003	1990	2003				
Belarus	46	66	44	70	12.2	22.0	1.1	22.8
China	18	34	14	32	5.1	2.5	1.6	42.8
Czech Republic	45	63	43	65	5.2	2.9	1.7	50.1
Estonia	60	75	54	83	19.3	4.2	2.4	29.5
Georgia	40	32	46	46	37.0	4.9	24.3	12.8
Kazakhstan	74	50	75	44	7.3	61.2	14.1	1.8
Poland	29	21	22	26	9.3	4.3	3.7	37.3
Russia	18	32	18	21	5.2	53.0	6.8	7.0
Slovenia	84	60	74	60	4.7	1.4	3.8	36.5
Ukraine[a]	28	53	29	48	14.9	9.2	8.6	14.1
Germany	25	36	25	32	5.1	1.6	2.1	50.2
Japan	10	12	10	10	1.0	0.4	1.3	66.9
Spain[a]	16	28	20	30	16.2	2.7	2.0	40.2
Sweden	30	44	29	37	8.0	3.0	2.3	42.1
United Kingdom	24	25	27	28	6.3	8.1	2.2	44.4
United States	10	10	11	14	10.5	2.0	2.0	48.6

Note: [a] Data on the structure of merchandise exports refer to 2002.

Definitions: (1) Exports and imports of goods and services represent the value of all goods and other market services provided to, or received from, the rest of the world. They include the value of merchandise, freight, insurance, transport, travel, royalties, license fees, and other services, such as communication, construction, financial, information, business, personal, and government services. They exclude labour and property income (factor services in the 1968 SNA) as well as transfer payments. (2) Merchandise exports are the fob value of goods provided to the rest of the world, valued in US dollars. Food corresponds to the commodities in the Standard International Trade Classification (SITC) sections 0 (food and live animals), 1 (beverages and tobacco), 4 (animal and vegetable oils and fats) and 22 (oil seeds, oil nuts, and oil kernels). Agricultural raw materials correspond to SITC section 2 (crude materials except fuels) excluding divisions 22, 27 (crude fertilizers and minerals excluding coal, petroleum, and precious stones), and 28 (metalliferous ores and scrap). Fuels correspond to SITC section 3 (mineral fuels). Ores and metals correspond to the commodities in SITC divisions 27, 28, and 68 (non-ferrous metals). Machinery and transport equipment corresponds to SITC division 7.

Source: World Bank (2005) *World Development Indicators 2005* (Washington, DC: The World Bank, available at <http://devdata.worldbank.org/wdi2005/index2.htm>); UNCTAD (2005) *Handbook of Statistics On-line* (New York and Geneva: United Nations, available at <http://www.unctad.org/Templates/Page.asp?intItemID=1890&lang=1>).

Table A.5 Financial depth and stock markets in selected countries, 1990–2004

Country	Domestic credit provided by banking sector		Stock market capitalization		Market turnover ratio	
	1990	2003	1990	2003	1990	2004
Belarus	–	21.2	–	–	–	–
China	90	177.9	0.5	48.1	158.9	113.3
Czech Republic	–	49.5	–	19.7	–	78.5
Estonia	66.7	54.8	–	41.7	–	17.5
Georgia	–	19.5	–	5.1	–	0.5
Kazakhstan	–	13.7	–	8.2	–	22
Poland	19.5	37	0.2	17.7	89.7	33.1
Russia	–	27.6	0	53.3	–	53
Slovenia	36.8	49.9	–	25.7	–	14.6
Ukraine	83.2	32.7	–	8.7	–	2.5
Germany	104.4	142.9	21.2	44.9	139.3	130
Japan	260.7	157.3	96.1	70.7	43.8	88
Spain	107	138.7	21.8	86.6	–	157.5
Sweden	139.2	110.7	40.8	95.3	14.9	113.6
United Kingdom	121	150.4	85.8	134.4	33.4	100.6
United States	174.5	261.8	53.2	130.3	53.4	122.8

Notes: Credit and market capitalization figures are percentages of GDP. The market turnover ratio shows the value of shares traded as a percentage of market capitalization.

Definitions: (1) Domestic credit encompasses credit provided by the banking sector to various sectors on a gross basis, with the exception of credit to the central government, which is net. Domestic credit refers to financial resources provided to the private sector that establish a claim for repayment. For some countries these claims include credit to public enterprises. The banking sector includes monetary authorities, deposit money banks, and other banking institutions such as savings and mortgage loan institutions and building and loan associations. (2) Stock market capitalization (also known as market value) is the share price times the number of shares outstanding as a percentage of GDP. Market turnover ratio is the total value of shares traded during the period divided by the average market capitalization for the period.

Source: World Bank (2005) *World Development Indicators 2005* (Washington, DC: The World Bank, available at <http://devdata.worldbank.org/wdi2005/index2.htm>).

Table A.6 Eastern Europe companies appearing in Europe 500 ranking, 2005

Eastern Europe rank 2005[a]	Company	Country	Sector	Market value US$ mn
1. (20)	Gazprom	Russia	Oil & gas	67,942.9
2. (66)	Surgutneftegaz	Russia	Oil & gas	30,102.2
3. (68)	Lukoil	Russia	Oil & gas	28,791.6
4. (139)	Mobile Telesystems	Russia	Telecommunication services	14,029.0
5. (164)	Norilsk Nickel	Russia	Steel & other metals	12,481.4
6. (165)	Unified Energy Systems	Russia	Electricity	12,472.5
7. (177)	Sberbank of Russia	Russia	Banks	11,567.0
8. (193)	CEZ	Czech Republic	Electricity	10,444.5
9. (212)	OTP Bank	Hungary	Banks	9,557.1
10. (214)	Telekomunikacja Polska	Poland	Telecommunication services	9,436.1
11. (230)	PKO Bank	Poland	Banks	8,796.9
12. (233)	MOL Magyar Olaj Gazi	Hungary	Oil & gas	8,728.3
13. (254)	Sistema	Russia	Diversified industrials	7,840.6
14. (267)	Bank Pekao	Poland	Banks	7,316.6
15. (281)	Vimpel Communications	Russia	Information technology hardware	7,044.0

(Continued)

Table A.6 (Continued)

Eastern Europe rank 2005([a])	Company	Country	Sector	Market value US$ mn
16.	Snp Petrom	Romania	Oil & gas	6,955.1
17. (303)	PKN Orlen	Poland	Oil & gas	6,171.6
18. (305)	Cesky Telecom	Czech Republic	Telecommunication services	6,056.4
19.	Hansabank	Estonia	Banks	5,568.0
20. (333)	Komercni Banka	Czech Republic	Banks	5,429.2
21. (356)	Severstal	Russia	Steel & other metals	4,966.7
22. (361)	Magyar Telekom	Hungary	Telecommunication services	4,891.4
23. (383)	Bank BPH	Poland	Banks	4,561.5
24. (461)	Tatneft	Russia	Oil & gas	3,464.1
25. (465)	Mechel Steel Group	Russia	Steel & other metals	3,417.4
26. (484)	Orenburgneft	Russia	Oil & gas	3,269.7

Note: [a] Relative position of the company in Europe 500 ranking, 2005.
No company registered in a central or south-east Asian post-communist country has appeared in the *Financial Times* Global 500 or Asia 100 companies ranking of 2005.
Source: FT 500 Report, *Financial Times*, June 2005.

Table A.7 Unemployment rates in selected countries, 1991–2004

Country	1991	1994	1997	2000	2004
Belarus	0.1	2.1	2.8	2.1	1.9
China	2.3	2.8	3.1	3.6	
Czech Republic		4.3	4.8	8.8	8.3
Estonia	1.5	7.6	9.6	13.6	9.7
Georgia				10.8	12.6
Kazakhstan					8.4
Poland		14.4	11.2	16.1	19.0
Russian Federation		8.1	11.8	9.8	7.8
Slovenia		9.0	7.1	7.2	6.1
Ukraine			8.9	11.6	8.6
Germany	6.6	10.3	9.8	7.9	11.0
Japan	2.1	2.9	3.4	4.7	4.7
Spain	16.4	24.1	20.6	13.9	11.0
Sweden	3.0	8.0	8.0	4.7	5.5
United Kingdom	8.4	9.6	7.1	5.5	4.6
United States	6.8	6.1	4.9	4.0	5.5

Note: Figures for Belarus are derived from the numbers registered at employment records offices. Figures for China are derived from figures for urban areas only. All others are derived from Labour Force Survey data. Changes in methodology occurred in Spain, Sweden and the USA, making figures not strictly comparable over the whole time period.
Definitions: The International Labour Organization (ILO) defines the unemployed as members of the economically active population who are without work but available for and seeking work, including people who have lost their jobs and those who have voluntarily left work. Reference periods, the age considered appropriate for employment, the criteria for those considered to be seeking work, and the treatment of people temporarily laid off and those seeking work for the first time vary slightly across countries. Labour force surveys generally yield the most comprehensive data statistics that are more comparable internationally.
Source: International Labour Organization (2005) *Laborsta Internet: An International Labour Office Database on Labour Statistics* (Geneva: The ILO Bureau of Statistics, available at <http://laborsta.ilo.org/>).

Table A.8 Distribution of income and consumption in selected countries: Gini indices, late 1980s–early 2000s

	1988	1995	1999	2003
Belarus	24.2	28.4	28.8	29.2[l]
China	33.1[a]	39.0[g]	40.3[i]	44.9
Czech Republic	19.8[d]	23.0[g]	23.2	23.4[l]
Estonia	27.8	35.5	37.0[i]	36.4[i]
Georgia	31.3	57.6[h]	50.3[i]	45.4[l]
Kazakhstan	29.1	53.0[g]	34.6[k]	31.8
Poland	27.5[d]	33.6[g]	33.4	35.3
Russia	26.4	43.2	37.4[i]	33.8[l]
Slovenia	23.5[c]	26.4	24.8	24.4[k]
Ukraine	24.8	49.4	32.0	32.7[l]
Germany	26.7[e]	27.8	24.8	28.0
Japan	31.2	31.6	31.9	
Spain	31.5[e]	33.2	32.7	31.0
Sweden	24.4[d]	25.6	26.0	25.7[l]
United Kingdom	31.7	32.9	34.1	34.2[l]
United States	37.2[b]	39.0[f]	40.5[h]	39.4[j]

Notes: Data refer to survey year; [a] 1985, [b] 1986, [c] 1987, [d] 1989, [e] 1990, [f] 1994, [g] 1996, [h] 1997, [i] 1998, [j] 2000, [k] 2001, [l] 2002, Belarus figure under 2003, Kazakhstan figures under 1999 and 2003 and the Russian figure under 2003 refer to consumption: these generally show less dispersion than figures for incomes.

Definitions: The Gini index provides a convenient summary measure of the degree of inequality. It measures the extent to which the distribution of income (or, in some cases, consumption expenditure) among individuals or households within an economy deviates from a perfectly equal distribution. A Gini index of 0 represents perfect equality, while an index of 100 implies perfect inequality. The data above use per capita household incomes.

Source: World Bank (2000) Making Transition Work for Everyone: Poverty and Inequality in Europe and Central Asia (Washington, DC: World Bank): appendix D; Asad, A., M. Murthi, R. Yemtsov, and others (2005) Growth, Poverty and Inequality: Eastern Europe and the Former Soviet Union (Washington, DC: World Bank), appendix; UNU-WIDER (2005) WIDER World Income Inequality Database (Helsinki: World Institute for Development Economics Research, available at <http://www.wider.unu.edu/wiid/wiid.htm>).

Table A.9 Main poverty indicators: selected post-communist countries, 1996–2003

Country		% of population below $2 a day	% of population below $4 a day
Belarus	2002	2	21
China	2001	47	n/d
Czech Republic	1996	2	1
Estonia	2003	5	26
Georgia	2003	52	85
Kazakhstan	2003	21	66
Poland	2002	3	27
Russian Federation	2002	9	41
Slovenia	1998	2	1
Ukraine	2003	1	22

Notes:
Definitions: Population below $2 a day and population below $4 a day are the percentages of the population living on less than $2.15 a day and $4.30 a day at 2000 international prices. As a result of revisions in PPP exchange rates, poverty rates for individual countries are not strictly comparable with poverty rates reported in earlier years (e.g. Czech Republic and Slovenia). The World Bank uses $2 a day (or, more accurately, $2.15 at 2000 PPP) as an intermediate absolute poverty line. It is exactly double its $1-a-day poverty line (later updated to $1.075 a day, using 1993 PPPs), which has come to be regarded as providing the absolute minimum standard of living and is typically used to assess poverty in developing countries. The higher $4-a-day ($4.30-a-day) poverty line represents a proximate vulnerability threshold to identify households that are not suffering absolute material deprivation, but are vulnerable to poverty.
Source: Asad, A., M. Murthi, R. Yemtsov, and others (2005) *Growth, Poverty and Inequality: Eastern Europe and the Former Soviet Union* (Washington, DC: World Bank), appendix; World Bank (2005) *World Development Indicators 2005* (Washington, DC: The World Bank, available at <http://devdata.worldbank.org/wdi2005/index2.htm>); UNDP (2005) *Human Development Report 2005: International Cooperation at Crossroads* (New York: UNDP), pp. 211–328. Definitions above are adapted from Asad *et al.* (2005) and World Bank (2005).

Table A.10   Health expenditure by source of funding in selected countries, 2002

	Total	Public		Private	Out of pocket	External resources
	% of GDP	% of GDP	% of total	% of total	% of private	% of total
Post-communist economies:						
Belarus	6.4	4.7	73.9	26.0	79.7	0.1
China	5.8	2.0	33.7	66.2	96.3	0.1
Czech Republic	7.0	6.4	91.4	8.6	100.0	0.0
Estonia	5.1	3.9	76.3	23.7	83.9	0.0
Georgia	3.8	1.0	27.1	60.3	98.7	12.6
Kazakhstan	3.5	1.9	53.2	46.2	100.0	0.6
Poland	6.1	4.4	72.4	27.6	100.0	0.0
Russian Federation	6.2	3.5	55.8	44.0	63.6	0.2
Slovenia	8.3	6.2	74.9	25.0	40.9	0.1
Ukraine	4.7	3.3	71.1	25.3	95.5	3.6
Advanced capitalist economies:						
Germany	10.9	8.6	78.5	21.5	48.2	0.0
Japan	7.9	6.5	81.7	18.3	89.8	0.0
Spain	7.6	5.4	71.3	28.7	82.5	0.0
Sweden	9.2	7.8	85.3	14.7	100.0	0.0
United Kingdom	7.7	6.4	83.4	16.6	55.9	0.0
United States	14.6	6.6	44.9	55.1	25.4	0.0

Notes:
Definitions: (1) Total health expenditure is the sum of public and private health expenditure. It covers the provision of health services (preventive and curative), family planning activities, nutrition activities, and emergency aid designated for health but does not include provision of water and sanitation. (2) Public health expenditure consists of recurrent and capital spending from government (central and local) budgets, external borrowings and grants (including donations from international agencies and non-governmental organizations), and social (or compulsory) health insurance funds. (3) Private health expenditure includes direct (out-of-pocket) spending by households, private insurance, spending by non-profit institutions serving households (other than social insurance), and direct service payments by private corporations. (4) Out-of-pocket expenditure is any direct outlay by households, including gratuities and in-kind payments, to health practitioners and suppliers of pharmaceuticals, therapeutic appliances, and other goods and services whose primary intent is to contribute to the restoration or enhancement of the health status of individuals or population groups. It is a part of private health expenditure. (5) External resources for health are funds or services in kind that are provided by entities not part of the country in question. The resources may come from international organizations, other countries through bilateral arrangements, or foreign non-governmental organizations. These resources are part of total health expenditure.
Source: World Bank (2005) *World Development Indicators 2005* (Washington, DC: The World Bank, available at <http://devdata.worldbank.org/wdi2005/index2.htm>). Definitions above are from the same source.

Index